BETWEEN
TERROR AND
TOLERANCE

T0346343

BETWEEN TERROR AND TOLERANCE

*Religious Leaders, Conflict,
and Peacemaking*

TIMOTHY D. SISK, EDITOR

Georgetown University Press/Washington, D.C.

Georgetown University Press, Washington, D.C. www.press.georgetown.edu

Library of Congress Cataloging-in-Publication Data

Between terror and tolerance : religious leaders, conflict, and peacemaking / Timothy D. Sisk, editor.
        p. cm.
    Includes bibliographical references and index.
    ISBN 978-1-58901-782-5 (pbk. : alk. paper)
1. Political violence—Religious aspects—Case studies. 2. Violence—Religious aspects—Case studies. 3. Terrorism—Religious aspects—Case studies. 4. Toleration—Religious aspects—Case studies. 5. Terror—Religious aspects—Case studies. 6. Religion and politics—Case studies. I. Sisk, Timothy D., 1960–
    BL65.V55B48 2011
    201'.7273—dc22

                                                                        2011004086

∞ This book is printed on acid-free paper meeting the requirements of the American National Standard for Permanence in Paper for Printed Library Materials.

18   17   16   15   14   13   12   11   9   8   7   6   5   4   3   2

First printing

Printed in the United States of America

CONTENTS

Acknowledgments

❧

The research on which this book is based was conducted with the support of a generous grant from the Henry R. Luce Initiative on Religion and International Affairs Program of the Henry Luce Foundation. Toby Volkman is thanked for her oversight and management of the award that made this project possible.

The project was administered through the Center for Sustainable Development at the Josef Korbel School of International Studies at the University of Denver. Former executive director of the center, Elizabeth Cox, did a masterful job of administering the project and of convening various project events in Colorado and New York. Also at Korbel, graduate students Fletcher Cox, Devin Finn, and Lauren Stackpoole all contributed in various substantive ways to the project over time through research assistance, reports on various colloquia and symposia, and help organizing project events. Lynn Backstrom-Funk of the University of Denver's Office of Sponsored Programs and Research provided impeccable professional administration of the Luce Foundation grant that made the project possible.

The contributors also thank a number of reviewers, policy-oriented participants, and expert commentators who have participated in various events related to this project. These include a number of University of Denver colleagues; leading academics in the field of religion, conflict, and comparative politics; United Nations officials; and representatives from human rights organizations. In particular, we would like to thank Tamra Pearson d'Estree of the University of Denver; Joyce Dubensky of the Tanenbaum Center for Interreligious Understanding; Anita Ernstdorfer and Gay Rosenblum-Kumar of the United Nations Development Program; Rama Mani of the World Future Council; Marc Sheuer, director of the Alliance for Civilizations; Massimo Tommasoli of International IDEA; Vanessa Wyeth of the International Peace Institute; and Valerie Rocher and Simona Cruciani of the Office of the Special Advisor on the Prevention of Genocide, United Nations.

Andrea Bartoli and an anonymous reviewer provided constructively critical, detailed comments on the manuscript during the review process, and these reviewers provided important conceptual and case-specific insights that are reflected in the book's pages. The editor would especially like to acknowledge the dedicated work of the book's contributors. David Little provided overall intellectual guidance throughout the project, and the case study authors in turn provided critical, complementary reflections that in turn helped develop Little's conceptual framework.

The contributors to the volume would like to thank Don Jacobs, acquisitions editor at Georgetown University Press, as well as the entire staff, for embracing the project and for their stewardship throughout the publishing process.

INTRODUCTION

∾

Religious Leaders, Conflict, and Peacemaking

TIMOTHY D. SISK

The horrific, coordinated terror bomb attacks on mass transit targets that rocked London during the morning rush hour of July 7, 2005—killing 52 and injuring more than 770—led to a quick and strategically considered response by the government of then–Prime Minister Tony Blair. With findings from investigations and the bombers' own videotaped statement that the bombers were British citizens, not al-Qa'ida from abroad, and that the bombings were inspired by radicalized Islamist clerics, Blair's government moved to expel the most inflammatory religious leaders believed to have preached "glorification" of violence.[1] This instance underscores a common understanding about the potential role of religious leaders in justifying or inciting violence, instances in which religious leaders may either provide a warrant for violence by professing intolerance on the basis of religion or belief, or may go further in articulating a specific injunction to action for violence against specific targets.[2]

Counterbalancing such situations are others in which religious leaders have played an opposite role: serving as an essential bridge between groups in conflict (see Gopin 2000; see also the rich essays in Coward and Smith 2004). In the midst of the violent and turbulent transition from apartheid to democracy in South Africa following a major upsurge in factional fighting in mid-1992, church leaders throughout the South African Council of Churches (and involving leaders of the previously isolated Dutch Reformed Church) stepped in to directly mediate the political crisis that had developed between antiapartheid fighter Nelson Mandela and President F. W. de Klerk.[3] The religious-leader mediation in South Africa

1

was an especially symbolic event in the peace process to move South Africa from apartheid to democracy; their moral stature bridged the distrust that had developed between Mandela and de Klerk over violence. In Iraq, Ayatollah Sistani has played a critical role as a "quietest" cleric in at times directly mediating in the deep sectarian rift that opened in Iraq following the 2003 US-led intervention (for example, in speaking against retaliation for attacks on Shi'a worshippers). At other times, Sistani has been seen as backing the sectarian political parties that divide Iraq (Rahimi 2007).

In other societies, too, religious leaders from virtually all major faith traditions have stepped to the fore as key agents of securing peace, tolerating the other's theology in pursuit of a shared goal (as they have in other pursuits, such as poverty alleviation) (see Sampson 2007).[4] However, peacemaking religious elites face an uphill battle. Scott Appleby observes, "While the religious extremist is often integrated into a well-organized movement, armed to the teeth, expertly trained, lavishly financed, ideologically disciplined, and involved in a kind of 'ecumenical' collaboration with other violence-prone organizations, the nonviolent religious actor is relatively isolated, underfinanced, unskilled in the techniques of conflict transformation" (Appleby 2001). [5]

Thus, there is a paradox regarding elite roles in conflict settings in general. And, more specifically, a clearly perplexing set of puzzles exists surrounding the role that religious elites in particular play in the complex dynamic of conflict escalation and de-escalation: religious leaders, at times, contribute to conflict escalation through their doctrinal and ethical interpretations and specific calls to action. At other times we see religious leaders directly appeal for tolerance and a deeper relationship of coexistence, organizing interfaith dialogue, and in some instances directly mediating peace. This juxtaposition of religious leaders' roles in exacerbation of conflict and the instigation of violence and their roles as direct and active peacemakers is simplistic—religions are "multivocal." Thus, there is need for a greater understanding of the contingencies and circumstances under which religious leaders may play a conflict-exacerbating or conflict-ameliorating role. However, the stark nature of these contrasting accounts helps illustrate the principal puzzle that is the focus of this book: Under what conditions do religious leaders justify or catalyze violence along identity lines that divide contemporary societies, and under what conditions do they lay the foundation for, advocate for, and sometimes mediate for peace?

This book presents the research and findings of an international team of scholars regarding religious leaders' roles in the thematic and case-study chapters on deeply divided societies. Since the period of rapid decolonization after World War II, a rich literature has developed on the nature of societies that are deeply divided: historically, these countries were considered "plural" or segmented societies in contrast to the either more putatively nation-state-based countries of Western

Europe or the complex, integrated, immigrant-based societies such as the United States.[6] This literature and our understanding of deeply divided diverse societies have come a very long way since the early work, focusing, for example, in the early post–Cold War period on "ethnic conflict" and more recently on the multidimensional challenges of diversity and difference.[7]

Religious difference within complex, deeply divided societies has long been at the heart of this analysis—from the early work on religious parties by Arend Lijphart in the Netherlands (Lijphart 1977) to Donald Horowitz's classic work, *Ethnic Groups in Conflict* (Horowitz 2000). Within this literature there is also a keen appreciation of the extensive role of elites—from analyses of how elites "play the communal card" to evaluation of the horizontal linkages between cultural, economic, and political elites and grass roots (Lederach 1997).[8]

Today there is a renewed focus on religion and conflict management in divided societies, seen poignantly in the literature on peacemaking and in contemporary "peacebuilding" (especially apropos of reconciliation processes).[9] Equally, understanding the role of religion is essential to US foreign policy, especially given that religion indeed shapes the US perspective of the world (Albright 2006). In the analysis of engagement with religious actors, two conundrums emerge: How can negotiation be conducted with those espousing higher-priority values? How can leaders achieve social transformation goals without being intolerant?

This book addresses four subsidiary questions in the analysis of religion and religious leaders in deeply divided societies.[10]

- What are the relationships among religion, national identity, and state character and authority, and how does religious belief affect the dynamics of conflict in deeply divided societies within the state?
- How do religious leaders affect social forces and, through social mobilization, help define intolerant or tolerant national identities?
- How do religious leaders rhetorically justify or mobilize for conflict in situations of violent struggle or affirmatively advocate for peace?
- What are the implications for the better understanding of the roles of religious leaders in peacemaking?[11]

The book's principal conceptual orientation is laid out by David Little in chapter 1, in which he analyzes the critical question of the complex relationships between religion, ethnonationalism, and intolerance. What religion can and does provide at times in divided societies is the "hateful motive" for intolerance that can lead to mass violence—at the extreme end, indiscriminate acts such as terrorism and genocide.[12] While religion is instrumental and manipulable in the application of most leading faith traditions toward or away from conflict, it cannot be a "cause" of conflict as such. Religious belief, however, constructively shapes the terms of conflict and provides an ideational framework through which conflict is interpreted. While root causes of conflict are often found in injustice, indignity, marginalization, inequality, deficits of basic needs, or the greed of a few, the state can be captured to be complicit in such mass violence. In Little's view, the critical question is the degree and nature to which religious identity blurs with ethnic identity and is fused with conceptualizations of the "nation" and the state. Little presents in the analysis two conceptualizations of religious interaction in divided societies: "tolerance" as a minimal form of interaction, subject to break-down in crisis, and a more extensive interpretation of tolerance, or "coexistence," in which religious difference is explicitly affirmed, protected, and, indeed, celebrated or affirmed by the state (through public holiday policies, for example). Little defines the distinctions between the minimalist forms of tolerance and a more extensive embrace of diversity. In divided societies, sustainable management of religious conflict over time requires the difficult process of moving beyond minimalist tolerance to a form of coexistence based on rights that reflect the global norms on freedom from discrimination on the basis of religion or belief. When this fails, as in Sudan, separation and the creation of a new "nation" may be the only solution.

This book then explores a number of case studies at the country level or, in the case of Sunni–Shi'a relations, at a more regional level. In chapter 2 Nader Hashemi investigates the complexity of the Sunni–Shi'a divide in Islam and considers its implications for conflict and coexistence in the Middle East. He underscores the importance of looking at the region in an integrated fashion and argues that, ironically, the social and political strife seen in the conflicts in Iraq, Afghanistan, and Israel/Palestine have created new opportunities for reconciliation and dialogue among Muslim religious leaders. In chapter 3 George Irani evaluates the role of the Vatican in its relationship with the Maronites in the context of the Lebanese civil war. Among the seventeen religious sects in Lebanon, the role of the Vatican in the conflict and into the post-Tai'f (1989) period sees its engagement in terms of efforts to secure the survival of Christianity in the Middle East. In chapter 4 Micheline Ishay explains the rise of extremism in Israel and in the Palestinian communities as a consequence of the uneven effects of globalization in recent years. She contends that "globalization, coinciding with the shift from an Israeli state-controlled economy to privatization of the Israeli economy in the mid-1980s, has in fact greatly exacerbated tensions within Israel and even more seriously within the Palestinian territories, and has forged the conditions underlying increasing religious and nationalist radicalism, spurring an ideological backlash which is now undermining peace efforts." In chapter 5 Scott W. Hibbard analyzes religion and conflict in Egypt, illustrating that leaders of ostensibly secular states have at times turned to religion to bolster weakening state legitimacy, which has in turn led to exclusion and conflict along intrareligious and sectarian lines.

Chapter 6 provides an authoritative look at the role of religion in Africa's longest-running war in Africa, which has at times been characterized principally, and simplistically, in Muslim versus Christian/Animist terms. Carolyn Fluehr-Lobban explains the role of religion in the conflict in Sudan in historical and contemporary terms. She reveals the myriad complexities and debates that swirl around mantles of religious authority, Arab-Muslim and African identities, and the role of interreligious councils in managing the still-unfolding process of defining a national identity in Sudan and newly independent South Sudan. In chapter 7 Rosalind Hackett explores the mixed record of religious conflict and cooperation in Nigeria. While there are areas of accord (particularly on socioeconomic welfare), there are deep divisions along Muslim and Christian lines and a history of religious-elite exacerbation of conflict. This mixed record is juxtaposed against a lively theater of interreligious peacemaking and an active civil society. Still, Nigeria remains deeply affected by intense local-level violence, as the religiously characterized ethnic riots of 2010 in Jos, Plateau State, attest.

In chapter 8 Mari Fitzduff explores the role of religion in Northern Ireland's twenty-seven years of "Troubles" and into the peace process that produced a power-sharing outcome in the celebrated Belfast Agreement of 1998. She describes the deeply religious dimensions of a conflict that appears on the surface not to be explicitly theological as such. The role of religious peacemaking has been limited, she argues, and her explanation focuses on social structures as an inhibiting factor in the ability of those religious leaders inclined toward peacemaking to be effective.

The rise of the Islamic Renaissance Party in Tajikistan in the early 1990s is the subject of Karina Korostelina's contribution in chapter 9. She describes how the Islamic resistance to the infant secular, postindependence state evolved in a troubled democratization process, the onset of civil war, and subsequent engagement of religious leaders in peace talks to end the conflict.

Susan Hayward, in chapter 10, delves into the role of Sinhalese nationalism and Buddhist conceptualizations of homeland in the civil war in Sri Lanka, and in particular the role of the monks in the peace process in the cease-fire of 2005 and the failed series of peace negotiations that fell to renewal of the conflict and a costly military end in 2009. In a case that is typically described in terms of conflict, not peace, she shows how various religious actors are working at the individual level to buttress interreligious coexistence on the blood-spilled island. In chapter 11 Sumit Ganguly and Praveen Swami explore the role of religion in Asia's longest-running conflict, Kashmir. They explore three episodes of crises over the history of the conflict, and they draw common conclusions about the various roles of religion in the dispute over the valley. They argue that "political leadership in Jammu and Kashmir drew its legitimacy, at least in part, as a representative and champion of religious causes. . . . Secular political mobilization and religious chauvinism were closely, often inextricably, enmeshed. As such, politicians—not priests—held the keys to the resolution of religion-driven conflicts, and continue to do so."

The book's concluding chapter ties together several threads in the analysis presented in these rich case studies. The first thread presents findings on the various types of religious leaders that have been seen in the case studies and makes some generalized findings about the conditions under which religious elites engage in speech that directly or indirectly incites violence and, in the worst instances, endorses genocide, terrorism, or other mass atrocities. With these findings the implications for international engagement to promote religious tolerance in deeply divided societies are drawn in two areas: the further evolution of norms on religious tolerance and the need to focus on norms against incitement to violence as opposed to efforts to declare the "defamation of religion" as against the norm of tolerance. However, the question of "defamation" remains in debate and is a special interest of the Organization of the Islamic Conference, for example. Thus, there is a difference in basic perceptions of tolerance that needs further exploration through the future interreligious dialogue. Second, the general principles of operational peacemaking are drawn to place emphasis on a core principle for peace in societies torn along religious lines: the need to go beyond mere tolerance to a higher standard of "parity of esteem," or coexistence, as an underlying basis for sustainable peace in societies now riveted along religious lines.[13]

NOTES

1. See the "Report of the Official Account of the Bombings in London on July 7, 2005," Report to the House of Commons," May 11, 2006; posted on the BBC News website at http://news.bbc.co.uk/2/shared/bsp/hi/pdfs/11_05_06_narrative .pdf. In 2004 then–French interior minister Nicolas Sarkozy also pledged to deport Islamist clerics who preach support for violence. In the immediate aftermath of the July 7 attacks, the House of Commons adopted the Terrorism Act (c.11, § 1(1)) (England) in 2006 that makes illegal the "glorification of terrorism," despite public and furtive debate in the House of Lords seeking to strip the bill of the term "glorification" on the grounds of an inability to render a precise definition of the term.

2. The distinction between "warrant" and "injunction to act" has been advanced by David Little (1994, 101) in his study of religion and intolerance in Sri Lanka, "There can be little doubt that religious belief has, for several reasons functioned in an important way as a warrant for intolerance so far as the Sinhalese Buddhists are concerned. There is also evidence, although it is more controversial and perhaps less pronounced, that the same is true for the Tamils."

3. Taylor describes the Council of Churches mediation as well as other denominational efforts such as those by the Quaker Peace Center (Taylor 2002).

4. The oft-cited case of the mediation by the Catholic lay society the Community of Sant' Egidio in Mozambique is exemplary.

5. See Appleby's book *The Ambivalence of the Sacred: Religion, Violence, and Reconciliation* (1999). For an additional recent analysis of religion and justification violence, see Juergensmeyer (2003).
6. For an evaluation of world attitudes on religion and politics, see Norris and Inglehart (2004); for an analysis of when religious issues make the political agenda in democracies, see Stepan (2001).
7. See, as one example of ethnic conflict, Moynihan (1993). These terms "diversity" and "difference" are preferred because they do not prejudice the existence of "primordial" terms such as "ethnic," "racial," or even "sectarian," and they take into account gender and other salient sources of difference such as disability. Today, there is richer understanding that the term "deeply divided societies" captures the difficulties of coexistence in countries sharply or institutionally segmented such as Bosnia, Nigeria, Lebanon, South Africa, or Malaysia. Societies that are ethnically "plural" in their structure share similar difficulties of coexistence that other less structured but multiethnic societies also face; post-Soviet Russia, postcolonial United Kingdom, postimmigration France, and multiethnic Australia, for example, have witnessed serious intergroup tensions and sometimes violent confrontations in recent years.
8. A 1995 Human Rights Watch report found that "the 'communal card' is frequently played, for example, when a government is losing popularity or legitimacy, and finds it convenient to wrap itself in the cloak of ethnic, racial, or religious rhetoric" (Human Rights Watch 1995, viii).
9. For an overview from contributors with Christian, Jewish, and Muslim perspectives, see Smock 2002a and 2002b.
10. These themes are drawn from an assessment of the principal issues that have arisen in interfaith interactions in conflicts such as those in India (Kashmir), Iraq, Macedonia, Nigeria, and Sudan. See Smock (2006).
11. Interestingly, it is clear that religious leaders can evolve in the roles over time, illustrated by the journey of Nobel Peace Prize Laureate Desmond Tutu, who moved from nonviolent resister to mediator to reconciler. The meeting of the Rev. Ian Paisley Jr. in Northern Ireland with Archbishop Séan Brady, Archbishop of Armagh and Catholic Primate of All Ireland, on October 9, 2006, is also symbolic of these transformation possibilities.
12. See Juergensmeyer (2003), for an evaluation of religious justification of terrorism across various religious traditions. See also Benjamin and Simon (2002).
13. The concept "parity of esteem" in divided societies is developed by du Toit (2004).

REFERENCES

Albright, Madeleine. 2006. *The Mighty and the Almighty: Reflections on America, God, and World Affairs*. New York: HarperCollins.

Appleby, R. Scott. 1999. *The Ambivalence of the Sacred: Religion, Violence, and Reconciliation*. Lanham, MD: Rowman and Littlefield.

———. 2001. "Building Peace to Combat Religious Terror." *Chronicle of Higher Education*, September 28. Available at http://chronicle.com/article/Building -Peace-to-Combat/11462.

Benjamin, David, and Steve Simon. 2002. *The Age of Sacred Terror*. New York: Random House.

Coward, Howard G., and Gordon S. Smith. 2004. *Religion and Peacebuilding*. Albany: State University of New York Press.

du Toit, Pierre. 2004. "'Parity of Esteem': A Conceptual Framework for Assessing Peace Processes, with a South African Case Study." *International Journal of Comparative Sociology* 45:195–212.

Gopin, Marc. 2000. *Between Eden and Armageddon: The Future of World Religions, Violence, and Peacemaking*. New York: Oxford University Press.

Horowitz, Donald. 2000. *Ethnic Groups in Conflict*, 2nd ed. Berkeley: University of California Press.

Human Rights Watch. 1995. *Playing the Communal Card: Communal Violence and Human Rights*. New York: Human Rights Watch.

Juergensmeyer, Mark. 2003. *Terror in the Mind of God: The Global Rise of Religious Violence*. Berkeley: University of California Press.

Lederach, John Paul. 1997. *Building Peace: Sustainable Reconciliation in Divided Societies*. Washington, DC: US Institute of Peace Press.

Lijphart, Arend. 1977. *Democracy in Plural Societies: A Comparative Exploration*. New Haven, CT: Yale University Press.

Little, David. 1994. *Sri Lanka: The Invention of Enmity*. Washington, DC: US Institute of Peace Press.

Moynihan, Daniel Patrick. 1993. *Pandemonium: Ethnicity in International Politics*. Oxford: Oxford University Press.

Norris, Pippa, and Ronald Inglehart. 2004. *Sacred and Secular: Religion and Politics Worldwide*. Cambridge: Cambridge University Press.

Rahimi, Babak. 2007. "Ayatollah Sistani and the Democratization of Post-Ba'athist Iraq." US Institute of Peace *Special Report* 187, June 2007.

Sampson, Cynthia. 2007. "Religion and Peacebuilding," In *Peacemaking in International Conflict*, 2nd ed., eds. I. William Zartman and J. Lewis Rasmussen. Washington, DC: US Institute of Peace Press.

Smock, David, ed. 2002a. *Interfaith Dialogue and Peacebuilding*. Washington, DC: US Institute of Peace Press.

———, ed. 2002b. *Religious Perspectives on War: Christian, Jewish, and Muslim Attitudes Toward Force*. Washington, DC: US Institute of Peace Press.

———, ed. 2006. *Religious Contributions to Peacemaking: When Religion Brings Peace, Not War*. Washington, DC: US Institute of Peace, *Peaceworks* series.

Stepan, Alfred C. 2000. "Religion, Democracy, and the 'Twin Tolerations.'" *Journal of Democracy*, vol. 11, no. 4 (October): 37–57.

Taylor, Rupert, 2002. "South Africa: The Role of Peace and Conflict Resolution Organizations in the Struggle against Apartheid." In *Mobilizing for Peace: Conflict Resolution in Northern Ireland, Israel/Palestine, and South Africa*. Oxford: Oxford University Press.

CHAPTER 1

RELIGION, NATIONALISM, AND INTOLERANCE

ᐢᐤ

DAVID LITTLE

The end of the Cold War and the collapse of the former Soviet Union reminded the world of the importance of ethnic and religious nationalism, a topic eclipsed in two ways by the Cold War. Countries such as Ukraine, long subjected to Soviet control, started in the late 1980s to mount an independence campaign that was, and still is, strongly colored by religion.[1] Something similar happened in the struggle between Azerbaijan and Armenia over Nagorno-Karabakh shortly after the two states gained national independence from the Soviet Union. The Bosnian war, from 1992–95, was the result of the disintegration of Yugoslavia, which was also an indirect outcome of the collapse of the former Soviet Union. Once liberated from the breakaway communist dictatorship of Josip Broz Tito, Yugoslavia's constituent ethnoreligious groups, principally the Serb Orthodox, the Croatian Catholics, and the Bosniak Muslims, fell into bloody conflict. The war in Kosovo in 1999 was simply a further consequence of the same circumstances. Again, religion served to symbolize and accentuate competing ethnic interests between the Serb Orthodox and Albanian Muslims of Kosovo after Tito's controlling hand had been removed.

If these examples illustrate the dramatic spread of nationalism after the decline of the Cold War, other examples demonstrate the way in which the Cold War distorted the understanding of nationalism. Cases such as Sri Lanka, Sudan, Israel/Palestine, Northern Ireland, Lebanon, Nigeria, and Tibet, not to mention Kashmir, Cyprus, South Africa, and India/Pakistan—all of them colored to a greater or lesser degree by ethnic or religious differences, or both—were there all along but were either unnoticed or were not seen for what they were until the 1990s. As long as such examples were viewed through the lens of the Cold War, they were understood either as functions of East–West rivalry or as incidental sideshows. These nationalist conflicts did not suddenly erupt when the Cold War ended; they were simply perceived in a new way.

To the extent that religious and ethnic identity affected post–Cold War nationalist conflicts, the influence was not only in the direction of violence and antagonism, though that influence was certainly there. In a powerful way, religious individuals and groups also helped guide the national transition from authoritarianism—whether communist, as in East Germany and Poland, or anticommunist, as in South Africa and the Philippines—toward greater democracy and ethnic and religious tolerance. These examples of the contribution of enlightened religious leadership (and, in South Africa, enlightened ethnic leadership) toward forms of nationalism that are inclusive and tolerant rather than exclusive and intolerant dramatically illustrates the variability or "ambivalence" (Appleby 2000) of the impact of religious and ethnic ideals on the culture and organization of the nation-state. The fact that religious and ethnic ideals are capable of encouraging both constructive and destructive forms of nationalism is a point of the greatest significance.

One other preliminary point of interest to students of nationalism might be referred to as the stubborn resilience of the nationalist impulse. In a world where the nation-state is insistently threatened from above by the transnational pressures of globalization and from below by the fissiparous pressures of multiculturalism, the persistence of the spirit of nationalism is nothing short of amazing. Still, there it is, typically reinforced by religious or ethnic consciousness, animating intense and sometimes hostile competition both within and among the nations of the world and regularly frustrating international efforts at political, military, economic, or environmental cooperation. Although there are some examples of progressive religious, ethnic, and other forms of leadership, the practical effects of the spirit of nationalism on the international scene at present, even among some of the more "liberal" countries, is generally weighted more toward impeding than advancing global collaboration. How such obstructionism can be overcome, both within and among nations, is one of the most urgent problems facing the world community.

RELIGION, NATIONALISM, AND INTOLERANCE

Nationalism is best understood in relation to the coalescence of nation and state. If a nation or people is taken to be a community defined by a common historical and cultural identity, and a state, at least in its modern form, is taken to designate those institutions officially responsible to direct and regulate the political order on the basis of a monopoly of legitimate and effective coercion with respect to the inhabitants of a given territory, then nationalism refers to the affirmation of national or popular identity as the basis of state legitimacy.[2] In the words of Anthony Marx and Benedict Anderson, nationalism is "a collective sentiment or identity, bounding and binding together those individuals who share a sense of large-scale political solidarity aimed at creating, legitimating, or challenging states" (Marx 2003, 6) and as such rests on the idea of a nation imagined "as a deep, horizontal comradeship" (Anderson 1991, 7).

The word "nation" is a synonym for "people," or "tribe," conveying the idea of an extended "birth community," from the Latin, *natio* ("nativity," "native"). The tie between birth and national identity is thus always salient in conceptions of the nation. However, we also emphasize that nationalism is a modern phenomenon— the term did not appear until the nineteenth century. That is because it is only in connection with the modern state that the idea of nation "as a deep, horizontal comradeship" makes sense. That the modern state is able to gain an effective monopoly of legitimate coercion by means of modern techniques of enforcement and standardization, and is thereby able to consolidate and regulate political and economic power, not to mention cultural life, makes possible "mass societies" within tightly regulated territorial boundaries. Ancient Israel combined the idea of a people with a political system, at least sporadically, but the arrangement was hardly bounded or centralized and regulated to anywhere near the extent modern states are.

Accordingly, a nationalist conflict is a contest, sometimes violent, between two or more groups claiming the right to rule within a given territory based upon competing conceptions of nationhood. In short, nationalist conflicts are contests over which national ideal will prevail in a given nation-state. Such conflicts are often described as ethnic or religious, or as ethnoreligious, because it is assumed that the competing ideals of nationhood are shaped or strongly influenced by considerations of ethnic or religious identity.

Nationalist conflicts typically involve the problem of ethnic and religious intolerance because beliefs about ethnic and religious identity, which shape the ideals of nationhood, are seen to be important in creating and maintaining a durable state. Beliefs that challenge the regnant ideals, that seek to make room for alternative conceptions of national life, are frequently perceived as undermining and destabilizing a given nation-state. Therefore, a strong incentive exists for both political and religious leaders to suppress and penalize competing religious or ethnic beliefs. I shall elaborate on this issue shortly.

There are two points of serious controversy about this way of characterizing nationalist conflicts that need to be dealt with, one terminological and the other theoretical or causal. The terminological problem is raised by the fact that in discussions of nationalism the conceptual differences and connections between "ethnic" and "religious" are not usually made clear. "Ethnic" denotes "origin by birth or descent," but it also denotes, in a more archaic but still potent usage, "a person not of the Christian or Jewish faith," as in "heathen," or "gentile"—namely, a spiritual alien or outsider.[3]

Consequently, "ethnic" can mean different things. It may designate membership in a group determined by inherited characteristics (genealogical lineage, language, manners and mores, etc.) that are not necessarily "religious" in the sense of reflecting adherence to a sacred authority, or other indicia commonly accepted as identifying a religion.[4] At the same time, "ethnic" may also, and often does, take on a distinctly "religious" connotation, a condition by no means restricted to Christianity or Judaism. In that case, groups are distinguished and evaluated depending on the degree to which they exhibit faithful adherence to a preferred religion. In combination with religion, then, genealogy, language, inherited manners and mores, and other ethnic characteristics all assume a strongly normative tone reflected in widely employed terms such as "chosen people."

The widespread tendency of ethnic groups in all cultural contexts to authenticate themselves religiously lends plausibility to the term "ethnoreligious." The tendency also explains why it is artificial to try to distinguish too sharply between religious and nonreligious ethnic attributes in particular cases. In those instances where religious identity becomes ethnically salient, language, customs, and even genealogy take on strongly religious overtones.

Furthermore, it is the central role of ethnic and religious impulses in forming the identity of a people or nation that directly ties these matters to discussions of nationalism and nationalist conflict. Although ethnic groups or peoples do not necessarily need a religious reason to seek to preserve and promote their identity by achieving political sovereignty, a claim of religious legitimacy is likely to strengthen and intensify such a campaign.

Still, with all this appropriate and generally not-well-appreciated emphasis on the conceptual distinctions and connections between ethnicity and religion, an important proviso should be emphasized. Significant "trans-ethnic" impulses exist in religious traditions alongside "pro-ethnic" ones. For example, there are references in the New Testament to the requirement of forsaking family and ethnic group in the name of new, higher obligations, as well as to the superiority of celibacy to marriage. Indeed, the whole idea—essential to Christianity—of being born again as a member of a new family, a new people in the sacrament of baptism, underscores this trans-ethnic dimension.

A belief in the superiority of "spiritual" to "natural" relations, including sexual relations, is, of course, central to all celibate monastic movements, not only in Christianity but in other religions such as Buddhism and Hinduism as well, and that belief obviously represents a direct challenge to the priority of biological heredity. A different form of the same emphasis can be found in all religions of conversion because, ideally, personal voluntary commitment to fundamental religious tenets supersedes the status of birth or ethnic membership. This would apply in general to Islam, even though "origin by birth" does bestow special status on certain direct descendents of Mohammed. The contrast and tension between "pro-ethnic" and "trans-ethnic" religious impulses, sometimes within the same religion, is occasionally an important dimension of nationalist disputes over the meaning of national identity.

The theoretical or causal problem is raised by the conflicting claims of social scientists and others that nationalist conflicts are not about ethnicity and religion at all but rather are about economic and political matters, or that they are at bottom more about ethnic than religious issues. As to the first claim, Paul Collier, former World Bank economist, has famously argued that national civil wars are basically the product of "greed, not grievance," presumably including ethnic and religious grievances (Collier 2001). Economic conditions, such as low national income connected with slow economic growth and accelerated population increase, together with the availability of unscrupulous entrepreneurs, make countries susceptible to nationalist conflicts. "Where rebellions happen to be financially viable, wars will occur" (154). Charges of cultural, economic, or political mistreatment by one or another party to a conflict are of no causal significance for the onset of violent conflict except, Collier concedes, in multiethnic societies where one ethnic or ethnoreligious group constitutes between 45 and 90 percent of the population—"enough to give it control but not enough to make discrimination against a minority pointless" (149).

The problem with Collier's argument, and with similar arguments by others, is that proponents do not prove what they set out to prove.[5] It is not just that Collier himself admits what turns out to be a huge and very consequential exception to his argument: All of the ethnoreligious majorities in the four very important cases of nationalist conflict—the Sinhala Buddhists in Sri Lanka, the Arabized-Islamized Northerners in Sudan, the Serbs in the former Yugoslavia, and the Shi'a Arabs in Iraq—constitute between 45 and 90 percent of the relevant populations and thus have reason to institute discriminatory policies against minority populations that, on Collier's own terms, would significantly affect the causes of violent conflict. In other words, Collier's thesis by his own admission has no explanatory power in regard to four of the most notable current nationalist contests.

Beyond that, Collier also admits that during the course of even unexceptional national civil wars, grievances (presumably including ethnic and religious grievances) and not just greed do become potent in influencing the direction and outcome of the war. He emphasizes the importance of a "sense of injustice" and a perception of discrimination in legitimating an insurgency and in rallying recruits to its cause, and he explicitly mentions that grievances concerning things like equitable government provision for education and health must be taken into account in any sustainable peace settlement (Collier 2001, 153). If that is so, then it is not simply economic factors that must be addressed in resolving nationalist conflicts, as his thesis about the priority of greed over grievance would seem to imply. Again, it appears that even in regard to the conflicts to which Collier believes his thesis does apply, ethnic and religious grievances, undoubtedly along with other concerns, eventually become very salient when considered in relation to the overall course of a nationalist conflict.

Another scholar, Ted Robert Gurr, while he assigns substantially more significance to grievance as a cause of nationalist conflict than does Collier, nevertheless plays down the causal importance of religion in contrast to the ethnic factor (see Gurr 1993, 2000; Harff and Gurr 2004). The difficulty is that some of his data and arguments do not support this conclusion. In *Peoples versus States* he writes: "The only conclusion drawn here [about the effects of group type on political action] is that religiously defined communal groups are not a relevant factor in a risk model of ethnorebellion" (Gurr 2000, 232). But fifty-five pages later, Gurr turns around and draws some large, ominous conclusions about the global risks of ethnorebellion in a revealing comment about intolerant Islamist political leaders. "Probably the greatest threats to [peaceful ethnonational relations] come from predatory, hegemonic elites who use the state as an instrument to protect and promote the interests of their own people at the expense of others. These and other sources of communal warfare and repression remain in many corners of the world and will continue to cast up challenges to those who would contain ethnic violence" (287). As the reference to the Islamist leaders suggests, religious identity appears after all, on Gurr's own accounting, to be relevant to the risks of nationalist conflict in regard both to minorities and to dominant state structures.[6]

Thus, the subject of religion, nationalism, and intolerance is very complicated, if only because it involves so many elements, and it is therefore in urgent need of a carefully conceived, sensitively applied multivariate approach, one that combines scientific and humanistic methods of investigation. In keeping with the canons of scientific inquiry, it needs rigorous definitions of terms and explicit standards of comparison, verification, and (where relevant) quantification. In keeping with the canons of humanistic inquiry, it needs the additional tools of historical, cultural, and legal analysis capable of identifying and appreciating the salience of "soft" factors, such as religious, ethnic, and other values that are so indispensable in constructing social and political legitimacy. The beginnings of such an approach are suggested in the next section.

THE DYNAMICS OF NATIONALISM

Building on the relation of the idea of nationalism to the coalescence of nation and (modern) state, taking into account the possible influence of religious and ethnic factors on notions of nationhood or peoplehood as the basis for state legitimacy, and, finally, recalling the variable implications of all this for tolerance and peace or intolerance and violence, we may suggest the following figure as a graphic sketch of the suggested approach.[7]

FIGURE 1   Relationships among Religious Tolerance, State, and Nation

	Regime Type *(Character of the State)*	
	Constitutional Democracy	*Non-Democratic*
Religiously tolerant, inclusive definition of the "Nation"	**Liberal Nationalism** *(high levels of democracy and high levels of religious tolerance)*	**Tolerant Non-Democratic Nationalism**
Type of Nationalism (Legitimacy of the State)		
Religiously intolerant, exclusive definition of the "Nation"	**Intolerant Democratic Nationalism**	**Illiberal Nationalism** *(low levels of democracy and low levels of religious tolerance)*

The general notion is that under the impulse of nationalism, nation and state coalesce in different ways, with variable consequences for the incidence of violence. The assumptions are that ethnic or religious values along with a variety of "external influences" are indispensable in constructing the ideals of the nation, that ethnic and religious attitudes vary as to how tolerant (inclusive) or intolerant (exclusive) they are, and, further, that national ideals, in legitimating the state, also vary as between supporting constitutional democratic states and states that are illiberal democracies or are weak, predatory, or authoritarian in character.[8] Given that states are understood to be the product of their own specific "external influences," and that they exert their own reciprocal influence on the ethnic and religious values that make up the legitimating national ideals, the interaction between nation and state is probably best described as "synergistic," so as to avoid reductionist or simplistic theories of social causation.

The critical idea is that the point of convergence on the figure between the type of state and degree of ethnic/religious tolerance associated with the national ideals determines the kind of nationalism—whether liberal (high degree of national tolerance combined with a strong constitutional democratic state) or illiberal (high degree of national intolerance combined with an illiberal democracy, or with a weak, predatory, or authoritarian regime), and its relation to the probability of violence. The supposition is that as the conditions of a given nation-state move toward the upper left-hand corner of the table, in the direction of liberal nationalism, the likelihood of violence will decrease. Contrariwise, as conditions move toward the lower right-hand corner, in the direction of illiberal nationalism, the likelihood of violence will increase. The approach obviously leaves open the possibility of a wide range of different combinations of national ideals and state type with variable implications for the incidence of violence as well as a broader range of causal factors bearing on the incidence of violence than has been elaborated here.

The approach builds on the work of Jack Snyder.[9] Snyder focuses on the conditions under which nations in transition from authoritarianism to democracy restrain or encourage violence. Violence is mitigated, according to him, by means of "thick versions" of liberal or constitutional democracy, which make up what Snyder calls, "civic nationalism" (or sometimes, "liberal nationalism," which is the term we choose.) It consists of an ample set of preconditions for "a stable, productive, peaceful society" (Snyder 2000, 316–17). These preconditions are "a certain degree of wealth, the development of a knowledgeable citizenry, the support of powerful elites, and the establishment of a whole panoply of institutions to insure the rule of law and civic rights" (316). "The findings of [Snyder's] book suggest that only thickly embedded liberal polities are well insulated from the risk of developing belligerent, reckless forms of nationalism in the course of democratization" (318).

Conversely, "democratization in weakly institutionalized settings often plays into the hands of nationalist demagogues and swaggering populists" (319). Of special worry in this regard is what Snyder calls "ethnic nationalism" ("illiberal nationalism," in our terms). Here appeals are made to "common culture, language, religion, shared [history], and/or the myth of shared kinship," and they are typically employed "to include [and] exclude members from the national group" (319).

Snyder is particularly attentive to the predictability of intolerance and violence in relation to illiberal democracies and weak states, precisely because the institutions of restraint associated with "thickly embedded liberal polities" are missing or badly enfeebled. Under those conditions, exclusionary "outbidding" is politically very effective. That is where leaders and elites outdo one another in making "legitimacy bids" favoring one religious or ethnic group and demeaning others, with great political benefit. Such an outcome, especially in a society with scarce opportunities, wealth, and resources, in turn readily fuels violence. A good illustration is the connection between the ongoing ethnic conflict in Sri Lanka and the distinctly illiberal form of democracy that has existed there since independence in 1948. It was exactly the unsavory combination of electoral democracy, unconstrained by adequate minority protection and other critical constitutional restraints, with the insistent chauvinism of the majority Sinhala ethnic group that led to a form of "majoritarian dictatorship" and eventually to civil war (Little 1994).

Snyder's conclusions may be extended to include predatory and authoritarian states. While the term "predatory state," introduced in a recent book by Larry Diamond (2008), appears to share some of the characteristics and effects of illiberal democracies and weak states, its key distinguishing feature is the widespread existence of corruption. Diamond's description bears importantly on our concern with the potential for violence of nation-states that deviate from the standards of a tolerant constitutional democracy.

> The predatory society is the inverse of the civic community.... There is no real community, no shared commitment to any common vision of the public good, and no respect for law. Behavior is cynical and opportunistic. Those who capture political power seek to monopolize it and the rents that flow from it. Thus, if there are competitive elections, these become a bloody zero-sum struggle where everything is at stake and no one can afford to lose. People ally with one another in the quest for power and privilege, but not as equals ... 'Corruption is widely regarded as the norm,' political participation is mobilized from above, civic engagement is meager, compromise is scarce, and 'nearly everyone feels powerless, exploited, and unhappy.' ...
>
> Very often, social fragmentation is reinforced by ethnic, linguistic, and other forms of identity cleavage that keeps the oppressed from collaborating and enables the privileged to rally ready political support. All too often, predatory elites mobilize ethnic tension or nationalism in order to direct public frustration and resentment away from their own exploitative behavior. Yet ethnic tensions and nationalist resentments have an independent origin, which is why elites often find such success when they inflame them. From Nigeria to the Congo, from Columbia to Kosovo, from Serbia to Sudan, ethnic violence, nationalist bloodletting, and civil war have been heavily mixed up with the corruption of cynical elites. (Diamond 2008, 298)

Our central contention that the violence potential rises as illiberal democracies and weak or predatory states combine with increasing degrees of national intolerance also applies to authoritarian states. Nazi Germany's combination of extreme authoritarianism and extreme national intolerance yielded exceedingly high levels of violence, at home and abroad, and thereby exemplified illiberal nationalism in its paradigmatic form, though there are other smaller-scale examples such as Serbia under Slobodan Milosevic. While the connection needs to be explored empirically, authoritarian states appear to draw life from ethnic or religious intolerance as a way of justifying the degree of violence required to maintain power.

At the same time, authoritarian states vary from dictatorial forms, such as Nazi Germany, to more paternalistic forms, such as present-day Singapore, with important consequences for the violence potential score. Singapore is unquestionably an authoritarian regime with pervasive, if subtle, forms of coercive repression (Diamond 2008, 209). But maintaining a system where the government "cater[s] to the welfare of all citizens" (211) takes into account both "its mass base to which it remains highly responsive" and the society's "elite[s] whom it works hard to co-opt" (209). Singapore does not rely on anything like the degree of coercion that was characteristic of Hitler's Germany or other strictly dictatorial regimes. Undoubtedly, an important part of the reason for the reduced violence potential is that "the regime has forged a national consciousness across the Chinese/Malay/Indian divide" (212) by ensuring racial balance in electoral procedures and by other measures. In other words, a significant ingredient of Singapore's paternalistic authoritarianism is the deliberate encouragement of national tolerance toward the different ethnic groups that make up the society. This does not mean, incidentally, that the present system is fixed in stone. "As education and income levels continue to rise, pressure will mount to free the press, make the electoral system fairer and more competitive, and reform the authoritarian 'mindset, ideology, and hierarchy' of the ruling party, which may constitute the most essential and most difficult reform of all" (212). The impact that efforts at constitutional democratic reform will have on national ideals of ethnic tolerance in Singapore will be something to watch.

The approach highlights certain key points of reference in the dynamics of nationalism that appear to affect the incidence of violence. It is of course far from being a rigorous causal theory, though there is some empirical support for the importance of the designated points of reference. The work of Gurr, mentioned earlier, concludes that since around 1995, "more effective international and domestic strategies for managing ethnopolitical conflict" and majority–minority relations have been developed. This trend is described as a "global shift from ethnic warfare to the politics of accommodation." Among the 275 minorities studied, more and more of them are turning to participatory politics and abandoning armed violence, thereby reversing a long-standing pattern (Gurr 2000, 275–77).

Gurr identifies two principles of special significance as comprising what he calls an "emerging regime of managed heterogeneity." One is "the recognition and active protection of the rights of minority peoples: freedom from discrimination based on race, national origin, language, or religion, complemented by institutional means to protect and promote collective interests" (278). The other is that of political democracy, "in one of its European variants," which is "as the most reliable guarantee of minority rights." "It is inherent in the logic of [constitutional] democratic politics that all peoples in heterogeneous societies should have equal civil and political rights" (279). Gurr does, however, caution that the process by which developing nation-states move toward constitutional democracies is typically not smooth but rather is fraught with difficulty and complexity. In such situations, he says, "a mix of democratic and autocratic features are somewhat better able to contain ethnopolitical conflict than new Western-style democracies" (163). This is an area that clearly calls for much more careful comparative study.

Another area requiring more extensive study is the impact of external influences on the state and the shape of national ideals in regard to the dynamics of nationalism. In cases of continuing ethnoreligious conflict, such as Bosnia, Sudan, and Iraq, it would be impossible to understand the current structure of the state without considering the role of international involvement. Apart from the Dayton Accords of 1995 in Bosnia, the Comprehensive Peace Agreement of 2005 in Sudan, or the impact of US intervention in Iraq beginning in 2003, present-day Bosnia, Sudan, and Iraq would have a very different character.

As to external influences on religious and ethnic ideals in these and other countries, considerable evidence exists concerning the consequences of colonial policies on postcolonial national identity. One of the best accounts remains Benedict Anderson's discussion in his classic study of nationalism, *Imagined Communities* (1991). He shows the ambivalent effects of European colonialism on the development of ethnic and religious tolerance in the nations of the "new world," conclusions that have been widely replicated by studies of other regions.[10] In addition to the impact of colonialism, a new body of literature has begun to emerge in the 1990s and the first decade of the twenty-first century that identifies the generally liberalizing effects on the spread of ethnic and religious inclusiveness produced by individuals and groups dedicated to what might be called transnational peace activism (see Little 2007b; Marshall and Van Saanen 2007; Coward and Smith 2004).

FURTHER THOUGHTS ON "TOLERANCE"/"INTOLERANCE"

A key theoretical assumption of this approach is that while attitudes of national tolerance and intolerance interact with and are no doubt affected by state structures in the process of establishing the type of nationalism and the violence potential score, such attitudes ultimately have, as Diamond put it, "an independent origin"—independent, that is, of political, economic, or other purely "material interests." That means, as Max Weber believed, that the "legitimating task"—the activity of justifying political, economic, and other social institutions—is logically distinct from the political, economic, and other human interests served by these institutions. Accordingly, such things as religious and ethnic ideals are taken to introduce their own "independent" stamp on the formation and maintenance of the nation-state, thus accounting in part for the degree of national tolerance or intolerance as well as the kind of state organization that results. Describing the relation between nation and state as synergistic, as we did, is intended to call attention to both the mutual interdependence and the mutual independence of nation and state.

The implication, as we have stressed, is that religious and ethnic traditions, sometimes separately, sometimes in combination, make their own distinctive contribution to whether the national ideals in a given case are tolerant or intolerant, and to whether the preferred state system is a constitutional democracy. Against simplistic views that religion and ethnicity invariably favors intolerance and anti-democracy (however much they do), we must emphasize some clear historical evidence to the contrary.

Strong religious influence on the rise of liberal nationalism appeared in seventeenth-century England and Colonial America. In those places, ardent Puritans such as John Milton and Roger Williams and the Levellers advocated an influential social and political ideal based on religious and ethnic inclusiveness, and on the equal freedom of all citizens, including the equal right of political participation and the freedom of conscience, the separation of church and state, the division of executive and legislative powers, due process protections, and regulations against arbitrary government interference in trade and business and in the confiscation of property.

An additional point of enormous importance is the fact that accompanying the establishment of the modern system of nation-states as the result of the Peace of Westphalia in 1648 there arose, under "strongly Calvinistic" influence, a new understanding of international law. The critical figure was Alberico Gentili, an Italian-born liberal Calvinist who taught international law at Oxford around the turn of the seventeenth century. He was arguably "as much as if not more than Hugo Grotius, the progenitor of the existing law of nations," (van der Molen 1937, 12) and his classic work, *Three Books on the Laws of War* (see Gentili 1933), had an incalculable influence on Grotius's doctrine of the just war. Building his theory on the idea of natural rights,[11] Gentili maintained as early as 1598 that "no man's rights are violated by a difference in religion, nor is it lawful to make war because of religion. . . . Therefore a man cannot complain of being wronged because others differ from him in religion" (41). Echoing a central, if frequently muted, emphasis in Calvin, Gentili writes that "religion is a matter of mind and of the will, which is always accompanied by freedom . . . . Our minds and whatever belongs to [it] are not affected by any external power or potentate, and the soul has no master save God only" (van der Molen 1937, 245–56). Accordingly, the only truly just causes for the use of force inside or outside national borders are enforcing the legitimate temporal and material interests of nation-states and their citizens. The assumption is that confining religion as a cause or inspiration for war, whether civil or international, is an indispensable basis for peace.

Nor should we forget the abiding impact of the Anabaptist wing of the Reformation on tolerance and on political organization and the regulation of force. Here was another group of fervent believers, many of them as opposed to any use of force by Christians (or anyone else) as they were to applying the "power of the sword" to religious affairs. In addition, many of them, at considerable cost, advocated the right of Christians to direct their own affairs based on voluntary and democratic deliberation rather than at the behest of political or unelected church authorities. The Anabaptists had considerable influence on the growth of religious tolerance in Holland and England, and on the legacy of nonviolent action that has in recent years become more and more respectable. Accordingly, the "Radical Reformation" deserves considerable credit for encouraging a culture of tolerance, peace, and nonviolence.

It is not, of course, argued that this distinctive "religious input" is all there is to the rise of modern constitutional democracy or modern liberal ideals of ethnic and religious tolerance. History is much more complicated than that. Still, we do wish to make the point that religious and ethnic ideals matter, both positively and negatively, when it comes to the type of nationalism that gets established here or there.

This legacy provides the backdrop for the modern human rights system with its special provision for the protection of religious and other forms of "tolerance and nondiscrimination." Human rights came into favor after World War II as a consequence of a direct, comprehensive, and systematic assault against the equal liberty of religious and ethnic groups by the Nazi regime. It is no wonder, therefore, that "belief rights," the special set of human rights provisions safeguarding religious and other forms of freedom of expression and exercise, came to occupy such an important place in the human rights movement.

Of special interest, incidentally, is the fact that human rights, including belief rights, apply both to state organization and to the attitudes and commitments pertaining to what we have called national ideals. That is, the human rights system clearly favors constitutional democracy, including, in Snyder's words, the "whole panoply of institutions to insure the rule of law and civic rights" (Snyder 2000, 316), and it obligates states to cultivate, through education, "understanding, tolerance, and friendship among all nations, racial or religious groups" (United Nations 1948, Art. 26[2]).

Drawing on the natural rights tradition associated with sixteenth- and seventeenth-century liberal Calvinists, human rights documents provide a list of five protections or belief rights. The principal right, as formulated by Article 18 of the International Covenant on Civil and Political Rights (ICCPR), is stated as follows:

> Everyone shall have the right to freedom of thought, conscience and religion. The right shall include freedom to have or to adopt a religion or belief of his choice, and freedom, either individually or in community with others and in public and private, to manifest his religion or belief in worship, observance, practice and teaching. No one shall be subject to coercion which would impair his freedom to have or to adopt a religion or belief of his choice (ICCPR, Art. 18 [1, 2]).[12]

Freedom to manifest one's religion or belief may be subject only to such limitations as are prescribed by law and are necessary to protect public safety, order, health, or morals or the fundamental rights and freedoms of others (ICCPR, Art. 18 [3]; cf. DEID, Art. 1 [3]).

The following four provisions elaborate the safeguards:

- "Respect for the liberty of parents and, when applicable, legal guardians to ensure the religious and moral education of their children in conformity with their own convictions" (ICCPR, Art. 18 ([4]).
- "No one shall be subject to discrimination by any State, group of persons or person on the grounds of religion or other beliefs" (DEID, Art. 2 [1]) This right includes provisions against "intolerance based on religion or belief" (see DEID). Discrimination has a clear legal meaning in the documents, namely, "any distinction, exclusion, restriction or preference based on religion or belief and having as its purpose or as its effect nullification or impairment of the recognition, enjoyment or exercise of human rights and fundamental freedoms on an equal basis" (DEID, Art. 2 [2]. Cf. ICCPR, Art. 2 and 27, and UDHR Art. 2 and 7). While intolerance is equated with discrimination in certain sections of the documents (DEID, Art. 2 [2]), elsewhere it is not (ibid., Art. 4 [2]).
- "Persons belonging to [ethnic, religious or linguistic] minorities shall not be denied the right, in community with other members of their group, to enjoy their own culture, to profess and practice their own religion, and to use their own language" (ICCPR, Art. 27; cf. UDHR, Art. 27 [1]).
- The right against "religious . . . hatred that incites to discrimination, hostility or violence" (ICCPR, Art. 20 [1]; cf. UDHR Art. 7).

The point is that these five belief rights begin to spell out in legal form the meaning of equal liberty for religious, ethnic, and other forms of belief that is appropriate in a constitutional democracy, and they provide the outlines of the spirit of tolerance appropriate for national ideals. In a word, these rights become a critical part of the legal and attitudinal basis for liberal nationalism, and their violation for illiberal nationalism.

Finally, in understanding the relation of fundamental religious, ethnic, or other beliefs to the meaning of tolerance/intolerance, it is necessary to distinguish two types of intolerance: belief as target and belief as warrant. The first sort of intolerance occurs when the beliefs of an individual or group are singled out for oppression or persecution, as in the case of Jehovah's Witnesses or members of the Baha'i faith, who in some countries are the targets of extensive abuse. The implication is that tolerance in this first sense would mean not treating religious or ethnic groups in that way. Intolerance as warrant occurs when individuals or groups are singled out for oppression or persecution not because of their beliefs but because of the beliefs of those doing the oppressing or persecuting. Thus, African Americans have historically been subject to abuse because their oppressors have believed (often on religious grounds) that people with dark skin are disqualified for equal citizenship.

This distinction turns out to be empirically very important in refining the incidence of tolerance and intolerance in different settings (see Little 1994). In examining the religious and ethnic ideals in a given case, the objective is to trace out the grounds in a religious or ethnic tradition for intolerance as target or as warrant, thereby appreciating with increased sophistication the way different traditions contribute to national ideals and the legitimation of the state.

PERTINENCE TO ACTS OF TERROR

In terms of our approach, acts of terror, or the perpetration of genocide and other mass atrocity crimes, such as murder, "extermination, enslavement, deportation or forcible transfer of population, torture, or various forms of sexual violence," "when committed as part of a widespread or systematic attack directed against any civilian population, with knowledge of the attack,"[13] are emblematic of extreme forms of illiberal nationalism (with obviously very high violence potential scores), insofar as such acts are committed by states. That is the case because our approach provides a way of analyzing nationalism, which by definition represents a coalescence of nation and state. Nonstate terrorists are only relevant to our approach insofar as they have as their objective the creation or transformation of a state. If they do not have that objective, they are not strictly nationalists and fall outside our concern.

In commenting on the meaning of genocide, as defined by the Genocide Convention, William Schabas emphasizes the importance of mens rea, or the "intent to destroy," in determining culpability for committing genocide. He continues:

Genocide is by nature a collective crime, committed with the cooperation of many participants. It is, moreover, an offence generally directed by the State. The organizers and planners must necessarily have a racist or discriminatory motive that is a genocidal motive, taken as a whole. Where this is lacking, the crime cannot be genocide. Evidence of [a] hateful motive will constitute an integral part of the proof of the existence of a genocidal plan, and therefore of a genocidal intent" (Schabas 2000, 255).

He emphasizes that the critical words in Article 2 of the convention, "with intent to destroy . . . a [designated] group as such," encompasses both intent and motive.

To plan deliberately to destroy, in whole or in part, a designated group on the basis of a "hateful motive"—a motive embodying murderous contempt for the targeted group as such—is essential. It would seem reasonable to expand Schabas's comments to apply to the broader category of mass atrocity crimes as well.

Schabas's observations about the centrality of the "hateful motive"—understood as "racist" or "discriminatory" attitudes—in proving that genocide or (we are assuming) other mass atrocity crimes have been committed indicates the point at which religious and ethnic ideals become particularly relevant to committing acts of terror. Investigation of the role of religion in provoking genocide and other mass atrocities in the cases of Nazi Germany, Bosnia, and Rwanda reveals unmistakably how salient are "ideal factors" in intensifying and reinforcing the motives for carrying out such acts (Little 2008). A further point is the relation of all this to the belief rights discussion, and particularly to the right against "religious . . . hatred that incites to discrimination, hostility or violence" (ICCPR, Art. 20 (1); cf. UDHR, Art. 7).

CONCLUSION

In the light of nearly twenty years of reflection on the problems of religion and nationalism, I draw three main conclusions. First, nationalism is best understood as the coalescence of nation and state around the modern idea of political legitimacy. A nation, defined as a "people" espousing a distinctive common identity and aspiring to political autonomy on the basis of a sense of "deep, horizontal comradeship," presents itself as justifying a political authority intended to preside over the inhabitants of a sharply circumscribed territory. Second, religion and ethnicity assume prominence—variously, to be sure, and along with other important influences—in shaping the character and ideals of the nation and the organization of the state. At the same time, religion and ethnicity are themselves reciprocally influenced by the character and practice of the state.

Third, because religious or ethnic ideals play such a constitutive part in the dynamics of nationalism, the issue of religious and other forms of tolerance and intolerance become extremely salient in relation to the occurrence or mitigation of violence. Where effective constitutional democracies combine with a high degree of national tolerance—examples of "liberal nationalism," in our terms—a very low incidence of violence is predicted. Conversely, where illiberal democracies or weak, predatory, or authoritarian regimes strongly lacking the characteristics of constitutional democracy combine with a high degree of national intolerance—examples of "illiberal nationalism," in our terms—a high incidence of violence is predicted. If this approach is well founded, then studying the complex interrelations of religion, nationalism, and intolerance in the way outlined makes considerable sense.

NOTES

1. See the recent article on Ukraine; Anne Barnard, "Slavic Rivals Embroiled in Church Rift," *New York Times*, July 30, 2008, www.nytimes.com/2008/07/30/world/europe/30ukraine.html.

2. For a more elaborate version of a community defined by a common historical and cultural identity, see MacCormick (1999, 191). Max Weber's famous definition of the modern state is in Gerth and Mills (1958, 176). I would add "effective" to Weber's definition of the modern state, to account especially for authoritarian states. While even the most dictatorial authoritarian regime is not without some degree of popular legitimacy, important segments of the affected population likely do not share such attitudes and will need to be held in check by a high degree of "effective," if (from their point of view) "illegitimate," coercion. Indeed, authoritarianism as a system depends by definition on a high degree of effective coercive repression. If repression is not effective, the regime collapses. See Little (1995, 287–93) for an elaboration of Weber's contribution to the study of nationalism.

3. This specification represents a composite of interrelated terms drawn from three dictionaries: *Oxford English Dictionary* (Oxford, 1986); *Webster's New International Dictionary* (Springfield, MA, 1928); and *Funk & Wagnall's Standard Dictionary* (New York, 1958).

4. We refer to the helpful list of the defining characteristics of "religion" found in Alston's well-known discussion in *Philosophy of Language* (1964, 8). Alston's list refers to attributes such as a belief in supernatural beings, a distinction between sacred and profane reality together with attitudes of reverence and awe, ritual practices including prayer, and a moral code and patterns of social organization that are all formulated in reference to the sacred beliefs. Alston holds, plausibly, that the list will apply selectively and in different combinations to different religions, but that all religions will be understood to manifest some mixture of the defining characteristics. Although there are of course penumbral cases, the list of attributes works well in general, and in various combinations certainly characterizes the religions of four of the cases of nationalist conflict considered, for example, in Little and Swearer (2006): Western and Eastern Christianity (Bosnia), Western Christianity (Sri Lanka, Sudan), Sunni Islam (Bosnia, Iraq, Sri Lanka, and Sudan), Shi'a Islam (Iraq), Sufi Islam (Sudan), and Theravada Buddhism and Hinduism (Sri Lanka).

5. See, for example, Fearon and Laitin (2003), which emphasizes political over economic deficiencies as causes of national civil wars. Although the authors, like Collier, start out making the same claims about the irrelevance of grievances to the onset of civil war, on careful inspection they introduce along the way a number of qualifications that concede the salience of perceptions of mistreatment and injustice on the part of insurgent groups for the direction and outcome of nationalist conflicts.

6. For a critique of the opposite claim that religion invariably fosters violence in nationalist civil wars, see Little (2007a).

7. We do mean "sketch." To make this approach rigorously applicable, it will be necessary to fill out much more than we do here the defining characteristics of the kinds of state mentioned, the standards for measuring how far they are or are not present, and what is meant by "national tolerance" and "intolerance" as well as how those notions are to be measured. We hope enough is suggested in what follows to lend initial plausibility to the approach.

8. The notion of "external influences" in regard to both the state and nation refers to the complexity of historical and international conditions that must be taken into account to understand the character and performance of given nation-states in particular times and places.

9. This section is adapted from Little (2007a). See also Snyder (2000) and Mansfield and Snyder (2005).

10. See Little and Swearer (2006, 15–21) for a summary of the impact of colonialism on the notions of national identity in Iraq, Bosnia, Sri Lanka, and Sudan.

11. "Now this is a just cause [for the use of force, if] our own rights have been interfered with . . . . Everyone is justified in maintaining his rights" (Gentili 1933, 8).

12. International Covenant on Civil and Political Rights, Art. 18, (1,2): "1. Everyone shall have the right to freedom of thought, conscience and religion. This right shall include freedom to have or to adopt a religion or belief of his choice, and freedom, either individually or in community with others and in public or private, to manifest his religion or belief in worship, observation, practice, and teaching. 2. No one shall be subject to coercion, which would impair his freedom to have or to adopt a religion or belief of his choice." At www2.ohchr.org/english/law/ccpr .htm. (Note: The same terminology appears in the DEID, Article 1 (1) at www2 .ohchr.org/english/law/religion.htm.

13. Rome Statute of the International Criminal Court, Art. 7; http://untreaty.un.org /cod/icc/statute/romefra.htm.

REFERENCES

Alston, William P. 1964. *Philosophy of Language*. Englewood Cliffs, NJ: Prentice-Hall.

Anderson, Benedict. 1991. *Imagined Communities: Reflections on the Origin and Spread of Nationalism*, rev. ed. London: Verso.

Appleby, Scott. 2000. *The Ambivalence of the Sacred: Religion, Violence, and Reconciliation*. Lanham, MD: Rowman & Littlefield.

Barnard, Anne. 2008. "Slavic Rivals Embroiled in Church Rift." *New York Times*, July 30. www.nytimes.com/2008/07/30/world/europe/30ukraine.html.

Collier, Paul. 2001. "Economic Causes of Civil Conflict and Their Implications for Policy." In *Turbulent Peace: The Challenges of Managing International Conflict*, edited by Chester A. Crocker, Fen Osler Hampson, and Pamela Aall. Washington, DC: US Institute of Peace Press.

Coward, Harold, and Gordon S. Smith, eds., 2004. *Religion and Peacebuilding*. Albany: State University of New York Press.

Diamond, Larry. 2008. *The Spirit of Democracy: The Struggle to Build Free Societies throughout the World.* New York: Times Books/Henry Holt & Co.

Fearon, James D., and David D. Laitin. 2003. "Ethnicity, Insurgency, and Civil War," *American Political Science Review* 97, no. 1: 75–90.

Gentili, Alberico. 1933. *De iure belli libri tres,* vol. 2, translated by John C. Rolfe. Oxford: Clarendon Press.

Gerth, H. H., and C. Wright Mills, eds. 1958. *From Max Weber: Essays in Sociology.* Oxford: Oxford University Press.

Gurr, Ted Robert. 1993. *Minorities at Risk: A Global View of Ethnopolitical Conflict.* Washington, DC: US Institute of Peace Press.

———. 2000. *Peoples vs. States: Minorities at Risk in the New Century.* Washington, DC: US Institute of Peace Press.

Huff, Barbara, and Ted Robert Gurr. 2004. *Ethnic Conflict in World Politics.* Boulder, CO: Westview Press.

Little, David. 1994. *Sri Lanka: The Invention of Enmity.* Washington, DC: US Institute of Peace Press.

———. 1995. "Belief, Ethnicity, and Nationalism." *Nationalism and Ethnic Politics* 1:287–93.

———. 2007a. "A Double-Edged Dilemma: The Odd Dilemma of Religion and Nationalism." *Harvard Divinity Bulletin,* Autumn, 87–95.

———, ed., 2007b. *Peacemakers in Action: Profiles of Religion in Conflict Resolution.* New York: Cambridge University Press.

———. 2008. "Religion, Genocide, and Mass Atrocity Crimes: Some Background," Paper presented at the Religion, Genocide, and Mass Atrocity Crimes conference, US Institute of Peace, Washington, DC, April 10.

Little, David, and Donald K. Swearer, eds. 2006. *Religion and Nationalism in Iraq: A Comparative Perspective.* Cambridge, MA: Harvard University Press.

MacCormick, Neil. 1999. "Nation and Nationalism." In *Theorizing Nationalism,* ed. Ronald Beiner. Albany: State University of New York Press.

Mansfield, Edward D., and Jack Snyder, 2005. *Electing to Fight: Why Emerging Democracies Go to War.* Cambridge, MA: MIT Press.

Marshall, Katherine, and Marisa Van Saanen, 2007. *Development and Faith.* Washington, DC: World Bank.

Marx, Anthony W. 2003. *Faith in Nation: Exclusionary Origins of Nationalism.* New York: Oxford University Press.

Schabas, William. 2000. *Genocide in International Law.* Cambridge: Cambridge University Press.

Snyder, Jack. 2000. *From Voting to Violence: Democratization and Nationalist Conflict.* New York: W. W. Norton & Co.

United Nations. 1948. Universal Declaration of Human Rights [UDHR]. 1948. December 10. www.un.org/en/documents/udhr/index.shtml.

van der Molen, Gezina H. J., 1937. *Alberico Gentili and the Development of International Law: His Life and Work.* Amsterdam: H. J. Paris.

CHAPTER 2

RELIGIOUS LEADERS, SECTARIANISM, AND THE SUNNI–SHI'A DIVIDE IN ISLAM

༽

NADER HASHEMI

U nder what social conditions do Sunni and Shi'a religious leaders justify or catalyze violence along identity lines, and under what social conditions do they lay the foundation for, advocate for, and sometimes mediate peace? These are the overarching questions that this chapter seeks to explore. The relevancy of this inquiry is supported by two objective facts about the contemporary Islamic world that give this topic a pressing new urgency.

Religion is a key marker of identity today in the Muslim world across the Sunni–Shi'a divide. While this has not always been the case, recent polling confirms that religion trumps ethnicity and national citizenship as the main source of self-identification across Arab and Muslim societies.[1] Consequently, religious leaders are ideally suited to play a critical role in influencing norms and values, shaping political behavior, regulating conflict, and promoting peace and reconciliation. The 2003 US invasion of Iraq has marked a new phase of Sunni–Shi'a tension across the Middle East. Beyond the loss of life that has already occurred in Iraq's civil war, a serious potential exists for a major human rights catastrophe in the aftermath of a US troop withdrawal that could rise to genocidal proportions.[2] Should the situation in Iraq implode in this direction, fears of a regional war would increase as neighboring states (principally Iran and Saudi Arabia) would certainly intervene, giving this conflict a distinct Sunni versus Shi'a character. Focusing attention, therefore, on Sunni–Shi'a relations, is highly relevant to future political trends and areas of possible conflict in the Muslim world.

Recent scholarship has also emphasized the pressing significance of this subject. In his critically acclaimed book, *The Shia Revival: How Conflicts within Islam*

Will Shape the Future, Vali Nasr has suggested that traditional concepts and categories used to explicate the Middle East, such as modernity, democracy, fundamentalism, and nationalism, no longer adequately explain the politics of the region. It "is rather the old feud between Shias and Sunnis that forges attitudes, defines prejudices, draws political boundary lines, and even decides whether and to what extent those other trends have relevance" (Nasr 2006, 82). Moreover, Nasr astutely observers that even though Shi'as comprise only 10 to 15 percent of the 1.3 billion Muslim population, in "the Islamic heartland, from Lebanon to Pakistan . . . there are roughly as many Shias as there are Sunnis, and around the economically and geostrategically sensitive rim of the Persian Gulf, Shias constitute 80 percent of the population" (34). Recent conflicts in Iraq, Afghanistan, Lebanon, and the Gaza strip, and the sectarian and regional tensions that have flowed from these events lend credence to Nasr's claim.

This chapter argues that the relationship among social conditions, religious leaders, and issues of peace and conflict in the Muslim world is not straightforward, clear, or uncomplicated. Social conditions vary across Muslim societies; Islamic religious leaders are not a homogenous group, and issues of peace and conflict vary in intensity, scope, and size. It will be argued, however, that one cannot understand Sunni–Shi'a tensions today and the accompanying behavior of religious leaders outside of the national, regional, and international context that shapes these tensions, fuels them, and contributes to their perpetuation. This is the critical analytical framework that informs this study and sheds light on how Muslim religious leaders can contribute to conflict resolution and peaceful relations among sectarian groups. Rather than a single or set of case studies, this chapter provides a broad overview of topic and seeks to frame how this topic can be approached and better understood.

The discussion begins with some theoretical considerations on the relationship between religious mobilization and sectarianism. Drawing on the literature on ethnic political mobilization, this scholarship is useful in understanding Sunni–Shi'a conflict in our contemporary world due to the functional similarities between ethnic and religious mobilization. Then the critical social question "why now?" is answered. Why have Sunni–Shi'a sectarian relations deteriorated at this point in time and not before, and what factors have contributed to this outcome? In pursuit of an answer, the national, regional, and international context that has shaped the political environment in which religious leaders must operate is discussed. The rise of ultraconservative form of Islam in Saudi Arabia is explored, along with the consequences of the 1979 Islamic Revolution in Iran on sectarian relations in the Muslim world. Finally, the chapter examines the actual attempts that have been made to reach an accommodation, reduce conflict, and promote toleration between Sunnis and Shi'as. What specific issues have been sources of recent conflict among religious leaders? Several examples illuminate this topic. The chapter concludes with a set of recommendations on how the international community can encourage Muslim religious leaders to play a more constructive role in promoting peace, conflict resolution, and intersectarian harmony.

RELIGIOUS SECTARIANISM AND POLITICAL MOBILIZATION

There are at least three schools of thought in the social sciences that explain ethnonationalist mobilization: primordialism, instrumentalism, and constructivism.[3] They are useful in explaining the rise of religious sectarianism and political mobilization in Muslim societies today given that most mainstream forms of political Islam are religious forms of nationalism whose actors have accepted the borders of the postcolonial state and are fundamentally concerned with the internal national politics of their home countries (Kepel 2002, 23–135; Ayoob 2007, 1–22). Moreover, Muslim sectarian discourses of power and their underlying paradigm of politics are "ethnic" in the sense they are concerned with the politics of group identity where the group in question self-identifies with religion as a key marker of its identity (Nasr 2000, 172).

Furthermore, as David Little reminds us, there are several other ways in which ethnicity and religion are connected. In his survey and analysis of nationalist conflicts, he observes that "the widespread tendency of ethnic groups in all cultural contexts to authenticate themselves religiously lends plausibility to the term, 'ethno-religious.'" He notes that in particular cases "it is artificial to try to distinguish too sharply between religious and nonreligious ethnic attributes in particular cases. In those instances where religious identity becomes ethnically salient, language, customs, and even genealogy take on strongly religious overtones."[4] This suggests that, functionally speaking, ethnicity and religion are deeply intertwined and often overlap and mutually reinforce each other. Aspects of the Sunni–Shi'a divide, particularly between Iranian Shi'as and Arab Sunnis, support this view, thus giving credence to the use of the social scientific literature on nationalism and ethnic politics in assessing religious sectarianism and conflict in Muslim societies today.

Returning to the three schools of thought on what we can now call "ethnoreligious" nationalist mobilization, the first school, primordialism, views ethnicity as a shared sense of group identity that is natural and deeply imbedded in social relations and human psychology. For primordialists, ethnicity is based on a set of intangible elements rooted in biology, history, and tradition that tie an individual to a larger collectivity. Ethnic mobilization is tied to emotional and often irrational notions of group solidarity and support (see Smith 1998; Connor 1993;

Lake and Rothchild 1998, 5; Stack 1986, 1–2). In societies where other forms of social solidarity around gender, labor, or class are weak, ethnoreligious mobilization is often an integral part of political life. One of the major criticisms leveled at primordialism is that it does not explicate the link between identity and conflict. While primordialism has utility in identifying where ethnic ties are prevalent, it does tell us how it can be a factor in mobilizing identify for conflict. The existence of multiple identities among social actors suggests that they are often manipulated as part of the mobilization process into cause-and-effect scenarios (Tiemessen 2005).

Instrumentalism, by contrast, suggests that ethnicity is malleable and is defined as part of a political process. The idea of manipulation is thus an inherent part of this school of thought. By emphasizing in-group similarities and out-group differences as well as invoking the fear of assimilation, domination, or annihilation, ethnic leaders can stimulate identity mobilization (see Laitin 1986; Lake and Rothchild 1998, 8; Brass 1979, 35–77; 1991). For instrumentalists, ethnic mobilization is a by-product of the personal political projects of leaders and elites who are interested in advancing their political and economic interests via social conflict. Placed within a larger context of conflict escalation, instrumentalism allows us to make cross-comparisons between societies with similar social cleavages.

Constructivism adopts a middle ground between primordialism and instrumentalism. Its proponents argue that ethnicity is not fixed but rather a political construct based on a dense web of social relationships (see Anderson 1983; Young 1993). Like primordialists, constructivists recognize the importance of seemingly immutable features of ethnic identity, but they disagree that this inevitably leads to conflict. Conversely, constructivists share with instrumentalists the view that elites and leadership play a critical role in the mobilization process; disagreement emerges, however, on the degree to which these identities can be manipulated. In brief, constructivists do not believe that ethnicity is inherently conflictual but rather conflict flows from "pathological social systems" and "political opportunity structures" that breed conflict from many social cleavages and that are beyond the control of the individual (Lake and Rothchild 1998, 6).

With this as a backdrop, religious sectarianism in the world today becomes more intelligible. Sectarian identities could not be politicized unless differences in beliefs, values, and historical memory compelled religious groups to collective action around particularistic identities. However, the critical question that demands an answer is, why now? What explains the outburst of ethnic/religious conflict at a particular moment in time and not before? Sunni–Shi'a relations, for example, were not always conflict-ridden nor was sectarianism a strong political force in modern Muslim politics until relevantly recently. What factors contributed to this change? While the role of elites and leadership is particularly salient here, in answering these questions, Vali Nasr has suggested that we must also take into account the agency of state actors in identity mobilization (2000, 173).

In the past, theories of ethnic conflict have generally treated the state as a passive actor in identity mobilization. The standard narrative held that competition from within society among competing ethnic groups would inevitably shift to the arena of the state as these substate actors would compete for control of various state institutions as a means of enhancing their power over rival groups. The intensification of these struggles would eventually lead to the weakness and failure of the state. However, drawing on research from South and Southeast Asia, Nasr has suggested that, "far from being passive victims of identity mobilization," states have a logic of their own and "can be directly instrumental in ... manipulating the protagonists and entrenching identity cleavages. Identity mobilization here is rooted in the project of power of state actors, not an elite or a community. These actors do not champion the cause of any one community but see political gain in the conflict between the competing identities" (173). Nasr's insight helps deepen our theoretical understanding of identity mobilization in that it pushes the conversation beyond primordial differences and elite manipulation and focuses attention on state behavior and state–society relations. This brings us to the national context that shapes sectarian differences in the Muslim world today.

NATIONAL CONTEXTS

While most Muslim majority societies are Sunni, comprising about 85–90 percent of the total global Muslim population, Iran, Iraq, Azerbaijan, and Bahrain are Shi'a majority societies. Significant Shi'a populations also live in Lebanon, Afghanistan, Kuwait, Yemen, Saudi Arabia, Pakistan, and Syria.[5] Critically, what these societies share in common is that most of their political systems are decidedly nondemocratic, and various forms of authoritarianism dominate the political landscape. It is this overarching fact that determines the ebb and flow of political life and influences the relationship between sects, the rise of sectarianism, and the behavior of political and religious leaders.

Authoritarian states in the Muslim world have several distinguishing features that influence sectarian relations. They suffer from a crisis of legitimacy; as a result, they closely monitor and attempt to control civil society by limiting access to information and the freedom of association of their citizens. Joel Migdal's concept of a "weak state" best describes these regimes (Migdal 1988, 3–41). In his formulation, based on an innovative model of state–society relations, "weak states" suffer from limited power and capacity to exert social control. They often cannot and do not control sections of the country, within both urban and rural areas, that they claim sovereignty over. Moreover, they confront highly complex societies made of up of a "mélange of social organizations" such as ethnic and religious groups, villages, landlords, clans, and various economic interest groups that limit the state's reach into society and compromise its autonomy. "Dispersed domination" describes these states where "neither the state (nor any other social force) manages to achieve countrywide domination" (Migdal 1994, 9). While the state is too weak to dominate society, it is often strong enough to manipulate and to effectively respond to crises that threaten national security and regime survival (Nasr 2000).

In weak states, politics revolves around "strategies of survival" (Migdal 1994, 206–37). State leaders and political elites are fundamentally concerned with both their staying power and staying *in* power. Thwarting rivals who might threaten them from within society as well as among various state organizations is a key political obsession that drives and informs political decisions. A common tactic to preserve and perpetuate political rule in a weak state is to manipulate social and political cleavages via a "divide and rule" strategy. This gives ruling elites greater room to maneuver in the short term but often at the cost of social cohesion in the long term. This dominant feature of the politics of weak states also suggests why "state actors are principal agents in identity mobilization and conflict in culturally plural societies, and the manner in which politics of identity unfolds in a weak state, is a product of the dialectic of state-society relations" (Nasr 2000, 174). Weak states, therefore, are more prone to sectarianism given that manipulating cleavages of identity is a dominant feature of their politics. As David Little has observed in his analysis of religion, nationalism, and intolerance, "authoritarian states appear to draw life from ethnic or religious intolerance as a way of justifying the degree of violence required to maintain power" (see chapter 1 in this volume).

During the 1960s and 1970s in several Muslim countries, political opposition to the ruling regimes was in the form of various socialist, communist, and left-wing political formations. In an attempt to pacify these oppositional currents, Islamic political groups were allowed greater freedom of movement and association in the hope that they would challenge the popularity of these secular oppositional groups, thus immunizing the state from criticism and scrutiny. The most dramatic case of this was in Egypt when Anwar Sadat released scores of Muslim Brotherhood members from jail and allowed exile leaders to return home (Sullivan and Abed-Kotob 1999; Kepel 2002). Similarly, in an attempt to enhance the capacity of the Pakistani state and solidify political control, Gen. Muhammad Zia-ul-Haq launched an Islamization program in the late 1970s that, despite its pretensions to Islamic universalism, was in essence an attempt at the Sunnification of political and social life of Pakistan. It was therefore viewed as a threat by religious minorities in Pakistan—the Shi'a community in particular, who considered these policies detrimental to their sociopolitical interests. The severe rupture in sectarian relations in Pakistan that soon followed was significantly shaped by this development, but as Vali Nasr has demonstrated, it was deeply influenced by regional and international variables as well (Nasr 2000).

SAUDI ARABIA AND SECTARIAN RELATIONS

The emergence of Saudi Arabia in the twentieth century as an independent state exists as a unique factor in explaining Sunni–Shi'a tensions across the Muslim world today. Due to its geographical proximity to the Islamic holy places and the presence of the world's largest energy reserves (and the immense profits that flow from its export), and buttressed by a close alliance with the United States, Saudi Arabia is today a regional power that can influence political trends both within the Middle East and far beyond its borders. The ruling ideology of the regime, Wahhabism, is central to this story.

Inspired by the work of the medieval Muslim scholar Ibn Taymiyyah (1263–1328), Muhammad Ibn 'Abd al-Wahhab, an eighteenth-century Islamic cleric and resident of central Arabia, developed an ultraconservative and puritanical interpretation of Islam that today dominates the Saudi peninsula. Responding to the general decline of Islamic civilization, 'Abd al-Wahhab was convinced that the roots of the social and political crisis facing Muslim societies was due to the importation of inauthentic practices, rituals, and beliefs into Muslim societies that were divorced from the original teachings of the Prophet Muhammad and the principles of the Qur'an. Sufism and Shi'a Islam were a core focus of his critique. In his view, they represented deviant and corrupt forms of Islam, and opposing their presence and manifestation in Muslim societies was deemed both a moral duty and a religious obligation (see Fadl 2007, 45–94; Algar 2002, 34–35; Abukhalil 2004, 58–59).

A political alliance developed between the clerical proponents of this creed of Islam and the House of Saud, one of the most powerful tribal groups in Arabia. It is this alliance that formed the foundation of the modern state of Saudi Arabia ensuring that Wahhabism would have a stable home to develop its theology and gradually spread its beliefs across the Muslim world (see Commins 2006, 104–29; Abukhalil 2004, 58–64). In the late twentieth century, students who came to Saudi Arabia for theological training, many of them on Saudi-subsidized scholarships, internalized Wahhabi ideology and began to spread this dogmatic and inflexible version of Islam upon return to their native countries. Gradually, with the assistance of petro-dollars, mainstream Sunni Islam came to unconsciously internalize Wahhabi norms and values, especially in terms of how Shi'a Muslims were viewed. For most of the twentieth century Sunni–Shi'a relations were relatively amicable as the themes of colonialism, imperialism, and nationalism provided a common theme of political interest that transcended sectarian divisions. The 1979 Islamic Revolution in Iran, however, marked a critical turning point.

The explicit radical, anti-American and revolutionary message that emanated from the Iranian Revolution sent out shock waves throughout the Muslim world. They were most alarmingly and immediately felt among pro-American allies in the Arab world where similar revolutions from below were feared. Saudi Arabia's close alliance with the West, the United States in particular, was portrayed as subservience and a form of neocolonialism by the Iranian revolutionaries. Leading Iranian clerics singled out Saudi Arabia for specific attack and critique. The Saudi royal family, feeling vulnerable to the populist fervor that was sweeping the region, responded by investing huge sums of money in promoting a decidedly anti-Shi'a and anti-Iranian politico-theological agenda. The universal pretensions and ideals of Iran's Islamic Revolution were undermined by portraying it as a distinctly Shi'a phenomenon that allegedly bastardized the original message of the Prophet Muhammad. Within a short span of time a new cold war had emerged between the Islamic Republic of Iran and pro-Western Arab regimes in the Middle East in which Sunni–Shi'a relations were a central battleground.[6]

During this period, leading Saudi clerics openly declared Shi'a Muslims as heretics and infidels. The chief mufti of Saudi Arabia, Abdul-Aziz Bin Baz, was very explicit on this point, and this tradition has been kept alive by his successor, Sheikh Abdul-Rahman al-Barrak, and by the new imam of the Grand Mosque in Mecca, Sheikh Adil Al-Kalbani (see Abukhalil 2004, 73–74; Trabelsi 2009). Moreover, in Saudi Arabia today, a broad-based and well-entrenched system of discrimination against Shi'a Muslims exists. For example, in 2007 the Saudi government canceled all Shi'a-sponsored blood drives in the eastern provincial region of Al Ahsa without explanation (Saudi Information Agency 2007; see also ICG 2005; Matthiesen 2009). The implication was that Shi'a blood was impure, and it should not contaminate the national blood supply. A year later a group of twenty-two leading Saudi clerics issued a joint statement attacking minority Shi'as while simultaneously claiming that Lebanon's Hezbollah was posturing against Israel to hide its anti-Sunni agenda. "Many Muslims have been fooled by the Shi'ites' claims to be championing Islam and challenging the Jews and Americans.... Those who believe their claims have not realized the reality of the infidel bases of their faith.... It is the rejectionist Shi'ites who began the practice of visiting graves and building shrines," the statement read, reflecting a major concern among Wahhabi clerics who deem such behavior as blasphemous.[7]

This anti-Shi'a animus has been a central theme in the speeches and the rhetoric of jihadi militants groups such as al-Qa'ida in Iraq. In September 2005 Abu Musab al-Zarqawi, head of al-Qa'ida in Iraq, declared an all-out war on Iraq's Shi'a population, drawing on images and ideas that go well beyond the traditionalist Wahhabi commentary that routinely describes them as apostates, blasphemers, and heretics. "[The Shi'a are] the insurmountable obstacle, the lurking snake, the crafty and malicious scorpion, the spying enemy and the penetrating venom. . . . They [have been] a sect of treachery and betrayal throughout history and throughout the ages. . . . I come back and again say that the only solution is for us to strike the religious, military, and other cadres among the Shia with blow after blow until they bend to the Sunnis" (quoted in Allawi 2007, 233).[8]

Iran's treatment of its Sunni population has given fodder to Sunni extremists and Wahhabi-inspired attacks on Shi'a Muslims. While there is no parity in the level of state-sanctioned vitriol and hostility meted out against Iranian Sunnis, the discrimination they face within Iran has added to sectarian tensions in the Muslim world. More importantly, theologically speaking, Shi'a Islam is inherently anti-Sunni in that it rejects the political, religious, and moral authority of the first three Muslim caliphs. Criticism and often ridicule of these deeply revered Sunni Muslim figures is "inbuilt" in Shi'a Islam and ensures a persistent level of tension between Sunnis and Shi'as that can act as a justification to legitimize and perpetuate conflict over political, economic, and social issues.[9]

THE REGIONAL CONTEXT

Regional conflict in the Middle East over the past thirty years has had a distinct sectarian dimension. It has been shaped by the rise of revolutionary Iran in 1979 and its attempt to influence the politics of the Muslim world versus a Saudi-led backlash that has sought to limit Iran's influence and to defend and spread its own interests within Muslim societies. This clash between Shi'a religious populism and Sunni–Saudi religious conservatism has varied in intensity and scope over the previous three decades, with the 1990s being a low point in regional and sectarian tensions. Today the alignment of political forces has changed very little. On the one hand are Iran, Syria, Hezbollah, and Hamas versus a pro-Western alliance composed of Saudi Arabia, most of the Gulf States, Jordan, Egypt, Morocco, Tunisia, the Palestine Authority, and half of Lebanon on the other side (with tacit support from Israel). Turkey and Qatar stand in between and often try to mediate tensions (see Hinnebusch and Ehteshami 2002, 1–27; Halliday 2005, 130–66, 193–260).

The key conflict during the 1980s that affected sectarian relations was the Iran-Iraq war. While Saddam Hussein's regime wrapped itself in the mantle of Arab nationalism and portrayed its conflict with Iran as a struggle against Persian nationalist hegemony, its key backers who subsidized the war, primarily Saudi Arabia and the Gulf States, fanned the flames of religious sectarianism by portraying Iran as the home of a heretical form of Shi'a Islam that was attempting to dominate the region. These tensions erupted in the most dramatic form in 1987 during the annual Hajj pilgrimage. Hundreds of Iranian pilgrims were killed in a clash with Saudi security forces after an attempted demonstration in Mecca. Both sides traded accusations, vilifying the other with very strong language. While this conflict was fundamentally political in nature, it revolved around and resulted in an expansion of Sunni–Shi'a tensions (Kifner 1987).

Regionally, as Trita Parsi has successfully argued, during this decade Israel had a pro-Iranian bias to its foreign policy orientation—notwithstanding revolutionary Iran's consistent and persistent calls for Israel's eradication. At this time, Arab nationalism was deemed the greater threat to Israel's survival, and any weakening or defeat of a major Arab power was welcomed in Israel even if this meant tacit support and aid for the Islamic Republic of Iran (Parsi 2007, 87–156).

The passing of Ayatollah Khomeini in 1989 and the rise of more pragmatic forces in Iran during the 1990s marked a turning point in regional conflict as well as a diminution in sectarian tensions. President Hashemi Rafsanjani sought to mend relations with Saudi Arab and the Gulf states. This decade began, however, with a major regional distraction that largely left Iran out of the political equation and completely overshadowed Sunni–Shi'a strife: Iraq's annexation of Kuwait and the subsequent Gulf War. Iran played no significant role in this inter-Arab (and Sunni) crisis, choosing instead a path of neutrality while focusing on economic reconstruction and mending its broken relations with the outside world. The Oslo Peace Process that also occurred during this period left Iran isolated with little influence over the Israel–Palestine conflict. Hamas at this time was just emerging as a political force, and its deeply Sunni conservative orientation and alliance with supporters in the Gulf states meant that they had more in common religiously and politically with Saudi Arabia and conservative Sunnism than with Iran and revolutionary Shi'ism.

Regional politics in the 2000s was deeply influenced by events related to the attacks on September 11 and the American decision to invade and occupy Iraq. These events greatly transformed the regional balance of power in large part due to the rise of Shi'a political Islamist parties in Iraq who were closely allied to Iran. The subsequent Iraqi civil war, which after 2006 had a clear sectarian dimension to it, further inflamed Sunni–Shi'a relations across the Middle East. These events were tied to the strength and popularity of Hezbollah—widely viewed on the Muslim street as an authentic national liberation movement. At the regime level, however, many Arab states viewed Hezbollah as a dangerous revolutionary force, controlled by Iran, which sought to upset the political status quo. In December 2004 King Abdullah II of Jordan, reflecting this concern, spoke of a "Shi'a Crescent" linking Beirut and Tehran and running through Damascus and Baghdad that was seeking to dominate the politics of region based on a new brand of Shi'a solidarity (Black 2007).[10]

The 2006 Israel-Hezbollah-Lebanon war inflamed regional and sectarian tensions once again. The pro-Western Arab regimes initially were critical of Hezbollah for instigating the conflict. When the casualty toll began to rise and popular sentiment rallied strongly behind Lebanon and Hezbollah, these regimes had to backtrack. The inability of Israel (and with the Bush administration support) to defeat Hezbollah despite a month-long bombing campaign resulted in Hassan Nasrallah emerging as a defiant and popular Muslim leader at the societal level, with Mahmoud Ahmadinejad coming in a close second. This serves to highlight that the concern about Shi'a expansionism and the rise of Iranian influence in Sunni Arab world is mostly relegated to the elite level because the masses in Arab world have no problem identifying Shi'a politicians as political heroes. Even in Lebanon, where the Sunni–Shi'a divide has erupted into conflict on several occasions in recent decades, according to a Beirut Center for Research and Information poll, the majority of Sunnis in Lebanon do not support sectarian attacks in Iraq, and the vast majority rejects the Shi'a Crescent theory (Saad-Ghorayeb 2007). The respectable Telhami-Zogby Poll in 2006 confirmed these findings. Specially, vast majorities in six Arab countries (Egypt, Saudi Arabia, Morocco, Jordan, United Arab Emirates, and Lebanon) viewed Israel and the United States as a greater threat to the Arab world than Iran, and the majority of those polled believed Iran had the right to develop nuclear power.[11]

A virtual replay of these events, with the accompanying divide between the pro-Western Arab regimes and the Arab masses, occurred in late 2008 and early 2009 in the context of the Gaza war. Sectarian tensions were inflamed when Egypt was strongly criticized by Hezbollah and Iranian leaders for maintaining the siege on Gaza. Egypt and its allies among the pro-Western regimes responded by accusing Iran and Hezbollah of fueling regional tensions and interfering in the internal affairs of neighboring countries. Morocco sided with Egypt and broke off diplomatic relations with Iran, accusing it of enflaming sectarian tensions by engaging in Shi'a proselytization (Slackman 2009; *Al Jazeerah* 2009).

THE GLOBAL CONTEXT

International relations over the past thirty years have exacerbated Sunni–Shi'a tensions. The regional alliances between a pro- and anti-Western bloc of countries has been buttressed by increasing American intervention and penetration in the Middle East. This intervention has been rejected by an Iranian-Syrian-Hezbollah alliance that lacks support from a major world power—but that has considerable popular support on the Arab street—and that strongly opposes US policies toward the Middle East.

In the aftermath of the Iranian Revolution, it was widely believed that Iranian Shi'a-inspired radicalism was the main threat to the Western interests in the region. The converse of this also applied: Saudi Arabia and Sunni Islam were viewed in the West as the more moderate sect that the United States could do business with and rely on to protect its interests. Events in Lebanon and Afghanistan during the 1980s seemed to confirm this conclusion. The US and Israeli attempt to create a pro-Western government in Lebanon after Israel's 1982 invasion was met with Shi'a resistance leading to the bombing of the American and French forces in Beirut in 1983 and the kidnapping of American hostages. Simultaneously, the West backed the ultraconservative Sunni Afghan Mujahedeen, whom Ronald Reagan repeatedly referred to as "freedom fighters," in their struggle against Soviet occupation. This Sunni-equals-good-guys versus Shi'a-equals-bad-guys approach to Middle East politics was severely challenged on the morning of September 11, 2001, when New York and Washington, DC, were attacked by Sunni militants, most of whom came from Saudi Arabia. The invasion and reconstruction of Iraq and the accompanying civil war and Sunni insurgency further complicated matters. It was now radical Sunni jihadi groups and al-Qa'ida who posed the main challenge to US interests globally while the Iraqi Shi'a political parties, whom the Bush administration was hoping would bring democracy to the Middle East, became the main allies of the United States.

The new Bush administration intervened in the Middle East after September 11, 2001, hoping to redraw the political map in favor of US interests (see Leverett 2005; Woodward 2004). This meant that Iran was to be challenged, albeit indirectly, and the Islamic Republic was described in a famous 2002 State of the Union speech as a member of the "axis of evil." The more the United States became bogged down in Iraq, caught between an Iraqi nationalist insurgency and a raging civil war, the more it sought to blame Iran for the turmoil (Tisdall 2007; Hirsch 2007). A preexisting Sunni alliance was solidified among pro-Western regimes with silent backing from Israel to confront Iranian involvement in Iraq, Lebanon, and Palestine. According to Martin Indyk, a senior State Department official in the Clinton administration who also served as ambassador to Israel, "the Middle East [was] heading into a serious Sunni-Shiite Cold War" (quoted in Hersh 2007).

The November 2010 WikiLeaks documents highlight the regional tensions between Shi'a Iran and its Sunni Arab neighbors. Many of these documents reveal private conversations of Arab heads of state sounding more hawkish on Iran than the prime minster of Israel. While much of the concern points to Iran's nuclear program, the real political concern stems from Iran's enhanced power, buttressed by its newfound influence in Iraq and its populist anti-imperialist rhetoric that undermines the legitimacy of pro-American Arab regimes (Sanger, Glanz, and Becker 2010; see also Cole 2010). To the extent that these documents are a reflection of actual policy directions from the leading countries of the Sunni Arab world, they suggest that, thirty-one years after the Islamic Revolution in Iran, the region has come full circle.

Sectarian relations have been deeply affected by these developments. The common fear of growing Iranian Shi'a influence was strongly encouraged by the Bush administration, affecting the national politics and foreign policies of many of the leading states in the Arab Middle East. Religious leaders on both sides of the Sunni–Shi'a divide were caught up in this debate. While some of the official clergy, especially in Saudi Arabia, publicly echoed the concern of a growing Shi'a ascendancy and Sunni vulnerability, greater US intervention and conflict between Israel and the Palestinians created an environment that facilitated cooperation and dialogue among religious leaders.

THE IRONY OF INTERNATIONAL INTERVENTION: GREATER SUNNI–SHI'A COOPERATION

Ironically, greater conflict in the Middle East after September 11, 2001, has led to greater cooperation among Sunni–Shi'a religious leaders (see Moussavi 2001, 301–15; Zaman 2002, 144–91). This is due to the perceived peril of a common enemy (i.e., the United States and Israel) and calls for great unity among Muslims in the face of familiar threats. Evidence of this is available from three major meetings between leading Sunni and Shi'a religious leaders where this theme emerged in Amman, Jordan (July 2005), in Doha, Qatar (January 2007), and in Mecca, Saudi Arabia (June 2008).[12]

The meetings, however, were not without tension. While the sectarian civil war in Iraq and perceived common threats generated calls for unity, there were fiery exchanges from senior religious authorities, in particular Sheikh Yusuf al-Qaradawi, the widely influential Egyptian cleric. He criticized "attempts to convert Sunnis to Shiism," Iran's role in allegedly orchestrating attacks on Sunnis in Iraq, and the continued Shi'a insult to the companions of the Prophet Muhammad. This is a long-standing bone of contention in Sunni–Shi'a relations, given the fact that these people are revered figures in Sunni Islam. "How can I shake hands with those who are swearing at the companions? It is the companions who brought Islam to Iran, so why the rudeness?" (quoted in Saad 2007). The leading Iranian religious leader at the meeting, Ayatollah Mohammad-Ali Taskhiri, fired back that colonial powers were trying to make Iran the enemy in the Muslim world, and the existence of Sunni–Shi'a disputes only serves the interests of Israel. He also complained that Sunnis were trying to convert Shi'as (ibid.).[13]

A year later, in a widely read interview in the Egyptian daily newspaper *Almasry Alyoum*, Qaradawi reiterated these themes; however, he went further by referring to Shi'a Muslims as heretics. A huge debate ensued in the Arab world in the aftermath of Qaradawi's remarks, with commentary varying from those who agreed with him, some partially and some entirely, while many others criticized and rejected his claims. Rather than backing down, he struck a more defiant tone. "I do not care and I am not shaken by this stir. I made this statement to answer to the dictates of my conscience and religion and responsibility. . . . I am trying to preempt the threat before it gets worse. If we let Shi'as penetrate Sunni societies, the outcome will not be praiseworthy. The presence of Shi'as in Iraq and Lebanon is the best evidence of instability" (quoted in Fleischman 2008).[14]

These views are significant for two main reasons. First, Qaradawi is very influential in the mainstream of the Sunni Muslim world as source of religious authority. He is often described as the spiritual head of the Muslim Brotherhood movement, and he hosts the popular television program on *Al Jazeera*, "Shariah and Life." Second, until these recent inflammatory comments on Shi'a Muslims, Qaradawi was widely known as a proponent of sectarian unity and reconciliation. For example, he signed the Amman statement in 2005 that recognized Shi'ism as a legitimate branch of Islam. His 2008 reference, therefore, to Shi'as as "heretics" whose "danger comes from their attempts to invade Sunni society" (Fleishman 2008) suggests a backtracking from his more moderate and accomodationist stance that bodes ill for sectarian reconciliation in the Muslim world.

CONCLUSION

Muslim religious leaders are not a homogenous group. Some are on the payroll of the political regimes under which they live; others have independent sources of income. Some are politicized; many are not. Some are in favor of sectarian religious toleration, accommodation, and dialogue. Others do not uphold these values while some, such as the influential Yusuf Qaradawi, have issued contradictory positions. Moreover, numerous regional, class, educational, historical, and generational divisions shape and differentiate clerical opinion in Muslim societies today.

In framing this inquiry in broad terms, it was argued that, during periods of state breakdown, social strife, and regional and international conflict, sectarian religious mobilization occurs in societies where the central state is weak, fragile, or suffers from a crisis of legitimacy. It is precisely during these moments of crisis that people are more susceptible to identity mobilization along religious sectarian lines. The political authoritarian nature of most of the regimes in the Muslim Middle East and the general absence of democracy are central to this dynamic. State elites can manipulate identities in pursuit of narrow gains of staying in power, perpetuating dynastic rule, deflecting pressure from civil society, and fundamentally blocking efforts at democratization. The behavior and political ideas of Muslim religious leaders on both sides of the Sunni–Shi'a divide are shaped by this enveloping context of authoritarianism.

Ironically, greater social and political strife connected to recent wars in Iraq, Afghanistan, and Israel-Palestine has created opportunities for reconciliation and dialogue among Muslim religious leaders. The intervention of great powers in the Middle East post–September 11, 2001, which has led to a civil war in Iraq plus the ongoing Israel-Palestinian-Arab conflict, has generated calls for unity and setting aside religious differences in order to face common threats. This is reminiscent of the early part of the twentieth century, when sectarian religious tension was diminished, coinciding with the domination of the Muslim world by various European powers. Thus, current social conditions actually provide a rare opportunity to build bridges and to promote peaceful strategies of conflict resolution among Muslims religious leaders, more than at previous moments in recent history.

Finally, in terms influencing the rise of Islamic militancy, Shi'a religious leaders are better able to contribute to conflict resolution than Sunni religious leaders. This might seem like a bold claim, but recent empirical evidence can be cited to substantiate this argument. Fundamentally, this issue is connected to the crisis of religious authority in Muslim societies and key doctrinal differences between Shi'a and Sunni Islam. While this topic needs further research, a preliminary argument would be as follows.

Shi'a Islam is hierarchical, and all practicing Shi'as are doctrinally required to follow the religious edicts of a learned religious scholar (*mujtahid*). This is known as the concept of *taqlid* (imitation), a long-standing tradition within Shi'a Islam. One political consequence is that it gives Shi'a religious leaders huge moral authority over their constituents. Moreover, the centralized nature of the Shi'a religious education and the existence of senior religious leaders who have achieved the rank of Grand Ayatollah (of which about twenty exist at this moment) streamline religious education and establish a consensus as to which religious leaders are qualified to issue edicts that command authority. In this sense with respect to religious authority, Shi'a Islam is very Catholic. The case in Sunni Islam is different. Using the same analogy, Sunni Islam has more parallels with Protestantism. Believers are not doctrinally obligated to follow the teachings of a senior religious scholar, and breakaway leaders without formal religious training are increasingly frequent and they can obtain a following from among the devout and the pious. Hence, controlling these offshoot or extremist groups who might resort to political violence is far more difficult in the case of Sunni Islam.

In Lebanon during the 1980s there were several high-profile cases of American and British citizens who were taken hostage by various Shi'a militant groups, some of whom had ties to Hezbollah. These hostages were eventually released in large part due to the intervention of senior Lebanese and Iranian religious leaders. Since this time, the existence of splinter groups among Lebanese Shi'a has been rare. The same situation existed in Iraq after the 2003 American invasion. Radical Shi'a splinter groups such as Muqtada Al-Sadr's Mahdi Army were eventually controlled and neutralized in part due to the intervention of senior Shi'a religious leaders, who command huge moral authority, such as Ayatollah Ali Sistani. This picture should be contrasted with the rise of al-Qa'ida in Iraq and Osama Bin Laden in Afghanistan. Notwithstanding the condemnation of mainstream Sunni religious leaders in the Arab world of al-Qa'ida, the network was generally undeterred by the intervention of senior Sunni religious leaders.

In the end, it is important to not exaggerate the role of religion and the effect of Muslim religious leaders on issues of peace and conflict. If the Muslim world was predominately Buddhist, I am prepared to argue there would be no substantive difference in the level of political turmoil and instability. This is because the primary divide in the region is not between Sunni and Shi'a but between the people and the authoritarian elites who rule over them. Until this fundamental chasm is bridged, meaningful progress in resolving Sunni–Shi'a tensions and reducing violence cannot be expected.

In this sense the international community can play a constructive role in terms of policy recommendations by emphasizing the problem of the persistence of political authoritarianism and the absence of democracy in the Middle East. This point has been strongly made and highlighted in the recent series of UN Arab Human Development Reports (UNDP).[15] Democratization is highly varied, fragile, and vulnerable to manipulation of religion by incumbent elites. The persistence of authoritarianism is the single biggest contributing factor that perpetuates sectarian conflict and affects the behavior of religious leaders. Until this issue is seriously tackled, meaningful progress in promoting peace and mitigating violence over the long term will be extremely difficult.

NOTES

1. See Telhami (2004); and Shibley Telhami's 2006 Annual Arab Public Opinion Survey available online at www.brookings.edu/views/speeches/telhami20070208 .pdf, where 45 percent said that "Muslim" was the most important aspect of their identity, compared to 29 percent who said "citizen of my country" and 20 percent who said "Arab." See also Esposito and Mogahed (2007), 5–6, 85–87.
2. After the American troop withdrawal from major Iraqi cities on June 30, 2009, there has been a huge increase in sectarian killings. This is a worrying trend that does not bode well for the future of Iraq. For details and casualty figures, see Nordland (2009). In terms of the overall civilian death toll, John Tirman estimates—based on all the leading studies on the topic—that the total number of Iraqis killed since 2003 are in the range of seven hundred thousand to eight hundred thousand—with approximately 3.5 million people displaced. See his website, "Iraq: The Human Cost," where all the major studies can be accessed: http:// mit.edu/humancostiraq/. The above figures are based on personal correspondence with him on August 22, 2008; however, it should be stated that the exact number of people killed as a direct result of religious sectarianism is below these figures and difficult to know with any precision. On a related note, the rise of a resurgent Taliban in Afghanistan and the future stability of this country will have consequences for Sunni–Shi'a relations given the sizable Shi'a population in Afghanistan and the anti-Shi'a orientation of the Taliban.
3. This section is informed by two excellent studies, Nasr (2000, 171–90) and Tiemessen (2005).

4. See David Little's chapter in this volume.
5. Statistics are taken from US State Department 2006 Report on International Freedom at www.state.gov/g/drl/rls/hrrpt/2006/, and CIA World Factbook at https://www.cia.gov/library/publications/the-world-factbook/.
6. There is imminently more to this story, including the Saudi, Kuwaiti, and other gulf monarchies' support for Saddam Hussein in the Iran-Iraq war. The role of Arab nationalism in generating anti-Iranian and anti-Shi'a sentiment must be factored into any comprehensive analysis as well. For a critical analysis of how this conflict was played out in Pakistan, see Vali Nasr (2000, 171–90).
7. "Saudi Clerics Attack Shi'ites, Hezbollah." *Reuters*, June 1, 2008. It important recognize that this statement was opposed by more moderate Saudi clerics who rejected the statement and used this occasion to reach out to Shi'a Muslims in the name of reconciliation and peace. For details, see "Sunni Saudi Cleric Visits Shi'ites to Ease Tension," *Reuters*, June 27, 2008.
8. Also see "Zarqawi in His Own Words," BBC News, June 8, 2006; and "Al-Zarqawi Declares War on Iraqi Shia," Al Jazeera.net, September 14, 2005. For background, see Hafez (2007, 70–78).
9. A core grievance of Iran's Sunni population, who compose about 10 percent of Iran's total population, is the persistent refusal of the state to grant permission for the building of new Sunni mosques. For a sense of these grievances, see the open letter to Iran's high religious authorities written by Sunni parliamentary deputies in July 2003 (Saba 2003).
10. The inclusion of Syria in this list might seem odd, given that the majority of Syrians are Sunni. The ruling Asad family, however, comes from the minority Alawi sect of Shi'a Islam. For background on the Shi'a threat debate, see Norton (2007).
11. University of Maryland and Zogby International 2006 Arab Public Opinion Survey, available at http://sadat.umd.edu/surveys/index.htm. The 2010 Arab Public Opinion survey revealed little change in these views. Asked which country threatened their security, the responses were 88 percent Israel, 77 percent United States, and 10 percent Iran.
12. For details, see the joint statement by Sunni and Shi'a religious leaders in Amman in July 2005, "True Islam and Its Role in Modern Society," available on the Embassy of Jordan in Washington, DC, website: www.jordanembassyus.org/new/pr/pr07062005.shtml. For a summary of the Doha meeting, see Saad (2007), and for the Mecca meeting, see Obathani and Imam (2008) and Latham (2008).
13. For more details on this conference, see the official website of the Dialogue Conference on Islamic Sects, www.qatar-conferences.org/mazaheb/english/viewlastnews.php?id=39.
14. For a summary of the reactions, see Qaradawi's follow-up interview with Majid al Kinani (2008).
15. The fifth UN Arab Development Report has just been issued in July 2009 under the title "Challenges to Human Security in the Arab Countries." It is available online at www.arab-hdr.org.

REFERENCES

Abukhalil, As'ad. 2004. *The Battle for Saudi Arabia: Royalty, Fundamentalism and Global Power*. New York: Seven Stories Press.

Algar, Hamid. 2002. *Wahhabism: A Critical Essay*. Oneonta, NY: Islamic Publications International.

Al Jazeerah. 2009. "Morocco Severs Relations with Iran," March 7, http://english .aljazeera.net/news/africa/2009/03/2009370303221419.html.

Allawi, Ali. 2007. *The Occupation of Iraq: Winning the War, Losing the Peace*. New Haven, CT: Yale University Press.

Anderson, Benedict. 1983. *Imagined Communities: Reflections on the Origins and Spread of Nationalism*. New York: Verso.

Ayoob, Mohammed. 2007. *The Many Faces of Political Islam*. Ann Arbor: University of Michigan Press.

Black, Ian. 2007. "Fear of a Shia Full Moon," *Guardian*, January 27.

Brass, Paul R. 1991. *Ethnicity and Nationalism: Theory and Comparison*. London: Sage.

———. 1979. "Elite Groups, Symbol Manipulation and Ethnic Identity among the Muslims of South Asia," in David Taylor and Malcolm Yapp, eds., *Political Identity in South Asia*. London: Curzon Press.

Cole, Juan. 2010. "US Embassy Cables: Verdict on the Leaks about the Middle East." *Guardian*, November 29.

Connor, Walker. 1993. "Beyond Reason: The Nature of the Ethnonational Bond." *Ethnic and Racial Studies* 16:373–89.

Commins, David 2006. *The Wahhabi Mission and Saudi Arabia*. New York: I. B. Tauris.

Esposito, John, and Dalia Mogahed. 2007. *Who Speaks for Islam? What a Billion Muslims Really Think*. New York: Gallup Press.

el-Fadl, Khaled Abou. 2007. *The Great Theft: Wrestling Islam from the Extremists*. New York: Harper Collins.

Fleischman, Jeffrey. 2008. "Egyptian Sheikh's Outburst against Shiites Roils Middle East." *Los Angeles Times*, September 28.

Halliday, Fred. 2005. *The Middle East and International Relations: Power, Politics and Ideology*. Cambridge: Cambridge University Press.

Hersh, Seymour. 2007. "The Redirection," *The New Yorker*, March 5.

Hinnebusch, Raymond, and Anoushiravan Ehteshami, eds. 2002. *The Foreign Policies of Middle East States*. Boulder, CO: Lynne Rienner Publishers.

Hirsch, Michael. 2007. "The Road to War, Part II." *Newsweek*, October 25.

International Crisis Group (ICG). 2005. "The Shiite Question in Saudi Arabia," Middle East Repot No. 45, September 19, www.crisisgroup.org/~/media/Files /Middle%20East%20North%20Africa/Iran%20Gulf/Saudi%20Arabia/The%20 Shiite%20Question%20in%20Saudi%20Arabia.ashx.

Kepel, Gilles. 2002. *Jihad: The Trail of Political Islam*. Cambridge, MA: Harvard University Press.

Kifner, John. 1987. "Iran and Saudi War with Fierce Words." *New York Times*, August 25.

Kinani, Majid al. 2008. "Al-Qaradawi Speaks to Asharq Al-Awsat." *Al Sharq Alwsat*, September 29.

Laitin, David. 1986. *Hegemony and Culture: Politics and Religious Change among the Yoruba*. Chicago: University of Chicago Press.

Lake, David, and Donald Rothchild, eds. 1998. *The International Spread of Ethnic Conflict: Fear, Diffusion, and Escalation*. Princeton, NJ: Princeton University Press.

Latham, Judith. 2008. "Mecca Conference Promotes Dialogue between Muslims and Followers of Other Faiths." *Voice of America*, June 12.

Leverett, Flynt, ed. 2005. *The Road Ahead: Middle East Policy in the Bush Administration's Second Term*. Washington, DC: Brookings Institution Press.

Matthiesen, Toby. 2009. "The Shia of Saudi Arabia at a Crossroads." MiddleEastDesk .org, May 6, www.merip.org/mero/mero050609.html.

Migdal, Joel S. 1988. *Strong Societies and Weak States: State-Society Relations and State Capabilities in the Third World*. Princeton, NJ: Princeton University Press.

———. 1994. "The State in Society: An Approach to Struggles for Domination." In *State Power and Social Forces: Domination and Transformation in the Third World*, edited by Joel S. Migdal, Atul Kohli, and Vivienne Shue. Cambridge: Cambridge University Press.

Moussavi, Ahmad Kazemi. 2001. "Sunni-Shi'i Rapprochement (Taqrib)." In *Shi'ite Heritage: Essays in Classical and Modern Traditions*, edited by Lynda Clarke. Binghamton, NY: Global Publications.

Nasr, Vali. 2000. "International Politics, Domestic Imperatives, and Identity Mobilization: Sectarianism in Pakistan, 1979–1998," *Comparative Politics* 32:171–90.

———. 2006. *The Shia Revival: How Conflicts within Islam Will Shape the Future*. New York: W. W. Norton.

Nordland, Rod. 2009. "Iraqi Shiites Show Restraint after Attacks." *New York Times*, August 11.

Norton, Augustus Richard. 2007. "The Shiite 'Threat' Revisited." *Current History*, December, 434–39.

Obathani, Sultan Al-, and Imam Mohammed Imam. 2008. "Interfaith Dialogue Conference Begins in Mecca." *Asharq Alawsat*, June 6.

Parsi, Trita. 2007. *Treacherous Alliance: The Secret Dealings of Israel, Iran and the United States*. New Haven, CT: Yale University Press.

Saad, Rasha. 2007. "Promoting Proximity." *Al Ahram Weekly*, January 25–31.

Saad-Ghorayeb, Amal. 2007. "What the Moderate Arab World Is." *Al Ahram Weekly*, April 26–May 2.

Saba, Sadeq. 2003. "Iran's Sunni MPs Speak Out." *BBC News*, July 21.

Sanger, David, James Glanz, and Jo Becker. 2010. "Around the World, Distress over Iran." *New York Times*, November 28.

Saudi Information Agency. 2007. "The Saudi Government Bans Shia from Donating Blood." January 25, www.arabianews.org/english/article.cfm?qid=196&sid=2.

Slackman, Michael. 2009. "Egypt Accuses Hezbollah of Plotting Attacks and Arms Smuggling to Gaza." *New York Times*, April 13.

Smith, Anthony D. 1998. *Nationalism and Modernism: A Critical Survey of Recent Theories of Nations and Nationalism.* New York: Routledge.

Stack, John F., Jr. 1986. "Ethnic Mobilization in World Politics: The Primordial Perspective." In *The Primordial Challenge: Ethnicity in the Contemporary World,* edited by John F. Stack Jr. New York: Greenwood Press.

Sullivan, Dennis, and Sana Abed-Kotob. 1999. *Islam in Contemporary Egypt: Civil Society vs. the State.* Boulder, CO: Lynne Rienner Publishers.

Telhami, Shibley. 2004. "A Growing Muslim Identity." *Los Angeles Times,* July 11.

Tiemessen, Alana. 2005. "From Genocide to Jihad: Islam and Ethnicity in Post-Genocide Rwanda," Paper presented at the annual meeting of the Canadian Political Science Association, London, Canada, June 2–5.

Tisdall, Simon. 2007. "President's Back Up Plan: Blame Iran." *Guardian,* January 12.

Trabelsi, Habib. 2009. "Sheikh Kalbani: All Shiite Clerics Are Heretics." *Middle East Online,* May 6.

Woodward, Bob. 2004. *Plan of Attack.* New York: Simon and Schuster.

Young, Crawford, ed., 1993. *The Rising Tide of Cultural Pluralism: The Nation-state at Bay?* Madison: University of Wisconsin Press.

Zaman, Muhammad Qasi. 2002. *The Ulama in Contemporary Islam.* Princeton, NJ: Princeton University Press.

CHAPTER 3

BETWEEN INTOLERANCE
AND COEXISTENCE

❧

The Vatican, Maronites, and the War in Lebanon

GEORGE EMILE IRANI

Lebanon is a very interesting and unique case to study the role that religious leaders, both Christian and Muslim, play in conflict escalation and mitigation. Throughout history, religious leaders have played a key role in mobilizing their communities in empowering their followers or inciting them against other groups. The other dimension to underscore is the interconnection that exists between local religious leaders and the transnational network linking to regional and global religious institutions. Most of Lebanon's major communities are associated with the large Lebanese diaspora living outside the country. The Maronites have been linked to the Vatican and the worldwide Catholic Church for centuries. The same applies to the Shi'as of Lebanon who have looked up to the Islamic Republic of Iran as a major backer and supporter since the advent of Ayatollah Khomeini in 1979.[1]

In his scene-setting conceptual chapter, David Little writes that "where effective constitutional democracies combine with a high degree of national tolerance . . . , a very low incidence of violence is predicted. Conversely, where illiberal democracies or weak, predatory, or authoritarian regimes strongly lacking the characteristics of constitutional democracy combine with a high degree of national intolerance . . . , a high incidence of violence is predicted." This approach is flawed and simplistic when it comes to societies or entities that are based on sectarian power sharing, which is the case of Lebanon. In Lebanon, a failed state par excellence, the state barely exists and functions mostly as a framework for various confessional groups to maintain a fragile equilibrium among themselves. This situation is made more dramatic with the current standoff between the two models of governance facing the country: a Swiss-type confederated liberal sectarian-based democracy or a Sparta-like Islamic republic receiving its orders from the mullahs in Iran. Little does not factor in his violence potential score the role played by external actors who intervene in fragile or failed states by manipulating various factions or ethnoreligious groups. A case in point is the role played by Lebanon's neighbors and other global actors (the United States, the former Soviet Union, France, Iran, etc.) during the civil war, thus rendering tolerance a more complicated quest.

In this chapter I focus on Lebanon, a country that, because of its pluricommunitarian constitution (there are in Lebanon more than seventeen religious sects, Christian and Muslim), has long been considered an example of coexistence of multiethnic and multireligious groups. Throughout its history, Lebanon has been a microcosm of changes—sociopolitical and religious—in the Arab world. As a land of refuge, enjoying a high degree of freedom and tolerance, the Lebanese polity became the testing ground on internecine struggles, opposing Arab regimes and ideologies.

Because of its pluricommunitarian constitution, Lebanon has long been considered an example of coexistence of multiethnic and multireligious groups. Nevertheless, there is an inherent corollary to this pluralism that has led some scholars to characterize Lebanon as "precarious," "improbable," and "fragmented."[2] As a federation of ethnoreligious communities, Lebanon cannot be considered a nation-state. Lebanese communities, each jealous of its socioreligious traditions and prerogatives, have never evolved from a confessional sectarian "mosaic" to form an integrated political system.[3]

The ecumenical and interfaith movements inspired by the Second Vatican Council (Vatican II) made the Lebanese formula of coexistence between Christians and Muslims of fundamental importance to the Vatican. In fact, in the eyes of the papacy, Lebanon was supposed to be a living example of how different groups can interact in the same social context. Moreover, with the exception of the Philippines, Lebanon is for the Catholic Church "the last citadel of Christianity in the whole Levant, at the crossroads of three continents" (Jabre 1980, 246).

I will focus on the role Christian leaders played in mitigating or exacerbating conflict during the Lebanese War (1975–89).[4] Religious leaders played and still play an important role in Lebanon's politics. To tease out their role in conflict management, this essay concentrates on the mediation role played by the Vatican and the Maronite Patriarchs (see Irani 1989).

MILITIAMEN AND WARLORDS

During the Lebanese War, Maronite Patriarchs had to contend with extremist elements in the Christian community. Maronite Patriarchs, with support from the Holy See, had to deal with Christian militiamen and warlords who were bent on destroying the example of Lebanon as a "message," to use the words of Pope John Paul II. The ecumenical and interfaith movements inspired by Vatican II made the Lebanese formula of Christian–Muslim coexistence of fundamental importance to the Holy See.[5]

Throughout the Lebanese War the Vatican has tried to maintain a balanced position vis-à-vis the various parties involved in the conflict. The war in Lebanon was a challenge to the Holy See's various attempts at conflict mitigation. It had to operate at three interrelated levels of feuds: inter-Christian, inter-Lebanese, and Lebanese–Palestinian. In a sense, this challenge faced other powers trying to mediate and find a solution to the strife. But for the papacy the problem was compounded by the deep misunderstanding that developed between the Holy See and some influential elements in the Christian Maronite community.

Throughout Lebanon's history Maronite Patriarchs have played a very important role in rallying the community around them. The Patriarchs, despite a certain reluctance to get involved in local politics, have made their voices heard, especially when tensions and divisions have wracked the Lebanese body politic. Moreover, the personality of the Patriarchs has been crucial to how successful their interventions for conflict management have been.

For instance, in 1958 the Maronite Patriarch Boulos (Paul) Meouchi played a key role in stopping the civil war that was raging in Lebanon at that time. Meouchi, who had a very strong personality, reached out to the Arab and Muslim communities against the wishes of the then–pro-Western Maronite president Camille Chamoun, who was opposed to the pan-Arab policies advocated by then–Egyptian gamal Abdel Nasser. Meouchi's pro-Arab nationalist sympathies led some government supporters and critics to assign him the epithet "Mohammad Meouchi."[6]

During the Lebanese War, the Patriarchs had to contend with clergy and lay Maronite militiamen who were opposed to the Holy See's policy supported by the Patriarchs: Save Lebanon as an example of Christian–Muslim coexistence in order to save the Christians. The radical Maronite monks and armed militant groups did not want to hear about this conciliatory message. Here we have a clear illustration of how religious leaders get involved in conflict mitigation and conflict exacerbation. I discuss this aspect of the Lebanese War in detail, focusing on the role the Vatican played in coordination with Maronite Patriarchs in managing the conflict in Lebanon.

The primary aim of some Christian leaders and their militias was to fight the Palestinians rallied around the Palestine Liberation Organization (PLO) and their leftist Muslim allies. Some Maronite radical leaders went on to advocate for the partition of Lebanon and the creation of a Christian state. This policy led to intra-Christian tensions and led the Patriarchs with the papacy to intervene, albeit in vain, to stop the onslaught.

THE LEBANESE WAR: ACTORS AND ISSUES

Throughout its history, Lebanon has been a microcosm of changes—sociopolitical and religious—in the Arab world. As a land of refuge enjoying a high degree of freedom and tolerance, the Lebanese polity became the testing ground of internecine struggles, opposing Arab regimes, and ideologies.

The war in Lebanon itself became a theatre of confrontation for the Arabs and the Israelis. By the end of the 1960s the increasing militancy of Palestinian nationalism trapped Lebanon in the Arab-Israeli-Palestinian struggle: first, passively, Lebanon gave asylum to waves of Palestinian refugees (1948, 1967, 1970, 1971); then actively, following the Jordanian subjugation in 1970 of the PLO. Moreover, with the involvement of regional powers (Syria, Israel, Iran, etc.), the Lebanese War escalated to the point where Lebanon became by proxy the center of confrontation between East and West.

The Lebanese War, which erupted in 1975 and was ended by the Taif Accord in 1989, is a very complex conflict involving several actors and issues. The strife—which was not of a religious nature—pitted the Maronite-dominated Phalangist Party and its allies against the Muslim-leftist coalition actively backed by Palestinian guerrilla organizations (Fatah, al-Sa'iqa) and those that rejected any peaceful settlement with Israel.[7]

Domestically, some of the major developments that led to the Lebanese War included a disruption of the demographic balance in favor of the Muslims, who called for a reallocation of government posts; social difficulties caused by soaring prices, housing problems, and student unrest; and an internal crisis inside the Maronite Church where the monastic orders contested the authority of the Patriarch.

At the regional level, the defeat by Israel of the Arab armies in 1967 led to marked disenchantment with the policies followed at that time by the champion of pan-Arabism, Egypt's president Gamal Abdel Nasser. Beginning in the early 1960s, the major issue in the Middle East became the question of Palestine and its resolution to the satisfaction of the Arabs. In the mid-1970s, following the fourth Arab–Israeli war (1973) and the United States–sponsored peace process in the Middle East, Lebanon became the battlefield for those favoring and those opposing negotiations with the Jewish state. To complicate the situation further, Palestinian commando groups were transformed into a symbol of righteous revenge.[8]

At the global level, the process of détente that characterized superpower relations in the late 1960s did not fully include the Middle East. A case in point was the shelving of the 1977 joint United States–Soviet statement for peace between Arabs and Israelis based on UN Resolution 242 and 338, and the exclusion of the former USSR from the Middle East peace process initiated by the United States. Finally, the oil crisis had an important effect on the policies of both producers and consumers, leading to a major but ineffective involvement of Western Europe and Japan in Middle Eastern affairs.

The major events that led to the Lebanese War began with the signing of the Cairo Agreements (1969) between the Lebanese government and the PLO. Palestinian fighters used the Lebanese south as a launching pad for guerrilla attacks against Israeli settlements in Galilee. The Israel Defense Forces retaliated after each PLO action, which in turn heightened tensions, first with the Lebanese Armed Forces, which clashed with the Palestinians, and then with the Christian militias after 1975. The turmoil in Lebanon also provoked a greater Syrian and Israeli involvement in Lebanese politics and resulted in their direct presence on the ground. Moreover, the Camp David Accords (1978) and the Egyptian–Israeli Peace Treaty (1979) destroyed what was left of Arab unity. This situation was reflected dramatically in the Lebanese arena. The Palestinians were left out of bilateral peace negotiations and had to obtain the backing of those Arab regimes that were willing to champion their cause.

In Lebanon itself, the Egyptian–Israeli entente led to polarization of the conflicting parties and increasing fear of the possibility of the permanent settlement of Palestinians in Lebanon and the partition of the country. By 1982 the major events in Lebanon included the emergence of Bashir Gemayel as a powerful Maronite leader; the Israeli invasion of Lebanon in 1982; and the massacres of Palestinian civilians in the camps of Sabra and Shatila.

Since the beginning of the Lebanese War, the role of the Holy See was guided by three major principles: no party in Lebanon should jeopardize the dialogue between Christians and Muslims; the behavior of some elements in the Christian community should not compromise the formula of coexistence sanctioned in the 1943 National Covenant (Mithaak al-Watani); and the Palestinians, who for years have suffered exile, should not fall victims to a "new injustice in Lebanon."[9] The Lebanese War constituted a threat to these objectives, and, to thwart serious attempts to disrupt the Lebanese formula, the Vatican dispatched several mediation and fact-finding missions to Lebanon (in 1975, 1976, 1978, 1980, and 1984).

Coexistence between Christian and Muslim communities was first sanctioned by the Lebanese Constitution of 1926 and by the unwritten National Covenant

(Mithaak al-Watani) of 1943. In Article 95 of the constitution, which was supposed to be only transitory, it is written that "the communities will be fairly represented in public jobs and the composition of the government."

The National Covenant of 1943 was more of a political act aimed at the "lebanonization" of Muslims and the "arabization" of Christians. It was based on the premise that the Maronites would renounce their allegiance to French protection, and the Muslims would forego their dream of unity with Syria. During the discussions on the National Covenant, it was agreed that the president of Lebanon would be a Christian Maronite, the prime minister a Sunni Muslim, and the speaker of the parliament a Shiite Muslim.[10]

The National Covenant of 1943 was the origin of the misunderstanding between Christians—mostly Maronites—and Muslims in Lebanon. In 1949 a prominent Lebanese journalist, Georges Naccache, writing about the covenant, said that "two negations will never make a nation." This is still applicable to the current situation in Lebanon.[11]

One of the major consequences of the modus vivendi worked out in the 1943 covenant has been that confessionalism thwarted any possibility for the creation of a solid Lebanese national identity. In fact, the unwritten agreement had institutionalized the heterogeneous aspect of the Lebanese polity. Unlike Western societies where the primary allegiance is toward the state, citizens of Lebanon have no bearing on the social system if they do not belong to a given religious community and pay allegiance to a *zaim* (leader), whether political or religious.

The communities that constitute Lebanon's basic population are, on the Christian side, the Maronites, the Greek Orthodox, the Greek Catholics, and the Armenians; and on the Muslim side, Shiite Muslims, Sunni Muslims, and the Druzes.[12]

Since 1932, when the last official population survey was undertaken in Lebanon, no formal census has been carried out to analyze the demographic weight of the Lebanese communities. The country has a population of nearly 4 million people. About 39 percent of the population are Christians, 59.7 percent Muslims (Shi'a, Sunni, and Druze), and there are Jewish and Kurdish minorities. Arabs make up 95 percent of the population while 4 percent are Armenian.[13]

The Maronites, the only group among Eastern Christians to have remained united, take their name from a hermit, Maroun, who lived in northern Syria where he died in 410. Following their persecution, the Maronites migrated to Lebanon where they settled in the mountains. There they have been able to maintain their identity as a people and develop a high degree of independence and cohesion. Maronite communion with the Holy See dates back to the period of the Crusades. The spiritual head of the Maronite community is the Patriarch of Antioch and all the East. Outside Lebanon, Maronite communities are found in Syria, Cyprus, Egypt, and Palestine. Following World War I, Maronites migrated to North America, Latin America, Africa, and Australia.

The political weight of the Maronite community goes beyond its numerical importance. In fact, the Maronites believe that Lebanon is their last refuge and that any threat to their presence and privileges would transform the country into another Arab-Muslim state. As an alternative to the failure of the National Covenant, several Maronite personalities advanced solutions ranging from the creation of a federal or a confederal state in Lebanon to the outright partition of the country.[14]

At the religious level, the Maronite Patriarch and some monastic orders have played an important role in Lebanese politics. Since the beginning of the twentieth century, the Patriarch has taken a leadership role in defending the Maronite presence in Lebanon. Since 1958 successive Patriarchs have spearheaded efforts to preserve the coexistence formula between Christians and Muslims. Throughout the Lebanese War, Patriarch Antonios Boutros Khuraysh (1975–86) and his successor, Patriarch Nasrallah Boutros Sfeir (1986–), have kept their distance from the more extreme elements—both religious and political—in the community.

They faithfully reflected the Holy See's stand of being a moderator and conciliator within the Maronite community and between the various Lebanese communities.[15] Nonetheless, since the Lebanese War began in 1975, and because of the reluctance of senior clergy to support openly the political objectives of Christian militias, the authority of the Patriarch was sidelined in favor of more militant Maronite clergy. This is one of the major reasons why the Holy See decided to use its mediation skills to mitigate the conflict in Lebanon.

Being large landowners, the Maronite monks have been the most active proponents of Lebanese and Maronite nationalism. During the war, some monks were actively involved in battling Palestinians and their allies in Beirut. One of the most influential institutions supervised by a Maronite monastic order was the University of the Holy Spirit in Kaslik. During the Lebanese War, a research group of the university issued several pamphlets and books dealing with the origins of the conflict in Lebanon and the monks' stand on the conflict.

One of these publications states that Lebanese Christians are opposed to "any idea of pacific existence in an Islamic state like the *dhimmis* living in Arab countries [Copts in Egypt, Assyrians and Chaldeans in Iraq, etc.]."[16] In the Qur'an, "peoples of the book"—Christians and Jews—are treated as "protected peoples," *dhimmis*, which literally means those on the conscience (*dhimma*) of the Islamic community. To be protected, non-Muslims had to pay a *jizya* (tax).[17] In this same pamphlet, the Maronite monks called on the "moral forces" of the earth, headed by the Holy See, to do their utmost not to allow Lebanon, "this unique refuge of all the Orient, where one lives, breathes, trades, thinks, worships, sings, and prays in total freedom," to be engulfed in the flow of Arab and oil politics.

One of the most influential ideologues of the Maronite monks was the late Father Sharbel Qassis, who was superior of the Permanent Congress of the

Lebanese Order of Monks. Qassis played a crucial role during the Lebanese War. He advocated a militant line in opposing the Palestinian-leftist alliance in Lebanon. Justifying the active role played by the Maronite monks in the war, Father Qassis said: "Monks are essentially and organically linked to the people.... In order to defend himself, every Christian has the right to be trained to handle weapons."[18]

In a personal interview with this author, Qassis stressed the difference in meaning between "tolerance," which is a condition that applies to the Christian communities in Egypt, Syria, and Iraq whereby "a majority tolerates a minority," and "coexistence," where all enjoy the same equal and reciprocal rights. In the case of coexistence, the state has no official religion. "The constitution is not inspired by the Qur'an." Qassis defined the formula agreed upon between Christians and Muslims in the 1943 National Covenant as a case of an "aborted coexistence." "If coexistence truly succeeds in Lebanon, we would have contributed as Christians to the creation of a new concept of society. In fact, societies at the end of the twentieth century tend to be less and less homogeneous."[19] In this same interview the Maronite monk stated that Lebanese Muslims have demonstrated, in their psychological and military attitude during the war, their "being capable of tolerance, not coexistence."

These views were not shared across the board within the Maronite community or Lebanese Christians in general. They reflected the feeling of despondency and fear that was predominant in some Maronite political and religious sectors. The Maronites, or some among them, wanted to maintain their political power and viewed the alliance between Lebanese Muslims and the PLO as a major threat to their status. This is what the Maronite Patriarchs and the Vatican had to contend with throughout the Lebanese War. By the mid-1980s, under pressure from the Vatican, Qassis and the monastic orders were forced to stop their direct involvement in Lebanese politics.

During the Lebanese War, the most important group that embodied and defended Maronite and Christian aspirations in Lebanon was the Phalangist Party.[20] The Lebanese Phalange Party (Hizb al-Kata'ib al-Lubnaniyya) was founded in 1936 by Pierre Gemayel, a leading figure in Maronite and Lebanese politics. From the Phalangist standpoint, the Lebanese entity is a historical fact, having its roots in the trade center of ancient Phoenicia. The pillars of Lebanese nationalism—the 1920 borders, the 1926 constitution, and the National Covenant of 1943—are incontestable facts that cannot be subject to question. Lebanon should cooperate with the Arab countries, provided that political relations are based on the principles of mutual respect and equality.

When the Lebanese War began in 1975, the Phalangists staunchly opposed the military involvement and political meddling of Palestinian guerrillas in Lebanese politics. In fact, they have called for the abrogation of the 1969 Cairo

Agreements (which allowed the PLO to operate freely from South Lebanon) and the relocation of Palestinian refugees (there are around 250,000 refugees spread in twelve camps in Lebanon) to the other Arab countries. Most Phalangist Party members are recruited from the Maronite community.

In 1976 the Phalangists joined a larger coalition of major Christian conservative parties known as the "Lebanese Front." The front included the National Liberal Party of former president Camille Chamoun, the Guardians of Cedars, the Permanent Congress of the Lebanese Orders of Monks, and other Christian personalities. The Lebanese Front charter stressed "the need to maintain the unity of Lebanon, to re-establish the authority of the law, and to respect private enterprise in the economic sector."[21] The militias controlled by the member parties of the Lebanese Front were unified in 1980 in the Lebanese Forces.

To preserve their presence and ensure their survival during the war, the Phalangists and their allies called first on regional powers, then on global intervention, to defend the integrity of Lebanon as a state. In the summer of 1976 the Syrian regime of Hafez al-Assad was invited to intervene in Lebanon. The Syrian army played a crucial role in boosting the morale of the conservative Christian militias with whom Damascus had sided to forestall victory by the Muslim-leftist-Palestinian coalition.

Strengthened by Syria's support, the Phalangists and their allies mounted an attack (June–August 1976) against the Palestinian camps situated in the Christian-dominated sector of Beirut. These camps surrounded an important area comprising 30 percent of Lebanon's industrial capacity. The most important and heavily populated of these camps was that of Tel al-Zaatar. It included Palestinian and Shiite refugees from southern Lebanon.[22]

The Syrian–Lebanese conservative Christian harmony did not last very long—less than two years. To counter the Palestinian and Syrian presence in Lebanon—the Syrian involvement was not favorably viewed by some leaders in the Maronite community—the Christian-dominated militia decided to establish close ties with the Israelis.

The Israelis came to the Lebanese Christians' rescue because of their status as a threatened minority in the Near East. The Israeli–Maronite connection goes as far back as the 1930s when some prominent Maronite leaders advocated the creation of a "Christian homeland" similar to the homeland promised to the Jews in the Balfour Declaration.[23]

Together with the Christian communities in Lebanon, Muslim communities have played an ever-increasing role in the country's politics. Unlike the Sunni community, which followed the mainstream teaching of Islam, the Shiites (derived from the Arabic for "partisans," the Shiites being partisans of Ali, nephew and son-in-law of the Prophet Muhammad) belong to the sect of the Twelvers, which is predominant in Iran. It was not until the 1970s that the Shiite community began playing an active role in Lebanese politics. The catalyst and leader of this community was Imam Mousa al-Sadr, who disappeared in the mid-1970s on a trip to Libya.[24]

Given their status as an underprivileged and docile community until the end of the 1960s, the Shiites then became more organized and challenged the status quo forced on them by the Sunni–Maronite domination of Lebanese politics. Two major institutions were established to channel Shiite demands: the Supreme Shiite Council, which was founded to advocate the community's case on a national level, and Harakat Amal, a politico-military force that became a significant group to be contended with, especially in west Beirut and southern Lebanon. Following the 1982 Israeli invasion of Lebanon, a third group, Hezbollah (the Party of God), emerged as a major player in Shi'a and Lebanese politics.[25]

During the war, the Muslim communities in Lebanon did not present a unified front. Nevertheless, both conservative and radical elements were in agreement on fundamental issues. Given the demographic changes that occurred in their favor since the formation of the Republic of Lebanon in 1920, Lebanese Muslims claimed that the distribution of power in Lebanon has been to their disadvantage. The other issue that united the Muslim communities was their total opposition to the partition of Lebanon and their stress on the Arab identity of the country as well as the consolidation of relations between Lebanon, the Arab countries, and the third world; solidarity with the Palestinian people, although rejecting its permanent settlement in Lebanon; the end of all cooperation with Israel; and the dismantlement of the militias. Furthermore, the Muslims in Lebanon advanced two requests: a major role for the prime minister, who until the Taif Accord in 1989 was considered a rubber stamp to the president's decision; and a better distribution of economic wealth.[26]

THE ROLE OF THE VATICAN IN CONFLICT MITIGATION

Since the establishment of diplomatic relations with the Holy See in 1947, Lebanon has always been considered by successive sovereign pontiffs as an example and model of coexistence between Christians and Muslims.[27] When the Lebanese War began in 1975, the Vatican followed a policy based on advocating the territorial integrity of Lebanon and the preservation of the Lebanese formula of coexistence with the required amendments. This meant that Rome was aware that the 1943 National Covenant had to be adapted to the changing realities of Lebanese society. Moreover, in their addresses and written statements, both Paul VI and John Paul II underlined their total support for the Patriarch and the central government in Lebanon. The Holy See reiterated its prescription that the Lebanese were alone capable of solving their problems and expressed its willingness to use its influence with friendly governments to defuse bloodshed.

The Maronites, or, more precisely, some influential politicians and clergymen, did not share the equidistant and conciliatory attitude that the papacy adopted in the clash between Lebanese and Palestinian nationalism. The main Maronite contention was that Lebanese Christians were being sacrificed on the altar of the dialogue between Christians and Muslims. Rome did not seem to take the necessary steps to soothe the fears of Christian minorities in the Levant to allow the Maronites to pursue dialogue with their Muslim counterparts.

Maronites in Lebanon thought that they could count on the total and unswerving support of the Vatican in their struggle against the Palestinians and their Muslim allies. However, it is the welfare of Christianity in the Middle East in general that dictates the Holy See's approach to Lebanese Christians—that is, to save Lebanon as a sovereign entity in order to save the Christians. This policy explains the Vatican's constant opposition to the partition or other similar schemes (federation, Swiss-type cantons, etc.) proposed for Lebanon. If Lebanon were to be carved up into small ethnoreligious entities, the creation of a Christian ministate would have negative repercussions on other Christian communities living in Arab and Islamic countries. These groups would be exposed to hostility, oppression, and isolation. The Vatican was most worried that, living in an autonomous entity, Lebanese Christians "would cut themselves off from the people with whom they are intimately linked by tradition and language, and would render their mission a dead letter."[28]

The militant stand adopted by some Maronite clergymen during the war led Vatican officials to talk about Christians in Lebanon as being "islamized." "The problem with Christians in Lebanon is that religious values are superseded by the fight for survival. Religion is used in an ethnic sense."[29] Maronite monks have always played a fundamental role in their community, and the Holy See could not but acknowledge the importance of this factor in its approach toward Lebanon.

Father René Chamussy, currently rector of the Lebanon-based Jesuit Université Saint-Joseph, compared relations between the Vatican and Lebanese Christians to Moscow's strategy toward communist parties in the Middle East: interstate relations were more important than the fate of communist parties in the area. The difference was, according to the Jesuit scholar, that the former Soviet Union "justifies its behaviour to the eyes of its followers. Rome did not have the same reflex; it praised the formula of coexistence but remained silent on the concrete problems facing the Christians."[30]

To assess the Vatican's conflict mitigation efforts during the Lebanese War, I will briefly assess some of the missions (mediation and humanitarian) that were dispatched to Lebanon in the course of the war, and the papacy's reaction to the Israeli invasion of Lebanon in 1982.[31] The Vatican's first mission (November 1975) to Lebanon was headed by Cardinal Paolo Bertoli, who had lived in Lebanon as apostolic nuncio from 1959 to 1960. He had previous direct experience with

Lebanese politics when he was sent to Lebanon on a mission during the 1958 civil war.[32] Cardinal Bertoli's mission focused on establishing a dialogue between the conflicting parties to find a formula to revive the pattern of Christian-Islamic coexistence in Lebanon. In addition, the purpose of this mission and the one that followed was to express the papacy's solidarity to the embattled Maronite Patriarch.

The papal emissary had to confront the claims and counterclaims of each side. The Maronites thought that Paul VI, through his envoy, was going to back their fight for survival against the Muslim-leftist coalition. Lebanese Muslims and their leftist allies thought that Bertoli had come to "disarm the Christians" and convince them to renounce their threat to partition Lebanon. Cardinal Bertoli stated that "a small Lebanon, a utopian idea, can never exist. If Lebanon cannot be reconstituted, Christians would suffer."[33]

Bertoli's statement expressed clearly the declared aim of the Vatican to save Lebanon as a sovereign entity in order to preserve a safe presence for the Christians. But this goal was very difficult to achieve given the wide gap that existed between the perceptions of the Maronites and the Holy See regarding the future status of Lebanon. Furthermore, the position adopted by the Holy See to link the conflict in Lebanon to the resolution of the Israeli–Palestinian dispute clashed with the stated aims of the Lebanese Front to isolate the Lebanese crisis from an overall settlement of the Palestinian question.[34]

Bertoli's mission was followed by another (April 1976) that had mostly pastoral and humanitarian aims. By 1976 the war was taking its toll on the Lebanese population. The Vatican's delegation, headed by Monsignor Mario Brini, secretary of the Congregation for Oriental Churches, met with major Lebanese political leaders and PLO chief Yasser Arafat. As in the preceding papal mission, the report after each meeting emphasized the Holy See's opposition to partition and the importance of the formula of Christian–Muslim coexistence in Lebanon.

The third Vatican mission to Lebanon in December 1978, headed by Cardinal Paolo Bertoli, came with the election of John Paul II in October 1978. The election of the new pontiff raised hopes among Lebanese that, because of his Polish background, he would be more sympathetic to the plight of their country. This mission came to Lebanon for conciliation purposes and denoted the continuity in the style of Vatican's diplomacy toward the conflict in Lebanon.

By 1978 the Lebanese War had provoked further fragmentation in the Lebanese arena. In addition to inter-Lebanese and Lebanese–Palestinian feuds, the Maronite leadership was also split by internal wrangling. This factor alone warranted the return of Bertoli, with strong international support.[35]

Bertoli came to inform the Christian community in Lebanon that the time was ripe to put an end to internal fighting and resume negotiations for a Christian–Islamic dialogue. However, the intricacies of the Lebanese conflict and the misperceptions that had deepened considerably between Lebanese leaders since 1975 had rendered impossible any attempt at reconciliation. Furthermore, regional factors became more pronounced and relevant to any solution of the Lebanese War. In some US and Israeli circles, the idea of settling some of the 250,000 Palestinian refugees already in Lebanon as an alternative to their return to Palestine had gained some support. This prospect alone paralyzed the Lebanese regardless of their party affiliation, and the Vatican could not by itself pacify their fears without major guarantees from regional and global powers.[36]

The fourth mission to Lebanon (1980) was headed by the Holy See's secretary of state, Cardinal Agostino Casaroli. It was mostly pastoral in nature and epitomized the deep concern that the Vatican had toward the Lebanese War. The Holy See's second-highest-ranking figure came himself to convince his Lebanese counterparts (clergy, warlords, and politicians) that the papacy could not sacrifice its regional concerns—the fate of Catholic communities in the Levant and the Palestinian issue, and the most important of these concerns was the unwillingness of the Lebanese to reconcile and settle peacefully their differences. The Holy See was ready to contribute to narrow the gap internally and ask for intervention by other powers, but it could not offer solutions that were beyond its sphere of competence.[37]

JOHN PAUL II, THE MARONITES, AND THE ISRAELI INVASION OF LEBANON (1982)

The Israeli invasion of Lebanon in June 1982 did not ease the tensions between the Vatican and radical political and religious players in the Maronite community. On August 23, 1982, Bashir Gemayel, commander of the Christian-dominated Lebanese Forces, was elected president of Lebanon. Prior to his election, Gemayel wrote in the official mouthpiece of the Phalangist Party, *al-'Amal*, that the "Vatican should understand that Christians in Lebanon are not guinea pigs for the Christian-Muslim dialogue in the world. Lebanon's mission as a bridge [between the West and the Arab world] was over."[38] In these few words, the Maronite warlord highlighted the cause of the differences between the Holy See and the Lebanese Forces since the war began in 1975. To survive in a Muslim environment, the Christians in Lebanon had no other choice but to resort to arms to defend themselves. Dialogue with Muslims was impossible unless from a position of strength.

Nevertheless, in his last speech as president-elect, refining his previous statements on relations with the Vatican, Bashir Gemayel said that the Maronite community still holds "respect and profound attachment to the Holy See." He also expressed the hope that his community "could always rely freely on the paternal support that the Vatican has always given us." For political purposes and to appear as a national leader, Gemayel had shed his more extreme views and replaced them with a conciliatory approach toward the papacy.[39]

On September 15, 1982, John Paul II granted an audience to Yasser Arafat. This meeting, coming one day after the assassination of Bashir Gemayel, caused a further deterioration in the Vatican's relations with several personalities in the Maronite community. One of these leaders, Sheikh Najib Dahdah, former ambassador of Lebanon to the Holy See, said that Arafat's meeting with the pope "was a plot against John Paul II mounted by pro-Palestinian sympathizers in the Roman Curia." Dahdah went on to assert that Arafat's followers "had killed Bashir Gemayel."[40]

One day after the meeting between John Paul II and Arafat, Israeli-sponsored Christian militias perpetrated a massacre against Palestinian civilians in the camps of Sabra and Shatila close to Beirut airport (September 16–18, 1982). Pope John Paul II reacted by saying that there were "no sufficient words to condemn such crimes, which are repulsive to the human and Christian conscience."[41]

This episode of the Lebanese War was the most dramatic illustration of the degree of hatred in some Lebanese Christian circles toward the Palestinians. The PLO in its attempt to create a state within a state in Lebanon had alienated large sectors of the Lebanese population. The bloodbath in the two Palestinian refugee camps was a warning to the papacy that something more radical had to be done to develop some sort of understanding among Lebanese, and between them and the Palestinians. However, a more radical approach could lead the Vatican to take sides in the war between Lebanese and Palestinian nationalism, which has always been regarded as going against the long-term interests of the Catholic Church.

The Holy See's approach toward the Lebanese War is guided by the view of Lebanon as a microcosm of the various conflicts that mar interstate and transnational relations in the Middle East. The success of the Lebanese formula of Christian-Islamic coexistence is crucial in terms of the fate of Christian communities in the Levant.

Throughout the conflict the Vatican has often repeated that only through dialogue can the Lebanese hope to solve their problems. The pope and his mediators have warned the Lebanese not to set high hopes on the concrete effects of papal diplomacy. The Holy See expressed its solidarity with Lebanon and its Christian communities by the mobilization of all resources available to the papacy—diplomatic and humanitarian. Since the beginning of the war, the pleas for peace advanced by the pope in favor of Lebanon were not unheeded by the leaders of temporal powers such as France and the United States. The content of papal appeals concentrated on helping the Lebanese free themselves from external pressures and interferences.

What is most painful for the Vatican is that unity among Christians in Lebanon is still unrealized and elusive. Given the independent and closely knit nature of their community, some Maronites in Lebanon have refused to see their country entirely absorbed in the Arab–Islamic environment. However, since the Lebanese War ended in 1990, radical religious elements lost their influence in the Maronite community. With Vatican support, the authority of the Patriarch has been reinstated. Still, Christian religious leaders have to contend with the lack of unity among Christian leaders and the increasing role and influence of radical Islamist-nationalist groups such as Hezbollah.

Lebanon and the preservation of its Christian communities constitute the most important lead regarding future trends in papal diplomacy toward the Arab–Israeli conflict. If the situation in Lebanon were to portend some kind of compromise among its major communities, then the fate of the Christians could be considered somewhat secure. If Lebanon were to break up as a result of precarious agreements and continuous turmoil, then the Holy See would be forced to muster all the resources available to its diplomacy to salvage what would be left of the Christian presence. In light of the intractable problems of the Lebanese situation, the papacy may well have to strike painful compromises and resort to concrete actions in order to prevent the Church in Lebanon and the Middle East from being "fossilized" by history.

NOTES

1. In this chapter I use the definition given by Ivan Vallier for transnational actors to describe the Catholic Church. "A nation-state that is closely linked with extra-national systems and that holds key positions of power and prestige in those international systems is, in fact, no longer a nation-state but a transnational actor." The same would apply to Iran and its connection and close relationship with Shi'a communities throughout the Middle East, especially in Lebanon and Iraq (see Vallier 1976, 150).
2. For instance, see Hudson (1968) and see also Meo (1965).
3. This point is raised by Gordon (1983). See Rabbath (1973) and the recently published first comprehensive history and contemporary politics of Lebanon in the modern period by Traboulsi (2007). Another important and scholarly source on the history and contemporary politics of Lebanon are the books of Lebanese historian Salibi. See his *Modern History of Lebanon* (1964); see also *Crossroads to Civil War: Lebanon* (1976); and his *A House of Many Mansions: The History of Lebanon Reconsidered* (1988).
4. In this chapter I define the 1975–89 conflict in Lebanon as the Lebanese War because it had not only an internal dimension but equally regional and global dimensions.
5. In this chapter the terms "Holy See," "papacy," and "Vatican" are used interchangeably.

6. On the role of the Maronite Patriarchs in Lebanese politics see Kerr (1973); see also Beggiani (2001) and Marini (2001). Although nominally subservient to Rome, the Patriarch is chosen by the Council of Maronite Bishops.

7. There is a large literature available on the Lebanese War. I have selected a few titles in Arabic, French, and English. An important and documented chronology of the war, published in Arabic, is the work by Khuwayri (n.d.). An objective French assessment of the first two years of the war (1975–77) can be found in Bourgi and Weiss (1978) and their other book, which covers the war from 1978 to the Israeli invasion in summer 1982 (Bourgi and Weiss 1983); see also Picard (1988). Primary sources written by two major protagonists of the Lebanese War include Joumblatt (1978) and Chamoun (1977). Among selected books written on the war by Lebanese, see, among other titles, Benassar (1978, 1983). A Phalangist perspective of the first two years of the war can be found in N. Nasr (1977) and J. A. Nasr (1977). A Lebanese-Marxist perspective can be found in Amel (1979, 1980).

8. For an interesting and in-depth analysis of Arab politics after 1967, see Ajami (1981).

9. *L'Osservatore della domenica*, October 2, 1975.

10. On the National Covenant and its implications, see Rabbath (1973). See also the excellent book by Messarra (1994).

11. "Deux negations ne font pas une nation!" (Naccache 1983, 52–58).

12. For further details on the communities in Lebanon, see Rabbath (1973, 1–144); see also Arberry (1969a, 1969b) and de Bar (1983).

13. CIA World Factbook. "Lebanon." https://www.cia.gov/library/publications/the -world-factbook/geos/le.html#People.

14. Former president Camille Chamoun had proposed the creation of a Swiss-like system of cantons, political decentralization, or a federal system for Lebanon. Pierre Gemayel, founder of the Phalangist Party, did not share Chamoun's proposed solutions.

15. For an excellent assessment of Patriarch Sfeir's tenure so far, see Antoine Saad's two volumes in Arabic, *Mar Nasrallah Boutros Sfeir* and *Al Sadis wal Sabooun*, available at www.entire-east.com.

16. See "Lumieres franches sur la crise libanaise," pamphlet no. 3 in *Question Libanaise* (Kaslik: Publications de l'Universite Saint-Esprit, 1975), 49–51. For a comprehensive study on Christian communities in the Middle East, see Valognes (1994).

17. Regarding the legal status of non-Muslim minorities, see Fattal (1958) and Braude and Lewis (1982a, 1982b).

18. Quoted in *Proche-Orient Chretien* vol. 26 (Jerusalem: White Fathers Monastic Order, 1976), 145.

19. Personal interview with Father Qassis, Jbail (Lebanon), April 11, 1983.

20. For an official history of the Phalangist (Kata'ib) Party, see *Tarikh Hizb al-Kataïb al-Lubnaniyya, 1936–1946*, 2 vols., put out by the party's publishing house, Dar al-'Amal lil Nashr (1979, 1981). See also Suleiman (1967, 232–49).

21. For further details, see Picard (1980).
22. Regarding these events and the issues surrounding the Palestinian camp of Tel al-Zaatar, see Khuwayri (1977, 784–86, 801, 809–10). For the Tel al-Zaatar events as seen from the PLO's perspective, see "Tall-Zaatar: The Fight against Fascism" (pamphlet, Beirut: PLO, Unified Information, Foreign Informsational Department, 1976).
23. For a detailed account of the Maronite-Israeli connection and the role of the Maronite Patriarch then, see Kerr (1973, 248–59).
24. Regarding the Shiite community in Lebanon, see de Bar (1983, 17–24). See also Norton (1987).
25. For an excellent account of Hezbollah, its origins, and its current role in Lebanon, see Charara and Domont (2004); see also Hamzeh (2004).
26. For further details, see Khuwayri (1978, 664–66).
27. For a historical background on the relations between the Vatican and Lebanon, see Khater (1966).
28. Personal interview with the late Monsignor John G. Meaney, regional director, Pontifical Mission, Lebanon, May 27, 1983.
29. Personal interview with Vatican official, Beirut, May 27, 1983.
30. Personal interview with René Chamussy, Beirut, March 29, 1983.
31. In addition to its intervention with successive US administrations, the Vatican coordinated its efforts toward Lebanon with the American Catholic hierarchy. The role of the US Catholic hierarchy has been of great value to the Holy See's policy in Lebanon. During the war, the US National Conference of Catholic Bishops issued several statements related to the Arab–Israeli dispute and the conflict in Lebanon.
32. See the special issue, "The Papacy, Lebanon, and the Arabs," *Al-Hawadess*, August 25, 1978, 73–77.
33. Personal interview with Cardinal Paolo Bertoli, Rome, June 14, 1983.
34. For further details, see Irani (1989, 126–31).
35. The Vatican's decision to send Cardinal Bertoli on a second mission to Lebanon was taken in coordination and agreement with international powers. Two weeks before dispatching Bertoli, the Holy See sent letters to US president Jimmy Carter, French president Valéry Giscard d'Estaing, British prime minister James Callaghan, and West German chancellor Helmut Schmidt. All of them expressed their support to the papal initiative, given the prestige the Holy See enjoyed. For further details, see *An Nahar Arab and International*, December 18, 1978, 3.
36. A former US ambassador to Lebanon, Richard Parker, is reported to have told Camille Chamoun, former Maronite president of Lebanon, that the solution "was for the Palestinians to stay in Lebanon and repatriate 100,000 to the West Bank and Gaza." For further details, see Khuwayri (1978, 654).
37. For further details on Casaroli's mission, see *Proche-Orient Chretien*, 30 (1980): 300–303.
38. Quoted in *al-Masira*, a publication of the Lebanese Forces, November 1, 1982, 12.

39. *La Documentation Catholique*, 1848, March 20, 1983, 305–7.
40. Personal interview with Sheikh Najib Dahdah, Beirut, April 1983.
41. *Proche-Orient Chretien*, 32, no. 3–4 (1982): 386.

REFERENCES

Ajami, Fouad. 1981. *The Arab Predicament Arab Political Thought and Practice since 1967*. Cambridge: Cambridge University Press.

Amel, Mahdi. 1979. *Bahs fi asbab al-harb al-ahliya fi lubnan*, vol. 1. Beirut: Dar al-Farabi.

———. 1980. *Al-qadiyya al-filastiniyya fi idiolojiat al-burjuaziyya al-lubnaniyya*. Beirut, Research Center, Palestine Liberation Organization.

Arberry, A. J., ed. 1969a. *Religion in the Middle East: Three Religions in Concord and Conflict*. Vol. 1, *Judaism and Christianity*. London: Cambridge University Press.

———, ed. 1969b. *Religion in the Middle East: Three Religions in Concord and Conflict*. Vol. 2, *Islam*. London: Cambridge University Press.

de Bar, Luc-Henri. 1983. *Les communautes confessionnelles du Liban*. Paris: Editions Recherches sur les Civilisations.

Beggiani, Seely. 2001. "The Patriarchs in Maronite History," *Journal of Maronite Studies* 5, no. 2 (July–December). www.maroniteinstitute.org/MARI/JMS/january01/index2.html.

Benassar. 1978. *Anatomie d'une guerre et d'une occupation: Evenements du Liban de 1975 a 1978*. Paris: Editions Galilee.

———. 1983. *Paix d'Israel au Liban*. Beirut: Les Editions l'Orient-Le Jour.

Bourgi, Albert and Pierre Weiss. 1978. *Les complots libanais*. Paris: Berger-Levreault.

———. 1983. *Liban: La cinquieme guerre du Proche-Orient*. Paris: Editions Publisud.

Braude, Benjamin, and Bernard Lewis, eds. 1982a. *Christians and Jews in the Ottoman Empire*. Vol. 1, *The Central Lands*. New York: Holmes & Meier.

———, eds. 1982b. *Christians and Jews in the Ottoman Empire*. Vol. 2, *The Arab-Speaking Lands*. New York: Holmes & Meier.

Chamoun, Camille. 1977. *Crise au Liban*. Beirut: n.p., 1977.

Charara, Walid, and Frederic Domont. 2004. *L'Hezbollah: Un movement islamo-nationaliste*. Paris: Fayard.

Fattal, Antoine. 1958. *Le statut legal des non-musulmans en pays d'Islam*. Beirut: Imprimerie Catholique.

Gordon, David C. 1983. *The Republic of Lebanon: Nation in Jeopardy*. Boulder, CO: Westview Press, 1983.

Hamzeh, Ahmad Nizar. 2004. *In the Path of Hizbullah*. Syracuse, NY: Syracuse University Press.

Hudson, Michael C. 1968. *The Precarious Republic: Political Modernization in Lebanon*. New York: Random House.

Irani, George Emile. 1989. *The Papacy and the Middle East: The Role of the Holy See in the Arab-Israeli Conflict, 1962–1984*. Notre Dame, IN: University of Notre Dame Press.

Jabre, Antoine. 1980. *La guerre du Liban: Moscou et la crise du Proche-Orient.* Paris: Pierre Belfond.

Joumblatt, Kamal. 1978. *Pour le Liban.* Paris: Editions Stock.

Kerr, David A. 1973. "The Temporal Authority of the Maronite Patriarchate, 1920–1958: A Study in the Relationship of Religion and Secular Power," PhD diss., St. Anthony's College, University of Oxford.

Khater, Lahd. 1966. *Al-Vatikan wa Lubnan.* Sidon, Lebanon: Manshuraat Majallat al-Risala al-Mukhlisiyya.

Khuwayri, Antoine. n.d. *Mausu'at al-harb fi Lubnan, 1975–1981,* 12 vols. Beirut: Dar al-Abjadiyya lil Sahafa wal Tiba'a wal Nashr, Sarba.

———. 1977. *Al-Harb fi Lubnan, 1976,* vol. 2. Jounieh, Lebanon: Al Bulisiyya Press.

———. 1978. *Hawadith Lubnan, 1977–1978,* vol. 6, *Wa akhiran harakuh* (Jounieh, Lebanon: Dar al-Abjadiyya.

Marini, Francis J. 2001. "The Role of the Patriarch," *Journal of Maronite Studies* 5, no. 1 (July–December). www.maroniteinstitute.org/MARI/JMS/january01/index2.html.

Meo, Leila M. T. 1965. *Lebanon: Improbable Nation. A Study in Political Development.* Bloomington: Indiana University Press.

Messarra, Antoine Nasri. 1994. *Theorie generale du systeme politique libanais: Essai compare sur les fondements et les perspectives d'évolution d'un systeme consensuel de gouvernement.* Paris: Cariscript.

Naccache, Georges. 1983. *Un réve libanais: 1943–1972.* Beirut: Fiches du Monde Arabe.

Nasr, J. A. 1977. *Mihnat Lubnan fi Thawrat al-Yasar.* Beirut: Dar al-Amal.

Nasr, Nicolas. 1977. *Harb Lubnan wa Madaha.* Beirut: Dar al-Amal.

Norton, Augustus Richard. 1987. *AMAL and the Shi'a: Struggle for the Soul of Lebanon.* Austin: Texas University Press.

Picard, Elizabet. 1980. "Role et évolution du Front Libanais dans la guerre civile," *Maghreb-Machrek* 90 (October–December): 16–39.

———. 1988. *Liban, état de discorde, des fondations a la guerre civile.* Paris: Flammarion.

Rabbath, Edmond. 1973. *La formation historique du Liban politique et constitutionnel: Essai de synthese.* Beirut: Publications de l'Universite Libanaise.

Salibi, Kamal. 1964. *Modern History of Lebanon.* New York: Praeger.

———. 1976. *Crossroads to Civil War: Lebanon 1959–1976.* Beirut: Caravan Books.

———. 1988. *A House of Many Mansions: The History of Lebanon Reconsidered.* London: I. B. Tauris.

Suleiman, Michael. 1967. *Political Parties in Lebanon.* Ithaca, NY: Cornell University Press.

Traboulsi, Fawwaz. 2007. *A History of Modern Lebanon.* London: Pluto Books.

Vallier, Ivan. 1976. "The Roman Catholic Church: A Transnational Actor." In *Transnational Relations and World Politics,* edited by Robert L. Keohane and Joseph S. Nye. Cambridge, MA: Harvard University Press.

Valognes, Jean-Pierre. 1994. *Vie et mort des chretiens d'orient: Des origins a nos jours.* Paris: Fayard.

CHAPTER 4

GLOBALIZATION, RELIGION, AND NATIONALISM IN ISRAEL AND PALESTINE

∾

MICHELINE ISHAY

As Western neoliberal economic architects were triumphantly remaking local and international politics in their own image after the Cold War, conservative and religious forces were preparing to crack the new edifice of globalization. Neoliberal economists and their proselytes were scarcely able to savor their victory over communism as they rushed to rearm themselves against the perceived dangers of fundamentalism after September 11. Images from the 1990s of "Jihad versus McWorld" or "the clash of civilizations" now seemed like sinister prophecies of an ever more fragile world left to its new laissez-faire destiny. Yet the more uncertain, greedy, and materialistic that world has become, the greater has been the appeal of religion. Religious movements have galvanized the poor and the disenfranchised, have fought to resurrect fragmented and desolated traditional communities, and are restructuring politics according to divine interpretations. That dark side of modernization had already been revealed during the Cold War struggle between left and right, and has grown bleaker under the reign of globalist conquistadors since the end of the Cold War. Politicized religious and fundamentalist leaders have challenged the dictates of globalization and sunk deep roots in places where political legitimacy has been eroded by chronic crises.

This volume focuses on the role of religion (fundamentalism) and nationalism in divided societies. This chapter addresses that issue by drawing on Antonio Gramsci's conceptual framework to assess these linkages in the Israeli and Palestinian context. It argues that while globalization has stimulated Israeli economic growth since the late 1980s, economic liberalization has simultaneously fostered greater social inequity within the Palestinian and Israeli communities and between Palestinians and Israelis. The blend and possible convergence of religious and nationalist extremism, discussed in David Little's chapter, has now moved into the void created by economic stress, unresolved security concerns, weak governments, and fragmented civil societies. Based on the analysis that follows, this chapter suggests ways to counter radicalism in the short and the long run that will require, among other things, governmental and international interventionism to redress the disparities that feed religious fundamentalism.

The revival of religious politics in our era of globalization can be illuminated by the work of Antonio Gramsci. One may wonder about the relevance of an Italian interwar Marxist thinker to the question of religion in today's divided societies. In fact, there is enduring value in Gramsci's critical analysis, which explores the relationship between capitalism, fragmented civil societies, and the rise of fascism—what Gramsci also called "statolatry" or the worship of the state (Gramsci 1971, 268). One needs only to replace the terms "fascism" with "belligerent fundamentalism" and "capitalism" with "globalization" to begin to apply Gramsci's insights to the emerging study of religion and international politics.

In this exercise, the purpose is not to blur the difference between fascism and fundamentalism; a focus on detail can always reveal distinctions shaped by historical contexts. While fascism has a more secular and nationalist character than fundamentalism, these terms are both defined in opposition to modernity, reason, and progress in their respective times and context. While the term "globalization" may signify a more advanced stage of capitalism, this concept is here employed to highlight how what has become a capitalist world economy fails to meet the needs of an important part of the world population (see Ishay and Goldfischer 2008; see also Sandbook and Romano 2004).

Further, the idea is not to fall prey to the simplistic equation of Islamism with fascism. Rather, this chapter is an effort to employ a conceptual framework that provides important insights into extremist antirationalist ideologues, violence, and capitalism during the interwar period to consider human rights alternatives for Israelis and Palestinians. Given this book's focus on the role of religion in conflict resolution, or the role religious leaders as catalysts of violence or as promoters of peace in divided societies, Gramsci remains highly relevant because the Italian scholar and politician was able to link local social dynamics to dominant economic forces in the international arena. After all, while religious leaders can be seen as potential agents of change, they can also be seen as pawns on a broad geopolitical and economic chessboard that shapes their moves and influence.

The revival of religious ideologues and the advance of globalization are not coincidental phenomena that occurred randomly worldwide but are dialectically related on three levels: the global economy, the institutional (state and civil society), and the ideological level. In other words, the growing of economic inequity, driven by globalization and Western culture, has shaken the stability of governments, eroded traditional communities, and fostered both secular and nonsecular extremist political reactions that are in turn shaping the scope and extent of globalization itself.

Let us consider Gramsci's analysis of fascism in terms of four related dimensions: First, his analysis is as an ultranationalist ideology beyond right and left, resulting from the incapacity of the capitalist system to deliver "food, housing and clothing to . . . a not insignificant portion of the population" (Gramsci 1925). Anti-Enlightenment ideologies, in fact, have become prevalent in similar circumstances; those of socioeconomically imperiled civil societies during the major economic crises of the interwar period, the postcolonial era, and the post–Cold War world. Second, fascism is an ideological response to the failure of a state or governmental entity to maintain its economic and cultural hegemony, coupled with the failures of dominant groups to create broad national consensus. Third, fascism is a force (such as Caesarism or Bonapartism) with a robust organizational capacity that enables it to fill an ideological gap in deeply divided civil societies. Fourth, it is a movement or a party whose leaders can be co-opted tactically or strategically according to stratagems that vary depending on the particular institutional and social terrain.

Without overlooking the historical and contextual differences that separate us from Gramsci's world, one can still draw striking similarities. Many postcolonial states are embedded in severe crises of legitimacy while experiencing the exclusionary dimension of globalization. Many such states are striving to contain the rise of religious politics and fundamentalism (beyond the traditional right and left divide). Yet defiant religious forces arrayed against the unfulfilled promises of modernization and globalization are gaining ideological and political leverage throughout the Middle East and beyond.

With the understanding that this trend takes different forms in different contexts, this chapter focuses specifically on the unfettered economic dimension of globalization as a critical precondition for the revival of religious fundamentalism and extreme nationalism in the Israeli–Palestinian context. It should be stressed that religion is not a sui generis cause of the Israeli–Palestinian conflict, yet observers of that region have witnessed how religion has been a growing component of the radicalization of Israeli and Palestinian politics. Just as the 2006 and 2009 elections in Israel have revealed the alarming influence of religious parties—notably Shas, the Ichud Leumi (the National Union) and United Torah, and the extreme right (Yisrael Beiteinu)—in shaping a more right-wing Israeli political scene, there has been an even greater radicalization of Palestinian politics by Islamist groups led by Hamas.[1]

The politicization of religion in Israel and Palestine is a not a new phenomenon. During the 1970s, well before the arrival of globalization in its neoliberal garb on the Israeli scene, the religious and radical right in Israeli society was on the rise. Extremist politics created together strange bedfellows as religious fundamentalists and some military hardliners combined to form the Gush Emunim (the Bloc of the Faithful) (Sprinzhak 1989, 173). The Gush Emunim were young, fundamentalist, and messianic living in or supporting settlements; they believed that Israeli prime minister Menachem Begin should never have returned the Sinai to the Egyptians or, with the secular ultranationalist party, Tehiya, rejected all territorial concessions from the post-1967 borders as a form of betrayal.

Well before the global market economy made its impact on the Palestinian territories, radical religious groups such as Hamas were also on the rise. Hamas grew out of the Muslim Brotherhood—a religious and political organization founded in Egypt with branches throughout the Arab world. Beginning in the late 1960s, Hamas's founder and spiritual leader, Sheikh Ahmed Yassin, preached and did charitable work in the West Bank and the Gaza Strip, both of which were occupied by Israel following the 1967 Six-Day War. In 1973 Yassin established al-Mujamma' al-Islami (the Islamic Center), to coordinate the Muslim Brotherhood's political activities in Gaza.

Hamas was founded in 1987 as the Muslim Brotherhood's local political arm and with Fatah fomented the first intifada, a Palestinian uprising against Israeli control of the West Bank and Gaza (Abu-Amr 1993). The conflict over the occupation of Palestinian land after 1967 is central to any account of rising religious and secular extremism on both sides. Yet this chapter argues that globalization, coinciding with the shift from an Israeli state-controlled economy to privatization of the Israeli economy in the mid-1980s, has in fact greatly exacerbated tensions within Israel and even more seriously within the Palestinian territories, and has forged the conditions underlying increasing religious and nationalist radicalism, spurring an ideological backlash that is now undermining peace efforts.

That argument is advanced in the hope that understanding the economic, institutional, and ideological sources of religious or ethnic violence can increase the possibilities for peace. Accordingly, it will conclude with a policy recommendation. In the near term, it argues for involving religious parties in the peace process to the extent that their leaders are willing to seek peaceful accommodation with their adversaries. Concomitantly, it calls for a long-term strategy that emphasizes a greater commitment to secular social and economic welfare mechanisms to fight poverty and outbid theocratic institutional entrenchment in Israeli and Palestinian civil societies.

Focusing on a Gramscian framework and on the Israeli and Palestinian contexts, this chapter is structured as follows: First, it uses broad strokes to depict the influence of the economic dimension of globalization on the local level, especially the shift from Israel state-management to neoliberal economic policy, Second, it considers the impact of globalization on the fragmentation of Israeli and Palestinian civil society (or what Antonio Gramsci referred to as the erosion of hegemony). Third, it assesses the rise of religious politics in the political vacuum formed by weak or "nonhegemonic" social structures. Finally, it considers (in terms of a Gramscian war of tactics) the conditions necessary for redressing the capacity of hawkish religious or nationalist leaders to obstruct peace while identifying the context in which moderate religious leaders may play a more constructive role.

FROM STATE-CONTROL MANAGEMENT TO PRIVATIZATION IN A GLOBALIZED AGE

Globalization, associated with incremental deregulatory economic policies, has shaped the new world hegemonic order since the 1970s. In the words of the neo-Gramscian scholar Robert Cox, a world hegemonic order "is expressed in universal norms, institutions and mechanisms which lay down general rules of behavior for states and for those forces of civil society that act across national boundaries—rules which support the dominant mode of production" (Cox 1993, 62). While lagging behind other Western industrialized countries, Israelis and Palestinians were not immune from the new global hegemonic trend toward privatization and post-Fordist forms of production (Filc and Lebel 2005).

The transition from a state-managed economy to liberalization had an important impact on both Israeli and Palestinian civil society. The end of the Labor's Party's dominance and the rise of the right-wing Likud Party, against the backdrop of economic crises of the 1970s and the 1980s, paved the road for a new economic stabilization plan (ESP). This 1985 plan marked a turning point toward liberalization and the emergence of a privileged class independent from the state. With inflation skyrocketing in the early 1980s, reaching hyperinflation (373.8 percent) in 1984, the ESP team adopted a plan to reduce government subsidies, devalue the currency, restrict wage growth, and open the economy to foreign capital and privatization (Hanieh 2003, 6).

It is worth noting that the people who devised this policy were initially members of the Labor Party, not neoliberals from the Likud. Indeed, Prime Minister Shimon Peres acted as a driving force behind the plan and later as the architect of the new Middle East Project.[2] With others, Peres was convinced that entering the global economy would lead toward regional prosperity, thereby strengthening as a way to strengthen peace efforts. If doves of the Labor Party advocated privatization and deregulation as an optimal way to promote peace, the Likud of Benjamin Netanyahu readily embraced the same economic policies as a way to promote Israel's power. Subsequently, the Israeli economy moved quickly to embrace high technology (Ram 2000, 221; Shafir and Peled 2000, 221). Foreign direct investment in the Israeli economy increased rapidly in the 1990s, as foreign multinationals in the high-tech sector, such as Microsoft, IBM, CISCO, INTEL, Motorola, and others, opened local branches for both production and research.

From 1967 through the early 1980s, the Palestinian economy grew in conjunction with Israeli state capitalism and occupation. That growth was initially driven by partial integration into the Israeli economy, along with opportunities resulting from the Persian Gulf oil boom. With the opening of the Israeli market to Palestinian manual labor, coupled with wage remittances from the Gulf and elsewhere, the Palestinian economy almost tripled in size. In the mid-1980s, along with the collapse of the regional oil boom and the corresponding decline in worker remittances from the Gulf, recession and hyperinflation in Israel reduced labor opportunities for Palestinians and weakened the dependent Gazan and West Bank economy (see Diwan and Shaban 1999, 2–3; Kleiman 2007). By the time of the outbreak of the first intifada, characterized by strikes and suppression of economic activity, the Palestinian economy was in decline while the Israeli economy continued to grow.

GLOBALIZATION AND THE ECONOMIC FRAGMENTATION OF ISRAELI AND PALESTINIAN CIVIL SOCIETIES

Economic globalization did not impact everyone equally within Israel and Palestine. In fact, globalization precipitated economic inequality and fragmentation within each respective civil society. That trend took different paths given the different degree of economic and social development in the Israeli and the Palestinian communities. While comparing developed states of the West with Russian civil society, Gramsci noted when a state within the West "trembled a strong structure of civil society was at once revealed." In Russia, conversely, where "the state was everything, civil society was primordial and gelatinous," social rupture within civil society was more devastating (Gramsci 1971, 238).

Replacing "the West" with Israel and replacing prerevolutionary Russia with the Palestinian territories, that comparison holds (with some historical license) insofar as it provides a context-based explanation for the different experiences of hegemonic (Israel) and nonhegemonic (Palestine) civil societies under conditions of crisis or transition. Despite the economic crisis, inflation, and the weakening of the state-owned sector, and as foreign capital poured into the Israeli market, a dominant class previously linked to the Labor Party emerged in control of new entrepreneurial activities in the late 1980s. Ten of the wealthiest Israeli families with that link to the past now accounted for more than 20 percent of Israel's gross domestic product (GDP). One analyst, Daniel Maman, estimates that the top eleven companies in Israel today control two-thirds of Israel's GDP (Hanieh 2003, 16). The success of such control during sharp economic transitions, Gramsci observed, attested to the capacity of a traditional ruling class to reacquire "the control that was slipping from its grasp" (Gramsci 1971, 210).

Notwithstanding the Israeli economic boom of the 1990s stewarded by an important segment of the old elite, Israel was entering one of the worst recessions in its history, with unemployment reaching 7.3 percent, leaving 1.65 million under the poverty line, according to a 2007 report released by Israeli government (Sinai 2007). Of that number, 30 percent are Arab Israelis, 30 percent are Haredim (religious orthodox), and a significant number are Mizrahim (Arab or Oriental Jews).[3] In Gaza and the West Bank, 67 percent of Palestinians live below the poverty line (World Bank 2008). These numbers reveal the darker side of Israeli economic growth and can help explain the resurgence of religious groups.

In short, the privatization of the Israeli economy showed two contradictory trends: rapid economic development that coincided with growing social disparities, inequality, and the descent of a significant segment of the population into poverty. Post-Zionist ideology associated with the liberalization of the economy was embraced by both Labor and the Likud, with the former as advocates of globalization qua peace and the latter as defenders of a stronger Israel within its post-1967 borders. This trend represented a renewed capacity for Israelis to reclaim independence from Palestinian labor. In that sense, the old left and the new right were embracing similar economic policies rooted in conflicting ideological perspectives. With repetitive failures on both the left and the right to deliver peace, the subsequent intifadas, growing social and economic gaps, and the debacle surrounding the war in Lebanon, the Zionist ideology of the Macworld age experienced an ever-deeper identity crisis. In the ideological void formed by conflicts, widening economic gaps, and social alienation, religious leaders began to increase their social and political influence.

Unsurprisingly, Palestinians outside the Green Line (temporary or interim borders established in the 1949 Armistice Agreements) experienced a more severe crisis of legitimacy. For a while, the Oslo agreement (1993) and the jubilation accompanying the arrival in Arafat in Jericho in 1994 seemed to promise a new life for Palestinians. Yet these popular sentiments would soon subside, leaving entrenched feelings of unresolved grievances and hatred, which erupted intermittently in increasingly brutal rebellions. Against this backdrop, one has to recall that soon after Israel occupied Gaza and the West Bank in 1967, Palestinian employment depended heavily upon the Israeli economy. Considered as second-class citizens, the Palestinian standard of living beyond the Green Line was far from adequate but not as dire as today. With newly opened economic frontiers, Israelis now had access to a new pool of workers—Filipino, Nigerian, Indian, and Chinese, among others—all of whom could compete with Palestinian labor without representing the security threat posed by Palestinians. At first, limited guest permits were issued, but with the onset of the first intifada, and the closure of the West Bank and Gaza after Desert Storm in 1991, Israeli employers pressed the government to address the labor shortage by issuing more permits. The government issued 8,000 permits in 1991, climbing to 68,900 in 1994. By 2006 there were nearly 200,000 foreign workers in Israel, including illegal as well as legal workers (Wagner n.d., 6; Friedberg and Sauer 2003). During the same period, Palestinian employment in Israel dropped from 110,000 to 50,000, even as the migrant workforce doubled (see Wagner n.d., 6).

In the context of the first intifada, Israel's increasing rejection of Palestinian labor precipitated the Palestinian descent into wretched living conditions. Following Arafat's arrival in the West Bank in 1994, the Palestinian Liberation Organization (PLO) struggled to keep in check a fragmented and impoverished Palestinian civil society. With more than half of its population living in poverty and the exposure of scandalous PLO political corruption at the expense of ordinary people, Palestinians were sinking into severe economic and ideological crises. Arafat's mythical image of heroic triumph was slowly fading at home and abroad. Upon Arafat's death, bloody infighting between Fatah loyalists and Hamas culminated in Hamas's ascension to power in 2006, completing its journey from a grassroots movement to a major player in Palestinian politics.

While it is true, as most commentaries have stressed, that pressure for a rapid transition from Palestinian labor to foreign guest workers was driven by security concerns over armed infiltration into Israel, this is arguably not the only critical component of a long-term shift toward guest workers. Growing labor mobility associated with globalization was making available a vast new labor pool of cheap labor, leading to growing reliance on non-Palestinian guest workers. Globalization was making available a labor force cheaper than Palestinians, and growing reliance on guest workers. In that sense, economic incentives and security concerns were working hand-in-hand to erode the living conditions of Palestinians in the West Bank and Gaza. The terrain was fertile for the ascension of religion, side-by-side with secular ultranationalism, to fill the new ideological vacuum.

INSTITUTIONAL CRISES AND THE RISE OF RELIGIOUS AND NATIONALIST CAESARISMS

Neoliberalism is not a purely "economic affair"; it can precipitate hegemonic political and institutional instability and generate collective identity crises. Endemic institutional crises, explained Gramsci, referring to France after World War I, "take the form of an ever increasing difficulty in forming governments. It has its immediate origin in the multiplication of parliamentary parties and in the permanent internal crises of each of these parties (one finds in each party what one finds in parliament as a whole: difficulty in governing and unstable leadership)" (Gramsci 1971, 80).

The 2009 Israeli and 2006 Palestinian elections offered a similar snapshot of well-ingrained institutional crisis. In Israel the formation of the governmental coalition under Likud, which includes a bizarre amalgamation of ministers across the spectrum from Labor, to the religious parties, to the extreme right-wing party, Israel Beiteinu, reflects Israel's recurrent inability to move beyond political deadlock. Similarly, the Palestinian election characterized a sharper Palestinian institutional division between Fatah, the sole acceptable representative of the Palestinians for the outside world, and Hamas, the winner of the elections, and the subsequent internecine fight between Hamas and Fatah over Gaza.

That kind of social malaise, explained Gramsci, often gives rise to the phenomenon of "Caesarism"—that is, a situation in which a great personality is entrusted with the task of reigning in conflicting political forces heading toward catastrophe. There can be, he added, a Caesarist solution even without a Caesar (Gramsci 1971, 222–23). If, as in the Israeli–Palestinian context, there is not such a Caesar or a clear Caesarist path looming in the horizon, such an "anti-democratic" dark force may well be in the making, considering the rise of religious and nationalist efforts to transcend or replace the old right and left divide.

Leaders of the Likud, religious parties, Shas, Israel Beiteinu, and HaIchud HaLeumi (National Union) have positioned themselves to provide a new cultural and strategic equilibrium leaning toward the right side of the political spectrum to fill an ideological vacuum created by reciprocally destructive political factionalism (Filc and Lebel 2005). Whether Hamas and Fatah leaders will be fully reunited after the 2007 fratricidal war in Gaza remains an open question, yet there is sufficient evidence to envision the emergence of an Islamist and secular nationalist modus vivendi despite the intra-Palestinian violence of 2007.

With Zionism gradually shedding its socialist skin during in the mid-1980s for a more capitalist worldview, the portion of the Israeli population that was left behind—in effect banished from the garden of globalization—was the poor community of Jewish Mizrahim, Haredim, and Arab Israelis. Add to that mix the one million Russian Jews who migrated to Israel starting in the 1990s, to a country that already had difficulties in integrating its poor, and the result is a cocktail of disenchanted people who seek nationalist pride in the parties of the right and, in religious parties, a sense of collective identity associated with economic welfare.[4]

One defender of that effort to form a new Jewish compact supplanting liberal secularism is the religious party Shas. Originally known as the Worldwide Association of Torah Keepers, Shas was founded under the leadership Rabbi Ovadia Yosef in 1984 (a former Israeli chief rabbi). Shas advocates Halakha (Jewish religious law), such as prohibitions on various activities on Shabbat. Its social agenda is conservative while its economic agenda supports welfare programs. It should be noted that its support for welfare helps sustain the viability of the high birthrate favored by religious families—which in turn adds a demographic factor to the growing political power of religion in Israel. While Shas has supported the idea of a Greater Israel under the crown of the Mizrahi Torah, it has never taken active measures to support the Gush Emunim movement and does not strongly favor the settlements. Shas has forged coalitions with secular parties across the spectrum of Israeli politics at different points in time. With the support of Haredim (orthodox) and low-income Mizrahim, Shas currently holds twelve seats in the Knesset and has emerged as the third force in Israeli politics. It is of interest that half of Shas voters, according to surveys, are not religious but are traditional or even secular (Cohen 2007, 325). Despite Shas leaders' early support of the Oslo Accords, Shas's constituency has slowly dragged the party toward a more hawkish stand regarding the Israeli–Palestinian question.

Another religious party, the National Religious Party (NRP), renamed the Jewish Home (Habayit Hayehudi) in 2008, despite a relatively early centrist political position in the past, has since 1967 moved to the political right (Tepe 2005, 290). The Jewish Home is a union of religious Zionist parties committed to furthering the security and integrity of greater Israel. While the Jewish Home believes in charity for the poor, its economic policy is closer to the neoliberal economy of Likud Party. Its political agenda is clearly associated with Israeli settlers and the Gush Emunim. The Jewish Home shrank steadily since the 1980s and slumped to just three seats in the last election, their worst electoral performance ever. Given the fact that the Jewish Home is more hawkish than Shas and less supportive of welfare for the poor, the shift among voters from the NRP to Shas represented in 2006 a more moderate trend regarding the compatibility of religion and peace. Yet, despite its decrease in votes, one should not underestimate the importance of the Jewish Home because its commitment, along with other orthodox parties (United Torah Judaism), to the expansion of the Jewish state beyond the 1967 borders coincides with the views of the radical right.

HaIchud HaLeumi (the National Union), for instance, represents an amalgamation of orthodox and non-orthodox parties. Created in 1999, the National Union is a coalition that includes Hardal and Tkuma, two national ultraorthodox parties that support the settlements and the reestablishment of Religious Zionism, and the ultranationalist party, Moledet, which has argued for transfer of the Palestinian population and has prided itself on being composed of both non-orthodox and orthodox elements. In the 2001 election HaIchud HaLeumi was doubled with the addition of Yisrael Beiteinu (Israel Our Home), a party that is largely backed by Jewish immigrants from the former Soviet Union.

Yisrael Beiteinu, a group that lacks a strong religious identification, is led by a charismatic leader, Avigdor Lieberman, who thoroughly opposes territorial concessions in the West Bank. He has also advocated "swapping" Israeli Arab communities for Jewish settlements—an open endorsement of ethnic cleansing.

This group ended up running on a separate list in the 2006 election, earning eleven seats in the Knesset. During the 2009 election, Yisrael Beiteinu moved from eleven seats to fifteen, becoming the third-largest political party in Israel, and Lieberman became foreign policy minister under the Likud-led government of Prime Minister Benjamin Netanyahu.

Overall, religious parties, including Shas and the National Union, have increased their seats in the Israeli Parliament since the onset of privation and deregulation. In the 1950s and 1960s, the religious parties won consistently fewer than twenty Knesset seats. Moreover, they were not essential to the securing of a coalition parliamentary majority due to Mapai's predominance. Today, religious Knesset representation—partly the result of large families among Orthodox Jews, and partly the result of economic deregulation—has reached thirty members, and religious factions are ever more essential to securing a parliamentary majority due to the disappearance of large party dominance (Cohen 2007, 343).

If the economic gap sharpened by deregulation in Israel initially strengthened Shas, two intifadas have fueled support for the nationalist right. Amidst an existential crisis of national identity, these religious forces are redefining secular Israelis as Jews and entrusting them with divine ownership over the greater Israel. Overall, under Likud governmental coalition, HaIchud HaLeumi, the Jewish Home, Shas, and Yisrael Beiteinu have swung the political pendulum to the populist right. Neither strictly right (from an economic perspective) nor left (from a universal human rights dimension) and despite their differences, these parties call on Israelis to transcend their selfish interests, either to reach higher Halakhic goals or to secure the survival and de facto expansion of the Jewish community in the post-1967 borders, regardless of the price imposed on Israeli democracy and human rights. Their subordination of human rights to faith in the state is reminiscent of the era of European extreme nationalism and fascism during the 1920s and 1930s.

On the Palestinian side, Arafat long represented the Palestinian Caesar, returning undefeated to his homeland in 1994 after years of relentless struggle against the Israeli state. Buoyed by a new jolt of hope over the Oslo agreement promising to end occupation, the beginning of a democratic political system, and a rapid improvement of living conditions, Arafat was seen as the hero unifying all existing Palestinian factions. Yet unemployment, corruption, and declining delivery of services brought Arafat's popularity down, from 65 percent in 1996 to 47 percent in 2000, with support for Fatah also dropping to 37 percent in 2000 and to 29 percent a year later (Khalil 2002, 89). The political center of gravity was shifting from Fatah to Hamas. As Hamas steadily became the leading grassroots organization, priding itself on its greater ability to offer basic human services to the poor delivered on a religious and armored plate, Islamism was taking center stage in Palestinian politics.

While Hamas did not field candidates in 1996, it shook the world when the party took seventy-four seats in the January 2006 ballots, with Ismail Haniyeh at its head, and left Fatah, the previous ruling party, with forty-five seats.[5] In an even more dramatic way than Shas's success in the Israeli 2006 election, Hamas did not merely enter the political arena; it won in a landslide. One cannot over-emphasize the importance to Hamas's success, of its capacity to provide extensive welfare assistance and services to all Palestinians—in the words of its early ideo-logue, Ahmed Yassin—"without distinction of religious belief or political affili-ation" (quoted in Hroub 2004, 22). While high Palestinian National Authority officials continued to live separately from their people in varying degrees of luxury, the popular reputation of Hamas's leaders was earned by living among the people and sharing their hardships without sinking into corruption. Hamas's principled posture, coupled with a refusal to negotiate with Israel or to recognize the Oslo agreement during a time of perceived humiliation and despair, contributed to the new theocratic party's rising popularity in Palestinian civil society at the expense of its secular and nationalist competitor, Fatah.

At first glance, nationalism and Islam can be perceived as contradictory; the former asserts earthly aspirations, the other pledges sacrifice for a better afterlife. Yet Islam is not defined in opposition to the state, as in the Western concept of separation between religion and the state. In fact, many Islamist leaders speak today in terms of Islamic nationalism, rather than in opposition to it (Israeli 2002). Against the national and secular aspiration of the Palestinians once personified by the PLO and Arafat, Hamas posited a viable Islamist Caesarist alternative, which gained momentum with the charismatic religious figure Sheikh Ahmad Yassin. Under Yassin's influence, the fusion between fundamentalism and nationalism filled a widening ideological hollow within Palestinian fragmented civil society. By fortifying Hamas's institutional base and strengthening its ideological plat-form beyond right and left, Hamas was catapulted to its 2006 victory.

In a sense, the fratricide of 2007 weakened both Hamas and Fatah, tear-ing apart secular nationalist Palestinians in the West Bank and Islamist follow-ers in Gaza, and one may wonder if religion will be used as a means to reconcile political differences among Palestinians during peace negotiations. Stressing the importance of prayer and faith in God during training of its new members is one of Fatah leaders' tactics to preserve their legitimacy (see Zelkovitz 2008). Should such policies be understood as a tactical move by a secular party seeking to reclaim the allegiance of all Palestinians, or does this trend signal a slippery slope towards a unified religious fundamentalist and nationalist collective worldview? While religious and nationalist forces are collaborating better in Israel than in the Pales-tinian territories, fundamentalism (even in its dovish iteration) and ultranational-ism represent a danger to any peace process. In such a context, the question arises:

can religious leaders (and their convenient ultranationalist allies) contribute to a constructive role in a peace process?

THE ROLE OF RELIGION AND RELIGIOUS LEADERS IN THE PEACE PROCESS

The stance of Israeli and Palestinian society toward globalization cannot be ignored. It has been a reaction against a classic case of McWorld, fostering religious extremism for both Jews and Muslims. Stronger efforts must be made to reconcile the pressures to succeed in a global market with the welfare and development policies necessary for maintaining the legitimacy of secular governance in each camp. Without such efforts, religious and nationalist zealots will be able to sabotage the Israeli and Palestinian search for peace. It is necessary, however, to discriminate among religious parties as possible peace partners based on their platforms and priorities. Obviously, those who call for a Jewish or Muslim theocracy from the "river to the sea" are open enemies of peace. Yet to the extent that their support is based on their welfare policies rather than on their political extremism, there may well be a path toward marginalizing some antiliberal appeal.

Because religious fundamentalism (in its moderate or belligerent form) is a response to social disparities, frustrated promises of peace, and insecurity, international or state secular intervention to address social issues offers the only hope of ameliorating the nefarious political effects of globalization. Ironically, religious extremism may be setting the stage for the reform of capitalism—a need that goes beyond the Israeli–Palestinian issue, and perhaps beyond even the broader challenges posed by radical fundamentalist movements. In that sense, assessments of this or that local religious leader in some arena of conflict should take into account the global challenge posed by the rippling effects of poverty, violence, and fundamentalism qua nationalism in divided and soon-to-be-divided societies.

To return to one of the specific questions addressed in this chapter, one could argue that Shas has thus far stood out as the best prospective partner for peace among the Israeli religious parties. Yet inclusion of Shas (or some other relatively dovish religious orthodox group) and nationalist parties such as Yisrael Beiteinu into a long-term partnership represents a serious dilemma for Israeli society from a human rights perspective. While a partnership with Shas may preserve some flexibility in current peace negotiations, it comes at the price of a steady incursion of fundamentalist rulings into Jewish civil society and political life. In that sense, whatever the value of such inclusion, it may represent a long-term setback for liberal Israelis and, overall, for a viable and durable peace.

With regard to Palestine, critics, including the Bush and Obama administrations, have condemned negotiations with Hamas, thereby recognizing Fatah as the legitimate representative of the Palestinian people. Yet ignoring Hamas is likely to strengthen its power. A better two-pronged strategy would be, first, to work toward the inclusion (or co-optation, to use a Gramscian term) of the more moderate Islamist leaders and, second, to pursue a gradual secular takeover of the provision of social services. In short, the tactical granting of recognition of Hamas would be coupled to a long-term strategy of marginalizing or delegitimizing the extremism of religious parties.

In conclusion, globalization has exacerbated the socioeconomic chasm within each side of the conflict and has intensified the conflict's intractability. A hegemonic crisis within Israeli and Palestinian society has led to the rising popularity of religious and ultranationalist parties. In the long run, even if one could imagine a peace settlement built on some modus vivendi or shared authority between these two ethnic groups, there would be good reason to worry about the status of Palestinian and, to some extent, Israeli women, and generally about the fair establishment of human rights in this region. These concerns, along with the prevalent antipathy to concessions by religious fundamentalist leaders in politics, suggest that a long-term approach to peace negotiations must aim at addressing poverty both by narrowing the gap between Israelis and Palestinians and by narrowing the gap between rich and poor within both societies. In that process, the religious parties' provision of welfare must give way to reinvigorated welfare policies by liberal and secular forces in both Israel and Palestine. In that effort, religious leaders in civil society should be encouraged to work alongside human rights nongovernmental organizations to create a climate of trust for future peace negotiations.[6]

Broadly speaking, that will require a strategy of state organization heading off the current descent from unfettered markets toward primordialism. The goal would be to preserve the progressive potential of globalization (economic growth, the liberation of traditional societies from parochialism) while addressing the association of globalization with widespread pauperization and the wholesale destruction of ethnic and religious identities. The new fundamentalist rebels of our time may well be inadvertently moving the wheel of history forward. Globalization, an agent of transformation, can in turn be transformed by the challenges posed by fundamentalism and ultranationalism. The key is to convert these ongoing changes into progressive action, advancing human rights and social justice as foundations for finally achieving peace.

NOTES

The author wishes to thank David Goldfischer, David Kretzmer, Raslan Ibrahim, the late Edmond Ishay, Claus Offe, and Joel Pruce for reading, commenting, or helping with research.

1. In the 1999 Knesset, Shas moved up to seventeen seats, the highest number since the 1984 inception of the party. In the 2009 elections it fell to eleven seats.
2. "Shimon Peres: Unplugged," *Middle East Quarterly* 2, no. 1 (March 1995): 75–78. www.meforum.org/article/245.
3. One should keep in mind that these numbers are relatively high due to the employment gap that exists between men and women. Women in Jewish orthodox communities and men in Palestinian communities tend to be compensated for their work outside home while their respective spouses study at Yeshivas or stay at home.
4. A section of the Russian population would ultimately contribute to the Israeli economic boom and achieve a high level of propaganda for themselves.
5. BBC, "Palestinian Election: Results in Detail," http://news.bbc.co.uk/2/ji/middle east/4654306, accessed July 14, 2008.
6. In this respect, it is worth recalling the interfaith Abrahamic communities seeking common religious ground between Islam and Judaism—such as in the Cairo (2002) and Alexandria (2004) summits. There are other venues in civil society in which one may envision religious leaders' contribution to a harmonious climate between Israelis and Palestinians. Rabbis for Human Rights is one such NGO known for its arduous work to promote social justice between Jews and Muslims within and beyond the 1967 borders. Another is Asatia, the first Islamic religious moderate party, which since its recent birth (2007) advocated a negotiated peace consistent with social democracy.

REFERENCES

Abu-Amr, Ziad. 1993. "Hamas: A Historical and Political Background." *Journal of Palestine Studies* 22:5–19.

Cohen, Asher 2007. "The Religious Parties in the 2006 Election." *Israel Affairs* 13:325.

Cox, Robert. 1993. "Gramsci, Hegemony and International Relations: An Essay in Method." In *Gramsci Historical Materialism and International Relations*, edited by Stephen Gill. Cambridge: Cambridge University Press.

Diwan, Ishac, and Radwan A. Shaban. 1999. *Development under Adversity: The Palestinian Economy in Transition.* Washington, DC: World Bank.

Filc, Daniel, and Udi Lebel, 2005. "The Post-Oslo Radical Right in Comparative Perspective: Leadership, Voter Characteristics and Political Discourse." *Mediterranean Politics* 10, no. 1 (March):85–97.

Friedberg, Rachel, and Robert M. Sauer. 2003. "The Effects of Foreign Guest Workers in Israel on the Labor Market Outcomes of Palestinians from the West Bank and Gaza Strip." Discussion paper no. 03.03, The Maurice Falk Institute for Economic Research in Israel, Jerusalem, October.

Gramsci, Antonio. 1925. "Controllo la legge sulle associazioni segrete," Speech to the Italian Parliament, May 16. Available at www.marxists.org/archive/gramsci /1925/05/speech.htm.

————. 1971. *Selections from the Prison Notebooks*, edited and translated by Quintin Hoare and Geoffrey Nowell Smith. New York: International Publishers.

Hanieh, Adam. 2003. "From State-Led Growth to Globalization: The Evolution of Israeli Capitalism." *Journal of Palestinian Studies* 32, no. 4: 5–21.

Hroub, Khaled. 2004. "Hamas after Shaykh Yassin." *Journal of Palestine Studies* 33:22.

Ishay, Micheline, and David Goldfischer, 2008. "Belligerent Fundamentalism and the Legacy of European Fascism." *Fletcher Forum of World Affairs* 32, no. 1: 63–82.

Israeli, Raphael. 2002. "State and Religion in the Emerging Palestinian Entity." *Journal of Church and State* 44:238–40.

Khalil, Shikaki. 2002. "Palestinians Divided." *Foreign Affairs* 81, no. 1: 89–105.

Kleiman, Ephraim. 2007. "The Conditions of Economic Viability." *Palestine-Israel Journal* 14, no. 3. www.pij.org/details.php?id=1103.

Ram, Uri. 2000. "The Promised Land of Business Opportunities." In *The New Israel, Peacemaking and Liberalization*, edited by Gershon Shafir and Yoav Peled. Boulder, CO: Westview Press.

Sandbook, Richard, and David Romano. 2004. "Globalization and Violence in Poor Countries." *Third World Quarterly* 25:1007–30.

Shafir, Gershon, and Yoav Peled. 2000. "Peace and Profits: The Globalization of Israeli Business and the Peace Process." In *The New Israel, Peacemaking and Liberalization*, edited by Gershon Shafir and Yoav Peled. Boulder, CO: Westview Press.

Sinai, Ruth. 2007. "Government Report: 1.65 Million Israelis Living below Poverty Line." *Haaretz*, May 9. Available at www.haaretz.com/.

Sprinzhak, Ehud. 1989. "The Emergence of the Israeli Radical Right." *Comparative Politics* 21:173.

Tepe, Sultan. 2005. "Religious Parties and Democracy: A Comparative Assessment of Israel and Turkey." *Democratization* 12, no. 3: 283–307.

Wagner, Roy. n.d. "Migrant Workers in Israel." Kav LaOved, Annual Report 2006. Available at www.kavlaoved.org.il.

World Bank. 2008. "West Bank and Gaza: Economic Developments and Prospects." March. Available online at www.worldbank.org/we.

Zelkovitz, Ido. 2008. "Fatah's Embrace of Islamism." *Middle East Quarterly* 15, no. 2: 19–26.

CHAPTER 5

EGYPT AND THE LEGACY OF SECTARIANISM

⤸

SCOTT W. HIBBARD

On January 6, 2010, three Muslim men armed with automatic weapons shot Christian worshipers as they left services celebrating the Orthodox Christmas Eve. Seven people were killed and several others wounded. The assault took place in Nag Hammadi, a city in upper (southern) Egypt, where tensions between the Muslim majority and Coptic Christian minority have long been an issue. Although the Egyptian government downplayed the sectarian motivations—arguing this was simply a criminal act—the attack sparked riots and intercommunal clashes in surrounding areas. It also shocked Christians throughout the country, resurrecting long-standing questions about their status in Egyptian society. Are Coptic Christians truly members of the Egyptian nation, or are they second-class citizens whose religion makes them a suspect population within a predominantly Muslim society?

The irony is that Egypt is not typically perceived as a "deeply divided" society, let alone a multiethnic one. This is because such tensions are relatively new. Animosity between Christian and Muslim is not endemic in Egyptian society, nor does it reflect "ancient hatreds." On the contrary, the denigration of Egypt's Coptic minority is a relatively recent phenomenon that corresponds with the rise of Islamic fundamentalism in the country since the 1970s.[1] To this end, the sectarianism of recent years reflects a changing attitude of both state and society toward religious tolerance and the norms of cosmopolitan citizenship. How this trend unfolded—and the role of political and religious elites in redefining the basis of national identity—is the subject of this chapter.

In the early and mid-twentieth century, Egyptian citizenship and identity was not rooted in religion but rather in a common language, culture, and history. Even during the Nasser era—which was very much anti-Western and illiberal in that sense—there was a conscious effort by government leaders to construct a religiously inclusive basis of social life. This was manifest in the liberal, and secular, vision of Arab nationalism. In the 1970s and 1980s, however, state policies toward religion, nationalism, and citizenship changed. During this latter period Anwar Sadat, Abdel Nasser's successor, abandoned the secular project and sought to chart a new direction for the country (Hibbard 2010). In doing so, the Sadat regime used the mechanisms of the modern state to promote a Saudi-inspired *salafist* (or fundamentalist) Islam in Egyptian public life.[2] The regime's support for an exclusive vision of religion was part of a larger effort to redefine the basis of state authority, one rooted in Islam, not Arab (or secular) nationalism.

The implications of these policies are evident in today's sectarianism. By embracing an overtly Islamic—and illiberal—vision of the nation, Egyptian political and religious elites undermined traditional conceptions of religious tolerance and, with it, the corresponding "rights . . . [to] participation and equal citizenship" that are the hallmark of an open society (Abdel-Fattah 1994, 19). The result is evident in discriminatory treatment of the Coptic minority and in the violence that has been directed toward them in recent years. The government's continuing support for an exclusive vision of religion and society has also affected intellectual and artistic freedom as well as the role of women in society as the misogynistic elements of Saudi culture have become equated with Islamic tradition.

This chapter examines these issues in their historical context. The primary focus is the changing attitudes of state (and religious) elites toward competing visions of religion and nation. The first part of this chapter traces the evolution of debates over religion and public life through the early twentieth century. At the heart of this debate is an ongoing question about whether one religion ought to be given precedence in the institutions of nation and state, or whether these institutions should be nondiscriminatory regarding matters of faith. In other words, should Egypt have a religious or secular state? The chapter also looks at the manner in which different leaders sought to answer this question, and how this changed over time. The latter part of the narrative then examines the implications of the state's support for an illiberal religious nationalism upon such issues as intellectual freedom, religious tolerance, and the Christian minority.

THE RISE AND FALL OF SECULARISM IN EGYPT

The question of religion in public life—that is, how to define the nation—has been a subject of debate in Egypt for much of the past two centuries. During the early modern period of Muhammad Ali (1805–63) and his successor, Khedive Ismail (1863–79), state leaders sought to rein in the influence of the ulema (religious scholars), whose authority rivaled their own. This tension between political authorities and religious authorities was not new in the Islamic tradition. What was different during this period was the ability of the former to exert control over the latter. As part of the early state-building enterprise, Ali and Ismail were able to separate the ulema from their source of independent income—tax farms and religiously endowed properties (*awaqaf*)—and to make them dependent upon the state. This paved the way for the introduction of Western-style education and legal codes, and for other similar reforms. The corresponding social revolution of the mid- to late-nineteenth century helped to establish the dominance of a political elite in areas traditionally controlled by religious scholars, and left to the latter only a very limited and reconceived realm of religion.

This early state-building project was very much intertwined with a program of secular modernization, and with the desire among Egypt's political elite to emulate the European model of development. The liberal political ideals of this era were similarly reflected in the religious reform movement led by Jamal al-Din al-Afghani (1838–97) and Mohammad Abduh (1849–1905). Abduh, who was mufti of Egypt (chief judge of the Sharia Courts), was particularly influential in shaping public attitudes toward religion and society. He and his supporters advocated a decidedly liberal interpretation of Islamic tradition—one that we will refer to as "modernist" in this chapter—and sought to break the hold upon society of an interpretation of Islam defined by "unquestioning imitation" (*taqlid*).[3] Instead, Abduh and his supporters advocated *ijtihad* (interpretation) as a means of changing Islamic thought and institutions. These early reformers also recognized that science and reason were essential for material progress, and argued that enlightenment norms were entirely compatible with Islamic tradition.

The political and religious ferment associated with this early modern era laid the foundations for Egypt's liberal experiment of 1922–52. It also provided a basis for the civic conception of national identity—one rooted in national, not religious, loyalties—that was embodied in the 1923 constitution. This liberal interpretation of both religion and nation would remain influential throughout the Nasser period.

The debate over religion and society, however, persisted throughout the first half of the twentieth century. Members of the Muslim Brotherhood (Egypt's oldest and most influential Islamist organization), traditional elites, and others argued in favor of a close association of religious and political authority. This view was based upon a belief that Islam is a source of morality and strength, and a symbol of the nation's commitment to its Islamic heritage. Many also believed that a more central role for Islam in governance was essential for the self-actualization of the dominant community. Conversely, supporters of a religiously neutral public sphere were concerned about the negative influence of religion upon politics as well as the corrupting influence that politics would have upon religion. Similarly, the Christian minority tended to oppose a close association of Islam and government because they feared becoming second-class citizens in their own society.

Hence, the argument was made that only a secular order—one that unlinks religious identities from civil status—could provide a nondiscriminatory basis to political governance.

At a deeper level, this debate over religion in public life reflected the division between liberal and illiberal conceptions of national identity discussed in the second chapter of this volume. Liberal (or civic) conceptions of nationalism are premised upon a nondiscriminatory cosmopolitanism that extends membership to all within the territorial boundaries of a given state regardless of religious or ethnic affiliation. Conversely, illiberal (or ethnic) nationalism explicitly links political standing to membership in one faith community or another. It gives priority to the dominant religious or ethnic communities at the expense of minorities. What is at issue in these debates, then, is whether the society (and, hence, the nation) ought to be defined by the values of inclusion and tolerance, or whether the will (and ethnic motifs) of a particular segment of the majority population ought to be predominant. In short, should public life be governed by the majoritarian tendencies of illiberal nationalism, or is there an obligation for state authorities to protect minority rights and cultural diversity?

Religion is central to these debates because it provides a moral basis to each of these differing visions of community. Liberal or "modernist" interpretations of religion, for example, commonly provide a foundation for liberal forms of nationalism and an inclusive basis to social life. By tolerating diverse peoples and opinions, liberal interpretations of religion support the kind of primordial compromise essential to the smooth functioning of multiethnic, multireligious societies. Conversely, illiberal interpretations of religion (or what I have referred to as fundamentalisms) commonly inform ethnic nationalism and the exclusive vision of social life that the latter embody (see chapter 1, this volume). Those who support an exclusive vision of the nation typically assume that collective self-actualization requires a public sphere defined by the ethnic or religious motifs of the majority community. From this perspective, freedom is a collective affair that requires a more central role for their religion in public life. The struggle to define the nation, then, is in essence a debate over how to construct modernity—inclusive or exclusive, liberal, or illiberal—and reflects both religious and political differences over how to interpret a shared tradition.

THE NASSER ERA

In July of 1952 a handful of young military officers led by Gamal Abdel Nasser overthrew the ruling government and sent Egypt's monarch, King Farouk, into exile. The military intervention ended months of political crisis and inaugurated a new period in Egyptian history. It was only after the military takeover, however, that the struggle to define the revolution, and the nation, began. Although much of the Nasser period is overshadowed by his effort to consolidate political power—and to transform an economically underdeveloped society—this period in Egyptian history was defined by a conscious effort to construct a basis of state authority that was both secular and modern. Secular in this context refers to non-discrimination in matters of faith and not hostility to religion. Nasser's modernist program, then, entailed breaking the power of the traditional elites that had dominated Egyptian politics in previous decades and promoting a liberal vision of religion and nation as part of a broader social revolution.

Nasser's modernist vision was embodied in the twin themes of Arab nationalism and Arab socialism. For purposes of this chapter, we are concerned only with the latter, which was the belief that the Arab peoples—defined by language, history, and culture—were a "nation" and ought to be politically unified. The emphasis upon an inclusive Arab identity was consciously nonsectarian and reflected the significant presence of Christians in Egypt and in the larger Arab world. There was, of course, a strong anti-imperialist, anti-European sentiment to this. Hence, Arab nationalism can be seen as politically illiberal in orientation—at least in terms of the regime's anti-Western bias—even if the ideology is premised upon a religiously inclusive notion of identity. In this latter regard, one can interpret Arab nationalism as a form of liberal nationalism.

A defining feature of the early Nasser period was the government's effort to eradicate residual elements of the old order. This was particularly evident in the regime's religious politics and in its effort to break the hold of a theologically conservative Islam upon the population. Although the Nasser regime is typically seen as "secular" and "modern," it was not above invoking religion for its own purposes. On the contrary, the regime sought to mobilize popular religious sentiments for their own purposes. It also took control of the Al-Azhar mosque and university complex—one of the leading centers of Islamic teaching in the Arab world—and other institutions of the religious establishment in Egypt. The regime placed the entire institution under the jurisdiction of the Ministry of Religious Endowments, and gave to the president of Egypt the power to appoint its director, the sheikh of Al-Azhar. The Nasser regime also abolished the historically separate Shari'a (Islamic law) courts and merged them into a unified court system (again, under state control).

The goal of these policies was to undermine the religious elite and to co-opt them into the service of the state. By bringing the institutions of religious authority under the direct control of a state bureaucracy, Nasser was able to exert influence over the *ulema* without having to eliminate them as a social force (Zeghal 1999, 374). The Nasser regime subsequently used the *ulema* to emphasize the compatibility of Islam with the socialist policies of the state and to promote a theologically liberal and modernist interpretation of Islam. This was done in large measure to counter the *salafism* of Saudi Arabia and traditional elites within Egypt, which were opposed to Nasser and his revolutionary policies. Those within Al-Azhar who opposed the Nasserist agenda were removed and replaced with those who were more supportive of the regime.

The Nasser regime also took a confrontational stance toward the Muslim Brotherhood, one of the most influential Islamist organizations (and political parties) in the Arab world. While the Brotherhood was initially supportive of the 1952 revolution, the relationship between the Brotherhood and the regime quickly soured. This tension was due in part to the inherent rivalry between both the Brotherhood and the Nasserists, and in part to fundamentally different conceptions of the nation. While Nasser and his allies sought to modernize Egypt along secular and socialist lines, the Brotherhood advocated a more central role of religion in public life. In short, the ideological division hinged upon whether the new government ought to create a religious or a secular state.

The debate over these competing visions of the nation was reflected in two books published during this period. The first was Khalid Muhammad Khalid's *Min Huna Nabda* (*From Here We Start*, published in 1950), which argues the secular position. This text echoed an earlier controversial argument by Ali Abd al-Raziq, who wrote that true Islam has little to say about the nature of political or social order (1925). On the contrary, the type of state structure adopted by the country was for the most part religiously immaterial. Accordingly, there was nothing inconsistent between Islam and a secular state as long as certain minimal prohibitions were upheld. Khalid further argued that secularism would be preferable given the danger of linking religious and political power too closely. As he argued in the book, a religious state would hinder Egypt's development since the unification of religious and political authority would be corrupting to both sides and would more likely undermine the development of liberty and justice than create it. What was truly needed, Khalid argued, was a social revolution. Such an alternative would be hindered, though, by a "priesthood" that "colluded with tyrants," and—in their pursuit of power—used religion to "keep the people poor and ignorant" (Hourani 1991, 353; see also Binder 1988).

Shaykh Muhammad al-Ghazzali represented the Muslim Brotherhood's position in this debate. Al-Ghazzali's book, titled *Min Huna Na'lam* (*Our Beginning in Wisdom*, or more literally *From Here We Learn*), was also published in 1950 and argued that Islam is a "comprehensive program" meant to regulate all facets of human existence, including the political and social realms of human life. To preclude Islam from a central role in governing the state would therefore be a violation of God's revelation. What this meant in practice remained vague. It was not clear what an Islamic state would look like or what specific policies it would pursue. Al-Ghazzali simply argued that "the duties of the state are clearly and precisely outlined in the Qur'an and the Sunna [tradition]" (Safran 1961, 235). More to the point, the need for an Islamic state, Al-Ghazzali argued, was clear. The return to Islam was a necessary requirement for a revived Islamic community, and this was all the more important given the imminent threat to Islam posed by a hostile, Christian West. In making this argument, al-Ghazzali appealed to the communal sentiments of a religious population and called upon them to defend their tradition. Not only was Islam "threatened with extermination" (236) from outside, but those within the community who argued for a secular political authority, such as Khalid, were betraying their faith and were, in al-Ghazzali's words, "puppets of the enemies of Islam" (237).

The conflict between the Brotherhood and the Free Officers Movement (a clandestine revolutionary group committed to overthrowing the monarchy) reflected not just different interpretations of religion but fundamentally different visions of society. This conflict came to a head in 1954, when an assassination attempt was made on Nasser's life, reputedly by a member of the Muslim Brotherhood.[4] Nasser used this event as an opportunity to confront the organization. Several thousand members of the Brotherhood (including the influential theorist Sayyid Qutb) were arrested, and individuals sympathetic to the organization within the military, the police, and other areas of Egyptian society were purged. A military tribunal subsequently convicted eight hundred members of the Brotherhood on charges of conspiring to overthrow the state, and six of its leaders were executed. With these actions, the Brotherhood's influence in Egyptian politics was greatly diminished, and Nasser had temporarily put an end to the debate over whether Egypt would have a religious or secular state.

SADAT'S REVOLUTION

Nasser's vision of Arab nationalism was enormously influential throughout the 1950s and 1960s. It came to an end, however, with the Israel victory over Arab military forces in the Six-Day War of June 1967. The Nasserist vision was dealt a second blow with Nasser's death in September 1970. These two events set the stage for a renegotiation of the basic issues of religion and society by his successor, Anwar Sadat. Sadat had become disaffected with Egypt's socialist experiment and sought to break with the legacy of his predecessor. The effort of the new president to change the country's direction, however, would thrust him into the heart of Egypt's religious debates.

Sadat's main rivals for leadership came from the secular left, including Vice President Ali Sabri, and his allies within the state bureaucracy. This latter group remained committed to the Nasserist project and to a secular (and socialist) vision of modernity. Sadat found an alternative basis of political support among the traditional elite who had been marginalized under Nasser's rule. Sadat also cultivated ties to the military and security services, many of whom shared a common antipathy for Sabri and his allies. The conflict between these two factions came to a head in May of 1971 when Sabri's supporters were accused of conspiring to overthrow the government. This led to the arrest of ninety members of the Sabri faction and their removal from key positions in government, the ruling party, and the military. These events came to be known as the Corrective Revolution.

This period marked the beginning of a fundamental realignment within Egyptian politics. Sadat abandoned Nasser's economic policies, committed his government to a more open political system, and actively promoted a theologically conservative vision of Islam in public life. Although Nasser had used religion to provide legitimacy to his rule, Sadat embraced Islam with much greater fervor. More importantly, the interpretation of Islam that would come to define Sadat's tenure differed dramatically from that of the Nasser era. Sadat embraced a more theologically conservative Islam as a means of supporting a more politically conservative set of policies. This shift reflected the increasingly close ties between the Sadat regime and Saudi Arabia, which was actively promoting a *salafist* interpretation of Islam with its newfound oil wealth.

The ultimate goal of the Sadat regime was to use Islam to sanctify his political power and to develop a basis of nationalist legitimacy that was more explicitly religious in nature.[5] Sadat consequently emphasized (and conflated) the ideas of religious morality and Egyptian nationalism in his speeches, and he used these themes to reinforce traditional patterns of authority and social order. The construction of an image of personal piety was a part of this strategy. Sadat was depicted as "al-Rais al-Mumen" (the believing president) and regularly had his participation in Friday prayers aired on state-run television. The regime also sought to promote a greater sense of personal religiosity, reflecting an assumption that a more religious population would be a more obedient one. The government subsequently provided millions of dollars for Islamic education and promoted a *salafist* vision of Islam through state-run television and radio. It also provided funding for the construction of thousands of mosques and gave favors (land, funds, television airtime) to popular sheikhs in return for their support (see Alam 1998).

The regime also supported Islamist (or fundamentalist) organizations in order to counter the influence of the secular left in Egyptian politics. This was particularly evident on Egypt's university campuses, where Islamist student groups—with the aid of government security services—undermined the traditional dominance of leftist student groups. The regime's antileft bias was similarly evident in the rapprochement between Sadat and the Muslim Brotherhood. As part of a negotiated agreement, the Brotherhood agreed to renounce the use of violence and promised not to engage in antiregime activities in exchange for the ability to peacefully advocate for Islam.[6]

Finally, the adoption of a new constitution in 1971 provided a greater role for Islam in Egyptian public life. Article 2 of the constitution designated Islam as the official state religion, and the sharia as "a principal source of legislation." Although the provision was vague, the fact that the sharia was mentioned so prominently represented a victory for the Islamists. The constitution was further amended in 1980 to make Islamic law "the principal (or primary) source of legislation" (*al-masdar al-ra'isi*). The reintegration of Islam into Egypt's legal codes was furthered by the National Assembly in the late 1970s. This was done to reconcile Egyptian statutory law with the requirements of Islamic law and was adopted largely under pressure from the Muslim Brotherhood. In conceding these issues, Sadat completed the project of disembedding secular norms in Egyptian public life. Islam was now the official state religion, and both political institutions and legal codes advanced the continued Islamization of the public sphere.

The regime's encouragement of Islamist groups, however, proved to be a double-edged sword. To begin with, the Muslim Brotherhood and the Islamic student groups proved to be unreliable allies. Although the Islamists generally refrained from overt criticism, this deference ended with Sadat's trip to Israel in 1977. The emergence of violence by Islamist militants in the mid to late 1970s—and the rise of sectarian tensions—was also indicative of the limits of this strategy. The fraying of Egypt's tradition of religious tolerance is commonly attributed to the politicization of religion at this time.[7] Sadat's embrace of a Saudi-inspired vision of Islam undermined the liberal conception of citizenship and national identity that was influential for most of the twentieth century. Moreover, specific policies intended to appease Islamic conservatives, such as the application of Islamic law to all Egyptians, created anxiety among Coptic Christians. While debates over the nature of Egypt's communal life—religious or secular—were conducted in largely theoretical terms, they had very real implications for the Coptic minority who became targets of discrimination and abuse.

By the end of the Sadat era, religious politics in Egypt had taken on a life of its own. Islamist groups had emerged as the dominant opposition to the state, a movement ironically facilitated by the regime's own policies. While Sadat had successfully marginalized the political left, he "had let the genie out of the bottle." And with his assassination in 1981 by members of Islamic Jihad, "the genie had struck him down" (Farag Foda, quoted in Ajami 1998, 206). Moreover, the message of both establishment Islam and the Islamist opposition was increasingly similar. While there remained divisions over the question of violence—both within the Islamist movement and between the religious establishment and the militants—the interpretation of Islam advocated by the Brotherhood, the official *ulema*, and other Islamists were all influenced by Saudi Wahhabism, a by-product of their common source of funding. Consequently, dominant religious figures, both those who supported the regime as well as those who opposed it, all sought a common goal of "bring[ing] Egyptian society back to Islam" (Zeghal 1999, 382) even if they differed over who should ultimately rule.

THE MUBARAK ERA

Egyptian politics over the last thirty years have been defined by this legacy. The government's approach to Islam, however, produced a confused and often contradictory set of policies. While Hosni Mubarak, Sadat's successor, characterizes his government as a bulwark against Islamic fundamentalism—and a defender of the secular vision of modernity—his government has in practice continued to promote an illiberal vision of Islam in public life. Moreover, the close association of religion and the state that emerged under Sadat has remained a hallmark of the Mubarak era. The regime has tolerated, though constrained, the Muslim Brotherhood while responding harshly to those who directly challenged the state. The Mubarak regime has also used the official religious establishment—including the *ulema* of Al-Azhar and the Dar al-Ifta (House of Fatwas) headed by the Grand Mufti—to sanction government policy. It similarly employed the media, the educational system, and other institutions of the state to promote a vision of Islam that was supportive of state authority and the continuation of military rule.

The regime's efforts to co-opt Islam in the service of the state has further entrenched an illiberal vision of religion and society within Egyptian public life. The government's struggle with the militant opposition during the 1990s, moreover, was not defined by competing visions of society but rather by a competitive religious populism. Each group claimed to be the legitimate defender of faith and nation, and each invoked Islam to sanction their rival claims to power. In pursuing such a strategy, the Mubarak regime effectively ceded the ideological debate over religion and culture to the Islamists (or at least to those members of the religious establishment sympathetic to the Islamist vision). Thus, even though the state was able to defeat Islamist militant groups in the mid-1990s, the ideas that animated the larger movement have become increasingly institutionalized in Egyptian public schools, the media, and the official religious establishment. What has subsequently emerged is an intolerant public sphere where the persecution of Christians and dissenting religious opinions occurred without official opposition and often with its complicity. The next section will examine the implications of this trend in two key areas: intellectual freedom and the treatment of the Christian minority.

INTELLECTUAL FREEDOM AND DISSENT

During the 1990s, debates over whether Egypt ought to have a religious or secular state were once again resurrected. At the heart of this debate was the conflict between those who advocated a society based upon a *salafiyya* (or Islamist) vision of social order and those who embraced a secular or liberal vision of the nation. The secular position was premised upon a commitment to liberal norms of tolerance, inclusion, and individual freedom. The Islamist position, conversely, promoted a vision of society defined by a high degree of cultural uniformity and the full application of Islamic law. While this latter view may be interpreted as a communitarian approach to social order, it nonetheless calls upon the state to regulate (and enforce) religious belief and practice (see Rutherford 2008). The religious motifs of the dominant community, moreover, inform this latter vision of community and, at least in practice, have provided a basis for discriminating against dissenting opinions, whether religious or political.

While the so-called Secular-Integralist (or Islamist) debate is not new, it had a very different outcome in the 1990s than it did in the 1950s.[8] Part of the explanation lies in the fact that the 1990s debate occurred in the midst of a militant insurgency—and state crisis—and part of it has to do with the willingness of the Mubarak regime to cede the ideological debate to retain control over the core functions of government (economic and foreign policymaking). Both of these issues were evident in the regime's alliance with the official *ulema* of Al-Azhar and the Dar al-Ifta, in opposition to the militant groups that threatened the government.[9] A tacit agreement was subsequently struck between the Mubarak regime and Gad al-Haq (then-Sheikh of Al-Azhar) in 1992: the Sheikh of Al-Azhar would support the government in opposition to the militants, and in exchange the conservative *ulema* would be granted greater opportunity to express their beliefs (Zeghal 1999, 389). The result of Egypt's conflict between the state security forces and the Islamic militants, then, was a highly ambivalent one. While the militants were decimated—most were killed, imprisoned, or driven into exile—the Islamist vision of social life became entrenched in Egypt's religious establishment, the media, and education.

The emerging dominance of an illiberal rendering of religious tradition created a climate in which those with dissenting opinions—religious or political—became targets of attack. Moreover, those carrying out such acts were commonly associated with, or had some degree of support from, state institutions. By setting the state up as the custodian of the faith and allowing state *ulema* to become the arbiters of religious belief, dissent of all sorts all sorts became subject to persecution. This was particularly evident in a series of court cases brought against secular intellectuals in the 1990s that redefined the limits of free thought. These legal cases were initiated by Islamist lawyers and journalists who targeted intellectual work that was deemed to be a violation of public morality. However, these Islamic activists relied upon conservative *ulema* within state institutions to either ban or censor such work, and upon sympathetic judges to rule in their favor. In effect, the state machinery was forced to uphold the religious ideas that the government promoted as a basis of its legitimacy.

The attacks on intellectual and artistic freedom took place largely through the court system, though they were associated with individuals within Al-Azhar who had the authority to ban books, films, music, and other forms of creative expression. This power was exercised through the Academy for Islamic Research (Majma al-Buhuth al-Islamiyya), an institution within Al-Azhar that has historically reviewed books and films with religious content.[10] The Mubarak regime expanded their jurisdiction in this area in a 1994 fatwa (religious ruling) issued by the Department of Fatwa and Legislation in the State Council.[11] The ruling extended Al-Azhar's review authority to all matters of public order and morality, and made these determinations binding.

A key basis of the State Council *fatwa* was the argument that "the unity of the nation can only be cemented by ensuring unity of thought" (Amin 1994). The fatwa also noted the centrality of Islam as both the religion of the state and the religion of the majority. Consequently, it is "regarded that Islam and Islamic principles and values permeate public order and morality and are therefore contained within the higher interests of the state."[12] Not only is Islam a basis of social order, the fatwa argued, but its proper interpretation is important in "building modern Egyptian society." The ruling goes on to argue that the Sheikh of Al-Azhar is the "final arbiter in all religious matters," and that it is within the purview of the Islamic Research Academy (which the Sheikh chairs) to "review all research and studies published on Islam and the *Turath* (tradition), at home and abroad, whether it contains sound opinion or, if not, to reply to it and rectify it" (EOHR 1994, 27).

The ruling thus affirmed the centrality of Islam for ordering Egyptian public life and identified Al-Azhar as the leading authority and interpreter of Islamic tradition. This move sparked controversy, particularly among members of the human rights community who viewed the government's actions as subordinating the civil rights of the population to the *ulema*. Many of these fears proved to be justified. The state's capitulation to the conservatives in Al-Azhar helped to validate the "integralist" position discussed earlier. It also sanctioned the attack on intellectual freedom by allowing the support for secularism to be viewed legally as a sign of disbelief. This was the basis of various lawsuits brought by Islamist lawyers against secular intellectuals, liberal Islamic scholars, and other critics of the *salafiyya* movements. These scholars were subsequently depicted as either apostates or agents of the West. Artists and novelists were similarly attacked, and many of their works were banned. The regime's unwillingness to defend these individuals reflected its continuing desire to portray itself as the protector of religious orthodoxy.

Infringements upon intellectual freedom were numerous; only a few, however, are mentioned here. Perhaps the most prominent case was that of Nasr Hamid Abu Zayd, a professor of Islamic Studies at Cairo University, who was declared a heretic (*murtadd*) based on his interpretation of the Qur'an and his effort to read the tradition metaphorically, not literally. Abu Zayd was forcibly divorced from his wife, since "being married to an apostate from Islam was a violation of the rights of God" (Sfeir 1998, 406). Muhammad Sa'id al-Ashmawy, the former chief justice of the Cairo High Court, found himself in a similar predicament for his criticisms of the *salafists*. An advocate of what he refers to as "humanistic Islam," al-Ashmawy argues that the politicization of religion by both state and opposition is contrary to the essence of Islam. Moreover, al-Ashmawy has been critical of the literal, selective interpretation of Islam advocated by official *ulema* and Islamist alike. Several of his books were banned in the 1990s, and a member of the Muslim Brotherhood called for him to be put on trial because "he has attacked the Islamic creed and maligned several Islamic values."[13] In 1996 a book he wrote on women and the veil was ordered confiscated by the Islamic Research Academy. Al-Ashmawy noted at the time that "this confiscation is like a religious order to instigate my assassination."[14]

Other scholars were similarly targeted, including Said Mahmud al-Quemny, whose book *The God of Time*, was banned by Al-Azhar's Scholars Front in 1997. The basis for the Front's action, and for al-Quemny's subsequent trial, was a report published on his work by the Islamic Research Academy. The report was critical of al-Quemny's depiction of the Third Caliph, Uthman, as well as his use of the Old Testament in characterizing the prophet Abraham's life (which, it was argued, was contradicted by Qur'anic sources). The attack on *The God of Time* was part of a broader campaign against 196 books that Al-Azhar deemed blasphemous. The case was submitted to a state security court upon the request of Al-Azhar, where al-Quemny was subsequently charged with "propagating ideas that denigrate Islam [under Article 198 of the Criminal Code]" (Ismail 1999, 40). The Islamic newspapers seized upon the case and immediately labeled him a *kafir* (unbeliever). Although he was ultimately acquitted on all charges (the judge's ruling specifically referred to provisions in the constitution ensuring freedom of expression), he, like Ashmawy, subsequently had to live with the threat of assassination.

A more recent dispute surfaced over the reissue of a book written in 1983 by Syrian author Haidar Haidar titled *A Banquet for Seaweed*. In the spring of 2000, the Islamist newspaper *al-Shaab* (*The People*) printed a scathing review of the book and argued that the text was an affront to Islam. It also criticized the government's ministry of culture for reissuing the book as part of its modern Arab classics series. The author of the article noted how shocked he was that the Egyptian government was promoting "rank atheism and blasphemy" (Rodenbeck 2000, 39). The review became the topic of fiery sermons and protests at Al-Azhar University in Cairo soon after it was published. *Al-Shaab* ran with the story and published denouncements of a number of secular literary figures, including Tayeb Salih, among others.[15] Despite a review committee's report that the book was a "valuable literary work that actually exalted the role of Islam," the Egyptian Parliament's religious affairs committee demanded that the book be burned. The government's response was to arrest several junior officials of the ministry of culture on charges of "assaulting revealed religion" and to shut down the newspaper that printed the review. The regime also banned the book after a committee at Al-Azhar pronounced it to be "a dangerous departure from accepted religious understanding and an assault on what is sacred in religion . . . and likely . . . to shake the solidarity of the nation" (Rodenbeck 2000, 38).[16]

The underlying debate in all of these cases—the limits of free expression and the ability to question revealed religion—is not new. As noted earlier, there has long been a debate over the degree to which Islam is open to interpretation. Historically, this has been between those who adopt a narrow interpretation of Islamic tradition and those who "perceive Arab-Islamic culture as a [more] a complex phenomenon" (Anis 2000). What was different during this period was that members of the state-supported *ulema* joined forces with non-Azharite Islamists in attacking the opinions of secular and liberal writers. The Azharites opposed what they perceived as unorthodox interpretations of Islam and have used their positions within state institutions to mobilize popular sentiments against such heterodoxy. More disconcerting, though, was the Mubarak regime's complicity in such attacks. The intolerance of alternative opinions on religious matters has been normalized by state policies designed to encourage religious piety and political quiescence. In promoting such policies, the state has helped to redefine religious orthodoxy in Egyptian public life, and has provided the basis for stigmatizing religious and political dissent alike (Farag 2000, 4).[17]

EGYPT'S COPTIC CHRISTIANS

The persecution of the Christian minority and the communalization of Egyptian politics were other consequences of the Mubarak regime's religious politics. Despite official commitments to equal treatment of religious minorities, the effort to appease Islamic conservatives has led state actors to tolerate abusive and discriminatory practices against Coptic Christians, the largest minority in the country. This type of discrimination is evident in a variety of issues ranging from the official population count to the systematic exclusion of Christians from positions of authority.[18] There are no Christian governors or mayors in Egypt, for example, or cabinet-level officials. Members of the Coptic community are also unrepresented in the upper ranks of the security services and are largely absent in academia. Other forms of discrimination are evident in matters of religious freedom and marriage. While a Christian may convert to Islam, Muslims who convert to Christianity have been subject to harassment by local law enforcement. An Ottoman-era law prohibiting church construction and repair without government approval is another source of contention. Although the law has been eased, it nonetheless remains in force. The result, as one Coptic activist noted, is that "it is easier to get license to open a nightclub than to fix a church."[19]

The communalization of the Egyptian polity, moreover, has deeply affected local government and security forces. Local police harass members of the Christian community and have been consistently slow to respond to intercommunal violence. In numerous instances, the government has done little to hold members of the majority community accountable for violent assaults upon the Coptic minority. During the Islamist attacks on Christian communities in the late 1980s and early 1990s, for example, state actors did little to protect the Coptic community and routinely depicted the assaults as the by-product of local disputes. This was the case even in the early 1990s when violence was carried out by Islamic militants. Moreover, the state-regulated press has done little in recent years to offset allegations made by Islamists that Copts were either converting or sexually abusing young Muslims. As such, Egypt's mass media contributed greatly to antiminority prejudice and to an environment "[that] provided a fertile staging ground for anti-Christian violence" (Fernandez 2001).

Such tensions have led to violence, as was evident in the 1999 incident at El-Kosheh. On New Year's Eve of 1999 violence in the southern city of El-Kosheh led to two days of rioting. During this period Muslims burned and looted Coptic stores and killed twenty Christians. Two Muslims were also killed. The violence reflected long-simmering tensions between wealthy Christians and less-well-off Muslims. When two Christians had been killed in the previous year, the government rounded up one thousand Copts—torturing many—convinced that Christians were behind the killings. An official organ of the Orthodox Church described this as "blaming the victim" (El-Magd 2000). The government's response to the 1999–2000 violence indicated a similar unwillingness to address the issues raised by the violence. The initial trial indicted ninety-six defendants—fifty-eight Muslims and thirty-eight Copts—but acquitted ninety-two of these. The remaining four were convicted of only minor crimes. According to one analyst, "the verdicts were intentionally light in order to avoid fanning the flames of sectarian strife."[20] Nevertheless, the verdicts outraged many in the Coptic community who felt that "the investigation and court deliberations were biased."[21] A subsequent retrial similarly freed all but two.

Behind the anger over the El-Kosheh affair was the continued sense of persecution that derives from the exclusive conception of national identity and the continued rejection of a minority "other." As Fahmy Howeidy, a prominent intellectual and journalist, described the situation, "what happened is not a crisis of a village or sect, but a crisis of a nation" (quoted in El-Magd 2000). While the Egyptian government refuses to recognize the Coptic community as a minority and argues that the Egyptian nation is entirely of one ethnic fabric, the government has nonetheless refused to allow for equal treatment of the Christian population.

This is reflected in the perception among members of the Coptic community that they are second-class citizens and, thus, not fully Egyptian. Moreover, the large amounts of Islamic programming on state-run television and radio have in the past either demeaned Christianity or emphasized the benefits of conversion to Islam (US Department of State 2004). Similarly, Islamist newspapers commonly denigrate Christianity and the Coptic community, as do the sermons at Friday prayers in mosques around the country. Each of these trends contributes to the further communalization of public life and has increased Coptic alienation. As one analyst noted, "you have to feel affiliation and respect in society, and this [the Copts] don't have."[22]

These issues resurface with each new incidence of violence. It is in this context, moreover, that the January 2010 attacks have been placed. The Nag Hammadi incident was not an aberration but part of a continuing series of assaults targeting the Christian minority. Between 2008 and 2010 alone there were fifty-three separate incidents of sectarian violence, the majority of which were in Upper Egypt (EIPR 2010). These recent attacks are perhaps more pernicious than those in the 1970 because they were not carried out by Islamist militants (as in earlier decades) but rather reflect the degree to which a sectarian mindset—and religious intolerance—has become entrenched within segments of the Egyptian population. It also demonstrates how religion both provides a warrant for action and identifies the minority population as a target for abuse. The Egyptian case also demonstrates how the connection between religion, illiberal nationalism, and political authoritarianism come together in a divisive combination. Despite the state's call for national unity, it is noticeably absent in addressing the root causes of the sectarianism it alternately denies and condemns.

CONCLUSION

The case of Egypt highlights several issues regarding the question of religion, tolerance, and violence. First, the case illustrates how differing conceptions of the nation affect basic issues of tolerance and intercommunal harmony. The case study also demonstrates how different interpretations of religion—modernist or fundamentalist—have alternately informed competing conceptions of the nation: liberal and illiberal, respectively. What is perhaps most interesting about the Egyptian case is the way in which these policies and attitudes changed over time. While political and religious leaders defended pluralist conceptions of social order and embraced the liberal or modernist religion in the 1950s and 1960s, this changed in the latter part of the century when state leaders abandoned their opposition to sectarian ideals and embraced a more explicit religious nationalism. During the Sadat period, state elites saw the Islamist tendency as a constituency to be courted, not a movement to be suppressed. The end result was that liberal and secular norms were delegitimized, and an illiberal vision of society (and the nation) became embedded in state institutions.

The changing nature of Egypt's religious politics also highlights the way in which different ideas reflect competing political interests. The modernist interpretations of Islamic tradition were closely associated with the leftist politics of the post-independence period and were caught up with the politics of the Cold War. In this context, fundamentalist interpretations of Islam were very much intertwined with traditional patterns of social hierarchy and reflected the interests and preferences of traditional elites (and land owners) within Egypt. The *salafist* vision of Islam was also promoted by Saudi Arabia and others opposed to the Nasserist program of social revolution and leftist change. The continuing promotion of an exclusive vision of religion and society today similarly serves the interests of those who seek to perpetuate the existing political order. As one commentator noted, in Egypt, "conservative Islam is wrapped up in political authoritarianism; it is an unholy alliance to keep people down."[23]

The Egyptian case also highlights the importance of religious and political elites in shaping popular conceptions of religion and society. Although the focus of this chapter has been the intolerance and violence in the country's religious politics, there are countervailing voices that remain important. One such person is the current mufti of Egypt, Sheikh Ali Gomaa, who is commonly seen as a moderate voice and sharp critic of the intolerance and utopianism associated with the Islamist vision. He is also perceived as progressive on issues of gender and governance, and he articulates a theologically liberal Islam. Similarly, the former Sheikh of Al-Azhar, Muhammad Sayyid Tantawi, was similarly known for his moderate—and modernist—views. Replacing the more theologically conservative Gad al-Huq in 1996, Sheikh Tantawi was the head of Al-Azhar until his death in 2010. Tantawi offered a progressive voice on such issues as female circumcision, militant violence, and the 9/11 attacks. Although Tantawi set a different tone than his predecessor, his ability to reshape the institution was limited. Moreover, even he accepted certain fundamental ideas about the necessity of a close association between religious and political authority.

Finally, one must recognize that there are elements within civil society that have sought to address the challenge of sectarianism through interfaith dialogue. Such initiatives represent a "bottom up" approach to intercommunal relations, though some talks have been supported by the government. While such dialogue is a crucial element in fostering better relations, it has faced a variety of challenges in Egypt. Part of the problem is that sectarian tendencies are actually reinforced by the fact that the government takes community issues up with the church leaders and not with secular representatives. Moreover, there are the tensions within communities over the merits of such dialogue. Although there are numerous Muslims and Christians willing to reach out to one another, they frequently face opposition within their own communities. For example, expatriate Coptic groups often differ with local leaders over how best to approach the many issues raised by their minority status. Similarly, the prevalence of sectarian views, particularly in Upper Egypt, has constrained Muslims and Christians who try to promote religious tolerance and mutual understanding. As one Coptic activist noted, "Sometimes what is needed is *intra-faith* dialogue; it is not the Muslim-Christian dialogue that is the problem, but rather getting each side to speak with one voice."[24]

NOTES

1. The term "Islamic fundamentalism" refers to a narrow reading of Islamic tradition that affirms certain fundamental beliefs within the tradition and the corresponding effort to transform society in light of these foundational principles.
2. Salafi means, literally, "of the ancestors." It refers to a literal reading of the tradition that looks to the early Muslim community as an example of piety. Given its influence on fundamentalism, the terms will be used interchangeably in this chapter.
3. By "liberal" or "modernist" interpretations of religion, I mean those who read scripture as metaphor, not literal truth, and who accept the use of reason as a guide for interpreting religion for a contemporary context. Modernist views on religion tend to be receptive toward religious pluralism.
4. Members of the Brotherhood deny involvement in the assassination attempt and argue that it was a ploy to give the state an excuse to crack down on the Brotherhood.
5. For more on the Sadat regime's political philosophy, see Beattie (2000, 168–72).
6. The outline of this rapprochement, including the contents of the six-point agreement between Sadat and the Muslim Brotherhood, is outlined in Guenena and Ibrahim (1997). See also Eshmawy (1993).
7. This view was conveyed to the author by a bishop in the Orthodox Coptic Church in July 2002.
8. The proceedings of this debate can be found in *Misr Bayn al Dawla al Diniya wa al Madaniya* (*Egypt: A Religious or Civil State?*) (Cairo, 1992). The Islamist position was represented by Muhammad Imara, Mamoun al-Hodeiby of the Muslim Brotherhood, and Shekh Muhammad al-Ghazzali of Al-Azhar. On the other side was Farag Foda, the founder of al-Tanwir, and Muhammad Ahmed Khallafa.
9. The Islamists criticized the official religious establishment as being too closely tied to the state and offered their own interpretations of Islam.
10. The Committee for Research and Publication is a subsidiary of the Islamic Research Academy. The process for banning books is irregular, with cases often being referred to the "Censorship Police" or to the State security. See Ismail (1999, 38). See also Egyptian Organization for Human Rights (EOHR, 1994).
11. The ruling was State Council Fatwa no. 58/1/63, which can be found in EOHR (1994). See also al-Tawaka (1994).

12. The *fatwa*, from which this quote is drawn, was issued by Judge Tarik al-Bishri, a noted Islamic scholar, and vice-chair of the State Council. EOHR (1994, 26).
13. The reference is to Mamoud al-Hodeiby, quoted in "Islamic Scholars Demand Waiving Immunity from Al-Ashmawy and Confiscating His Books That Malign Islam," *Al-Nour, Arab Press Review*, January 29, 1992.
14. Associated Press, "Writer Condemns Confiscation by Police," June 1996.
15. Salih is the author of *The Season of Migration from the North*. Several human rights groups issued a joint statement depicting the affair as a "fascist attack against freedom of expression." The statement (in Arabic) is available through the Cairo Institute for Human Rights Studies.
16. The quote is from the report by the Islamic Research Academy of Al-Azhar.
17. Farag quotes the editor-in-chief of *Sawt al-Azhar* (*The Voice of Al-Azhar*) as saying "those who want to be atheists can do so . . . but they do not have the right to publish such ideas."
18. There is dispute over the size of the Coptic population. Government figures place the number at 6 million, or roughly 5 percent of the population, while Coptic activists claim a much higher figure, around 10 million. Independent sources place it at 7 to 8 million.
19. Conversation with Mahmoud Nahkleh, October 14, 2002, Cairo Egypt.
20. "Kosheh File Re-Opened," *Al-Ahram Weekly*, March 20–26, 2003.
21. Ibid.
22. Conversation with Dina Al-Howega, Center for the Study and Documentation of Economic, Juridical, and Social Affairs, Cairo, Egypt, October 8, 2002.
23. Conversation with an Egyptian scholar who spoke on a nonattribution basis with the author in October 2002.
24. Conversation with Samir Ruca, Christian Evangelical OSS. August 25, 2002, Cairo, Egypt.

REFERENCES

Abd al-Rizik, Ali. 1925. *Al-Islam wa Usul al-Hakum* (*Islam and the Principles of Government*). Cairo: Aufq Press.

Abdel-Fattah, Nabil. 1994. *Veiled Violence: Islamic Fundamentalism in Egyptian Politics in the 1990s*. Cairo: Khattab Press.

Ajami, Fouad. 1998. *The Dream Palaces of the Arabs: A Generation's Odyssey*. New York: Pantheon Books.

Alam, Anwar. 1998. *Religion and State: Egypt, Iran and Saudi Arabia*. Delhi: Gyan Sagar Publications.

Amin, Samir. 1994. "Pluralism Spurs Innovation." *Al-Ahram Weekly*, April.

Anis, Mona. 2000. "Intellectuals' Dilemma." *Al-Ahram Weekly*, May 11–17.

Beattie, Kirk J. 2000. *Egypt during the Sadat Years*. New York: Palgrave.

Binder, Leonard. 1988. *Islamic Liberalism: A Critique of Development Ideologies*. Chicago: University of Chicago Press.

Egyptian Initiative for Personal Right (EIPR). 2010 *Two Years of Sectarian Violence: What Happened, Where to Begin? An Analytical Study of Jan 2008–Jan 2010*. Cairo, Egypt: EIPR.

Egyptian Organization for Human Rights (EOHR). 1994. *Freedom of Opinion and Belief: Restrictions and Dilemmas*. Cairo: Egyptian Organization of Human Rights.

El-Magd, Nadia Abou. 2000. "The Meanings of Al-Kosheh." *Al-Ahram Weekly*, February 3–9.

Eshmawy, Ali. 1993. *The Secret History of the Muslim Brotherhood Movement*. Cairo: Dar al-Hilal.

Farag, Fatemah. 2000. "Re-Drawing the Line." *Al-Ahram Weekly*, August 3–9.

Fernandez, Alberto. 2001. "In the Year of the Martyrs" Anti-Coptic Violence in Egypt, 1988–1993." Paper presented at the Middle East Studies Association Annual Meeting, San Francisco, November 18–20.

Guenena, Nemat, and Saad Eddin Ibrahim. 1997. *The Changing Face of Egypt's Islamic Activism*. Unpublished manuscript, US Institute of Peace, September.

Hibbard, Scott W. 2010. *Religious Politics and Secular States: Egypt, India and the United States*. Baltimore: Johns Hopkins University Press.

Hourani, Albert. 1991. *Arabic Thought in the Liberal Age: 1798–1938*. New York: Cambridge University Press.

Ismail, Salwa. 1999. "Religious 'Orthodoxy' as Public Morality: The State, Islamism and Cultural Politics in Egypt." *Critique: Critical Middle Easter Studies* 14 (Spring): 25–47.

Rodenbeck, Max. 2000. "Witch Hunt in Egypt." *New York Review of Books*, November 16.

Rutherford, Bruce. 2008. *Egypt after Mubarak: Liberalism, Islam and Democracy in the Arab World*. Princeton, NJ: Princeton University Press.

Safran, Nadav. 1961. *Egypt in Search of Political Community: An Analysis of the Intellectual and Political Evolution of Egypt 1804–1952*. Cambridge, MA: Harvard University Press.

Sfeir, George N. 1998. "Basic Freedoms in a Fractured Legal Culture: Egypt and the Case of Nasr Hamid Abu Zaid," *Middle East Journal* 52:402–14.

al-Tawaka, Abdel Sattar. 1994. "Ayna yaqaf ulema al-azhar?" ("Where do the Ulema of al-Azhar stop?"). *Ruz al-Yusef*, April.

US Department of State. 2004. "2004 Report on International Religious Freedom." www.state.gov/g/drl/rls/irf/2004/.

Zeghal, Malika. 1999. "Religion and Politics in Egypt: The Ulama of al-Azhar, Radical Islam, and the State (1952–94)." *International Journal of Middle East Studies* 31:371–99.

CHAPTER 6

RELIGION, WAR, AND PEACEMAKING IN SUDAN

⁀

Shari'a, Identity Politics, and Human Rights

CAROLYN FLUEHR-LOBBAN

Sudan has attracted global attention for its chronic conflicts, history of repressive rule, and human rights violations. Few African nations are as deeply divided or have experienced as much chronic war and conflict since its independence in 1956. Indeed, decades of war and poor governance have brought the country to the brink, and the South will separate in 2011. However, this oft-mentioned fact fails to mention the nearly permanent state of war and the suppression of rebellion that characterized the prior colonial period, 1898–1956. Notably, the Sudan was the only African region to defeat and expel initial British colonization efforts in 1885 when the Sudanese Mahdi overran Khartoum and executed Major-General Charles "Chinese" Gordon. General Gordon had suppressed the Taiping Rebellion (1863–64) securing British occupation before coming to Sudan in 1873 (Lobban, Kramer, and Fluehr-Lobban 2002, 113). The post–Cold War new world order noted by Little in his chapter in this volume affected the newly independent Sudan. During the Cold War, Sudan was more often aligned with the Soviet Union than the West, and presaging the new enemy of the West, it embraced Islamism in 1983 shortly after the Iranian Revolution in 1979. Today Chinese influence has engaged in ways unimaginable in the heyday of European colonialism with deep economic interests in Sudan's oil and complex political support for one of the world's pariah regimes.

While prominent in human rights campaigns, Sudan has generally escaped the attention of the United States and the West for its booming economy (now Africa's eighth largest) and the dramatic growth and demographic transformation of its primate city, Khartoum, now estimated at 8 million, making it one of Africa's largest cities. In a reversal of colonial history, Sudan is gaining attention for the likely permanence of Chinese dependence on Sudanese oil (7 percent of its total import) and the "China model" for African development and bilateral relations. This loss of perspective in the West results from nearly two decades of boycott, sanctions, and a nonexistent or weak diplomatic presence that has left the United States unengaged and poorly informed. After the 2005 signing of the Comprehensive Peace Agreement (CPA), which ended Africa's longest civil war between the central government and the South, a trickle of scholars began to return to study the complex effects of four decades of war, twenty-five years of Islamism, the state of human rights on the ground, and the fragile implementation of peace in one region of this vast nation equal to one-third of the continental United States.

Khartoum as a major African conurbation now holds as many as one-quarter to one-third of the nation's population, perhaps half of whom are the internally displaced (at least 2 million in IDP [internally displaced person] camps that ring the city) who fled decades of conflicts in the South, or more recently, in Darfur. One-quarter are non-Muslim. This is not only a major demographic transformation of the primary city but of the nation. Uncounted economic male migrants have left the northern towns and villages for work in the Persian Gulf, leaving the vast areas north of metropolitan Khartoum predominantly composed of the female, the very young and very old, and male internal economic migrants from the South, the West, and from nearby Chad and Nigeria. Since most Western researchers stopped coming to Sudan after the 1989 Islamist coup with its brutal suppression of dissent in the North and intensification of the war in the South, these dramatic changes have not been studied.

After more than fifty years of independence, Sudan has known only eleven years of relative peace. Generations of Sudanese have grown up only knowing civil war and chronic conflict. Its decades of chronic military rule by an elite of Northern Arab-Muslims place it in Little's category of "illiberal" states characterized by high degrees of intolerance and authoritarian rule. Untold millions of persons have died, have been internally displaced, or have fled to neighboring countries to live for extended periods in refugee camps or as exiles in Kenya, Egypt, Ethiopia, or Uganda. A smaller and more fortunate North American and European diaspora has developed but has yet to perform the vital role it might play in future conflict management, resolution, and stability of the nation. This chapter assesses the various factors in the complex Sudanese equation that lead to exacerbation of conflict or its relative amelioration in this deeply divided society. It also specifically examines the multiple roles that religion and religious leaders have played, or might play in a future postconflict society and in the precipitation of conflict and its management.

CAUSES OF WAR: MANTLES OF RELIGIOUS AUTHORITY

A partial list of the root causes of Sudan's chronic conflicts in the recent past would include the emergence of an Islamist religious establishment that hijacked the state and its traditional Sufi religious base, and effectively used a religious mantle of authority through the primary vehicle of Shari'a to legitimize its rule. Added to this are the fundamental problem of its huge boundaries created by British colonialism without regard to ethnicity, its poor governance since independence by self-serving elites, and its chronic militarism that has crippled or crushed democratic alternatives. As Little notes in chapter 1 of this volume, ethnic-religious majorities who have ruled Sudan from independence to the present have merged their identities to justify their rule as popular and legitimate while, in fact, they have been authoritarian and repressive to minority populations.

Douglas Johnston's (2003, xviii–xix) adaptation of a model from Joseph Hanlon's *Peace without Profit* (1996) for the root causes of Sudan's civil wars argues that wars in Africa have erupted when internal tensions are exacerbated by intervention of external interests. For Sudan, of relevance to the role of religion in the conflict are the following:

* The Sudanese religious center and periphery were established in the development of the Sudanic Islamic states before the nineteenth century.
* The introduction of militant Islam in the late nineteenth century sharpened growing divides between persons by economic status and citizenship within the state.
* A narrowly based ethnoreligious nationalist movement from the North (Umma Party and Khatmīyya Sūfi order) claimed leadership of Sudan as their entitlement after independence.
* Militant political Islam reemerged as a major force, both nationally and internationally, and placed limitations on non-Muslim citizens.

These summary points may help to explain selected religious factors in Sudan's chronic conflict, but they do not explain why other Sahelian Muslim states in Africa have not experienced a similar length and degree of chronic, unresolved conflict. Nigeria is a case in point. Although Nigeria's history is far from being conflict-free, its only civil war, over Biafra in the early 1960s shortly after independence, was short-lived and was resolved in favor of unity of the state, but Sudan's nearly continuous civil war from independence places it on the verge of imminent separation of the South. Other Sahelian nations along the tenth parallel have been identified as zones of conflict between Christians and Muslims and have been targeted by Evangelical Christians for proselytizing (Cooper 2006), while some predominantly Muslim West African nations, Senegal and the Gambia, have been relatively free of ethnoreligious conflict and war. These examples are worthy of further examination and analysis.

For a majority of the 35 million Sudanese, the conflicts in the South and now in Darfur are remote. They exist in Sudanese consciousness at the margins because the regions in which the wars are waged are themselves marginalized. However, the May 2007 attack by the Darfuri Justice and Equality Movement (JEM) on Omdurman resulting in a considerable loss of life has brought the war from the margin to the center.

RELIGIOUS DEMOGRAPHY AND IDENTITY

The number of Muslims in Sudan is estimated at 65 percent of the 35 million population, or about 22.7 million. Christians—Coptic, Eastern Orthodox, Catholic, and Protestant denominations—are estimated at 10 percent of the population, or 3.5 million. The remaining 25 percent, 8.7 million, practice indigenous African faiths, described in the 1972 constitution as "heavenly faiths." Indigenous religions are mentioned in both the 1998 "Permanent Constitution," and in the 2005 "Interim National Constitution," drafted after the CPA. However, there is a significant difference in the wording describing "the Nature of the State" in the 1998 and postpeace 2005 interim constitution:

- 1998: The state of Sudan is an embracing homeland, wherein races and cultures coalesce and religions conciliate. Islam is the religion of the majority of the population. Christianity and customary creeds have considerable followers.
- 2005: The Republic of the Sudan is an independent sovereign State. It is a democratic, decentralized, multicultural, multilingual, multiracial, and multireligious country where such diversities coexist.

The seriousness of religion in Sudan's North–South wars is reflected in the fact that religious identity appears at the beginning of each constitution, yet Islam and Christianity are not mentioned anywhere in the 2005 "Introductory Nature of the State." A small but significant estimated population of 23,500 in 1976 of southern Muslims (Wani 2006) has likely swelled to double or triple that size under the influence of forced or opportunistic conversions during the decades of imposed Islamization and Arabization in government schools, IDP camps, and locations of war resettlement of southerners in the North. The estimated and decimated postwar population of the South is 2.7 million.

The dominant northern political parties have been religiously based while the major southern movements have been secular. This fact speaks volumes regarding Muslim majority and non-Muslim minority politics in Sudan. Both of the two major northern parties—Umma Party and the Democratic Unionist Party—descend through hereditary lines where the mantle of religious legitimacy meshes with political entitlement. The line of the nineteenth-century Mahdi to the present Sadiq al-Mahdi informs the origins of the Umma Party, and the Khatmīyya religious brotherhood led by the Mirghani family informs the origins of the Democratic Unionist Party. Both power and allegiances are hereditary. Two important religious leaders have stood outside of this pattern—Mahmoud Mohamed Taha, leader of the Republican Brothers and Islamic reformer who was hung for apostasy in 1985, and Hassan al-Turabi, who likely signed Taha's execution order. The strength of the issue in the Muslim North is such that the once-powerful Sudanese Communist Party did not oppose Shari'a as state law in 1983, nor did the northern-dominated secular National Democratic Alliance after the 1989 Islamist coup.

Historically the bedrock of Sudanese Islam has been a Sufi folk system, decentralized, tolerant, and for some a transcendental mysticism expressed through various *turūq* religious brotherhoods, Qadirīyya, Tijaniyya, and others. This was fundamentally changed by top-down Islamism, imposed and institutionalized by two military regimes (Generals Numeiri and al-Bashir, respectively) who were greatly influenced by the Muslim Brotherhood, later the National Islamic Front (NIF) created by Hassan al-Turabi. This politicized Islam required implementation of a strategic cultural agenda that would transform the historical Sufi social order into a new Islamic "moral order" (*Nizām al-Am*) imposed top to bottom, penetrating every institution, and eventually displacing the old order through terror and fear.

The New Public Order was the most visible face of the Islamist Civilization Project (*Mashrū' al-Hādari*) instituted by the al-Bashir Inqāz ("Salvation") regime. Public order and morality were enforced primarily through the new penal code, a Saudi-like public morality that was enforced through a series of laws and its own Public Order Police (*Shortat Nizām al-Am*). Initial fear and intimidation among the populace eventually gave way to acquiescence as well as subtle and overt forms of resistance to a public order that was essentially foreign to Sudanese ways. During the 1990s, the decade of the strictest application of these laws, an entire generation grew up in the changing cities and towns of the country that has created lasting effects and has become the identity of the new Sudanese Muslim. A newly socialized generation now asks me, a veteran Sudanese researcher, what it was like in the old days when women could dress as they please and men could openly enjoy their local brew, '*aragi*, in the company of equally devout Muslim friends.

With this heavy investment of religion in political parties, there has never been a mass, religiously based peace movement. Moreover, most religious leaders have not positioned themselves to be agents (more than just voices) for peace. With religion co-opted by the major political players and with repression and violence used to silence critics, religious leaders have been neutralized as moral critics of the chronic militarism that has fueled and perpetuated wars plaguing the country and decimating parts of it.

The southern resistance movements—the Sudan People's Liberation Army/ Movement (SPLA/M) from 1983, and its predecessor Anya-Anya—eschewed religion, although their leaders were often educated Christians. The movement evolved from a program of separation to one of national unity as a secular democratic state, envisioning a "new Sudan" where religion and state are constitutionally separated. That dream and possibility ended with the tragic death (or possible assassination) of John Garang just six months after the signing of the CPA and two weeks after he was sworn in as national vice president.

ARAB-MUSLIM AND AFRICAN IDENTITY

Construction of a cohesive national identity has bedeviled the Sudanese polity since independence—for which both British and Sudanese leaders are responsible in colonial times and since independence in 1956. A racial hierarchy in the Nile Valley was established by British colonialism in an effective system of divide and rule and through a sophisticated manipulation of race by phenotype and putative proximity to "Arab identity" (Fluehr-Lobban 2004). The complexity of social-racial formations in the two major Nile Valley countries is explored by Eve Troutt Powell (2003). Racialized references separating "Arab" from "African," and brown from black, are embedded in the colonial system erected by politicians and anthropologists to offer a scientific veneer. Delta Egyptians were ranked over Nubians of Egypt and Sudan, but the system offered Arabized Nubians of Northern Sudan superiority over the peoples of the South and the Nuba Mountains.

This system descends to the present in a homogenized, monolithic use of "Northern Arab Sudanese." In the twenty-two-year civil war between North and South Sudan, it was alleged that Muslim Arabs were pitted against Christian Black Africans, and this confusion, or misrepresentation, was mirrored again in the Western press, which described the conflicting parties in Darfur as Arab against Black African, dropping the religious referent since Darfur is an overwhelmingly Muslim region. These terms are highly contested in contemporary public discourse. "African" is as much about geography as race, and "Black" is a moving target in the social construction of race. "Northerner" and "Southerner" in Sudanese discourse have become akin to the black–white binary in the United States where people with complex social, ethnic-racial histories are homogenized and categorized as one or the other.

Scores of domestic and foreign nongovernmental organizations (NGOs) operate freely in the capital city, probably the majority of which are indigenous in name and leadership. Some are devoted to nonviolence, some to enhancing the role of women in peacebuilding, and many to the use of religion in peacebuilding. The seeking of David Little's "Tolerance Level II" (reacting to beliefs and practices and disapproval but worthy of respect and/or engagement; see chapter 1, this volume) is appropriate at this moment, where the maintenance of peace is still fragile at best, where violent encounters are still the norm in Darfur and Abyei, South Sudan. Tolerance has been criticized as merely sufferance but not real acceptance in hierarchical societies such as Sudan, where dominant social groups have bestowed and withdrawn tolerance over the tortured years of conflict since independence. Constitutional pluralism, embedded in law and enforced by government institutions, is the clear legal remedy to the still ambiguous and uneven levels of tolerance in contemporary Sudan (An-Na'im 2006).

Defining Sudanese nationality as exclusively Arab and Muslim has been a cornerstone of the central Northern ruling elites. Arab-Islamic identity was asserted by nearly every postindependence regime, except for a brief period of negotiated peace during 1972–83, when an alternative "Afro-Arab" identity was adopted as an inclusive concept intended to meld northern and southern regions. General Jaafar Nimeiri (1969–85) initially seized power as a Nasserite "Arab nationalist" and then squandered the first Peace Accords (signed at Addis Ababa, 1972–83) by initiating Sudan's Islamist agenda decreeing Shari'a as national law in 1983. This move, more than any other, brought about resumption of civil war, and aggressive Arabization and Islamization programs were pursued. Afro-Arab identity was rendered a cynical cliché, and the discourse on identity shifted inside the country to a derogatory usage of "Arab" as racial oppressor by southerners, and "African" used by northern chauvinists to mean "primitive" or "slave" (*'abd/abīd*), the most potent racist term.

In the United States, the simplistic rendering of the civil war as "Muslims" waging jihad against "Christians" dominated the media, drawing the attention of American Christian evangelicals. In the mid-1990s allegations of Sudanese Arab slavers abducting African Blacks energized an abolitionist campaign to emancipate southern Christian slaves, eventually bringing the case to the Bush administration. These efforts by the Christian right put Sudan on the US political agenda.

In the declining years of the war, during the decade of stalled peace negotiations, Arab identity was denied by prominent Islamist leader Hassan al-Turabi, who emphasized that Sudanese are all "African." Some northern and southern intellectuals employ the term "Arabized Africans" for northern Muslims, especially targeting the ruling elite whom they see as being in denial of their African identity. Since the CPA, the African character of the South was affirmed in multiple political-cultural details of the negotiated peace, and the demographic transformation of the capital city is turning Khartoum into a recognizably more "African" city.

The issue of race has become more central in Sudanese political discourse as the sharp contrast between the Arab center and the marginalized regions of the South directly threatens the unity of the Sudanese state. In fairness to the government of Sudan, the Darfur conflict erupted in 2003 when rebel movements attacked the government airbase in El Fasher, which reacted with force. Quickly depicted as a war of Arab against Black African, the well-known folk categories of ethnic identity with neutral references to difference in skin tone and color have been replaced by a politicized discourse of race and identity. The citizenship status of the millions of internally displaced and expatriate Sudanese in exile was tested in the 2009 national elections, as was the 2011 referendum on southern statehood, both negotiated in the CPA.[1]

RELIGION, POLITICS, AND THE STATE

In medieval times Sudanese Christian Nubia forged one of the longest treaties in history with Muslim rule in Egypt from the seventh to the fifteenth centuries known as the *baqt* (Arabic corruption of *pactum* from Greco-Roman treaties with Nubians in pre-Christian times). This treaty was based on mutual interests of trade and nonaggression, including a supply of slaves, ivory, ostrich feathers, and other exotic goods for which the Nubian elite received cloth and foodstuffs, wine and beer, and horses. The *baqt* held long after the dramatic spread of Islam into North Africa and across the Sahara so long as Nubians accepted and did not challenge their tributary status (Lobban 2006, 15). The *baqt* could be examined as a model for future North–South Sudanese relations.

Since independence, except for brief and gloriously remembered periods of democratic rule, Sudan has been governed by military regimes, each of which has manipulated religion for their political legitimacy. At first Muslim religious identity was presumed yet kept officially at the margins as governments proclaimed a secularism derived from their Arab nationalist bent. After the 1983 installation of Shari'a as national law, the separation of religion from politics was erased, and neither military nor democratic governments dared to remove Shari'a as it too became melded with political identity.

The present regime of General Omar al-Bashir (1989–present) institutionalized and codified Shari'a as the base for all Sudanese law as the country became a de facto Islamic republic. The question has been raised as to whether an Islamic state, or any theocratic state, can be nondiscriminatory (Sisk 1992; An-Na'im 2006). In theory, the answer is yes, but the track record of contemporary Islamic states, including Sudan's, has not supported this in practice. Al-Bashir's government, the longest of any since independence, has been described as a combination of brutality and pragmatism (Jopson 2008), a strategy that might have been admired by Machiavelli but has drawn the wrath of the international community, as witnessed in the indictment of al-Bashir by the chief prosecutor of the International Criminal Court in The Hague as a war criminal in July 2008.

MANIPULATION OF RELIGION USING THE INSTRUMENT OF SHARI'A: WAR AND PEACE

The most overt manipulation of religion in Sudanese politics was the instrument of Shari'a to launch, implement, and eventually partially withdraw Sudanese Islamism. The "September Laws" (which made Shari'a the only source of law) introduced the application of criminal *hūdūd* penalties. This was especially evident in the ready use of amputation for theft in the early years, 1983–84, which forcefully revealed the "new order" demonstrating that Islam's religious law could be used as a means of terror and suppression. The propagandistic use of jihad waged against the southern unbelievers (*kufār*) also began in 1983 but was most vigorously pursued after the Bashir/Turabi coup of 1989, until 1999 when the relaxation of the Islamist "civilization" experiment coincided with the commercial flow and export of oil. Within a decade 7 percent of China's total import of oil flowed from Sudan.

The decade or more of peace talks stalled over the issue of Shari'a. The Abuja I and II talks in the early 1990s acknowledged the multiethnic, multireligious Sudan, but the government of Sudan insisted on the right to retain an Islamic constitution for the Muslim majority while the Southern Peoples Liberation Movement (SPLM) rejected the application of Islamic law to southern Christians and animists, adding the right of southern self-determination and separation. The government of Sudan conceded the removal of the *hūdūd* punishments from southerners but not from the remainder of the Shari'a. With the signing of the CPA, Shari'a was withdrawn from the South and from non-Muslims in the North. A central compromise leading to the signing of the CPA was the agreement at Machakos, Kenya, in 2002 that the South would be secular and the North would retain its religious base, with Shari'a as its source of law. Thus, a model of "one state: two systems" was created.

SHARI'A AND HUMAN RIGHTS: TOLERANCE LEVELS I AND II

Human rights during the decades of war, peace, and the installation and partial withdrawal of Shari'a as state law are complex, varied, and nuanced. Sudan experienced an extremist application of the Shari'a with hundreds of amputations and thousands of lashings carried out on Muslims. *Hadd* criminal sentences were applied incorrectly to non-Muslims for theft, morals and alcohol infractions, and an imposed Islamist public moral order that intimidated all citizens. Little (2008) has noted that highly authoritarian societies can be relatively nonviolent. Such was the case for the often rebellious northern Sudanese who had previously risen up and overthrown military regimes in 1964 and 1985. During the decade of extremist Islamism and intolerance lasting from 1989–99, popular unrest was crushed and most democratic opposition leaders were imprisoned (and many tortured) while others fled into exile. This repression may have given the impression of acquiescence, but Sudanese post-1999 authors tell a different story as they hailed the failure of the Civilization Project (al-Mubarak 2001; Ibrahim 2003; al-Tigani Mahmoud, 1993–present).

However, most of the civilization project repression has been relaxed in the wake of the flow of oil and the signing of the CPA without any official national withdrawal of Shari'a. Indeed, in the aftermath of the CPA, reassurances were issued by the president about its continuation. Since the cessation of violence between the North and South, the present conflict zones, in Darfur and Kordofan, and the IDP camps remain the most vulnerable to extremist abuse. David Little (see chapter 1, this volume) has proposed the following model for assessing a nation's movement away from a state of intolerance toward greater tolerance:

- Tolerance Level I: "Reacting with disapproval or disagreement to beliefs and practices but without incitement to discrimination or violent acts."
- Tolerance Level II: "Reacting to beliefs and practices and disapproval but worthy of respect and/or engagement."

It is axiomatic that nations in a state of civil war are creating an atmosphere of mutual intolerance. This was the case during the decade of the 1990s when the opposing government of Sudan and the SPLM/SPLA (SPLM/Southern People's Liberation Army) made almost no progress at the peace table. Intolerance of Southern cultural and religious autonomy by the government of Sudan was matched by a campaign of intolerance of Islam, Muslims, and Shari'a as the source of conflict. As the extremist regime wore itself out, eventually acknowledging that the war in the South was unwinnable, the politics of pragmatism and of oil revenues shifted the course of the nation toward official tolerance in 1999 by winding the war down and finally negotiating a set of comprehensive peace accords in 2005. The transition from authoritarian intolerance to peace between North and South was brokered by the warring parties, and succeeded due to significant strategic intervention and pressure by international actors, especially the United States; the African nations of Kenya, Ethiopia, and Uganda; and the European Union nations of Norway and Sweden. With an end to the civil war, the CPA moved Sudan toward Tolerance Level I at the official level. Religious and ethnic discrimination were effectively outlawed with the following:

(Section 1) State and Religion: [The CPA] Recognizes that Sudan is a multi-cultural, multi-racial, multi-ethnic, multi-religious and multi-lingual country and confirms that religion shall not be used as a divisive factor . . . all personal and family matters . . . may be governed by the personal laws (including Shari'a or other religious laws, customs or traditions) of those concerned. (CPA, 6.4)

And the rights of local self-determination and equitable participation in the national government were enshrined in a promised democratic system of governance where the cultural, ethnic, racial, religious, and linguistic diversity and gender equality of the people are reflected (ibid., sec. 1.3; 1.4).

Postconflict specialists recognize that the transition phase is precarious. This is surely the case for Sudan, particularly since the conflict in Darfur erupted just as the civil war in the South was ending. Most experts agree that there is a close relationship between the two (deWaal and Flint 2008), and that Sudan's future rests on its ability to accommodate the increasing demands of its peoples at the margins.

Human rights violations negotiated in the CPA have lessened since 2005. From my recent research in 2007–8 funded by the US Institute of Peace, prosecution of southern non-Muslims under Shari'a has stopped in the capital city, but it continues in the IDP camps. Southern women beer brewers were finally released from prison in 2007, and a CPA-mandated committee for the status of non-Muslims in the capital and city non-Muslim courts were established in 2007 and 2008, respectively. A possible effect of the international human rights campaigns highlighting human rights abuse in Sudan might be evident in the words of Ali Osman Yassin, the chief judge of the Sudan judiciary, upon the withdrawal of a stoning sentence imposed on a Christian woman in 2002 as "incorrect" while describing stoning as "excessive and cruel" and flogging as a "humiliating punishment" (Sudan Organization Against Torture Annual Report 2004).

In the post-CPA environment as new human relations are evolving in the multiracial capital city, there are signs that Little's Tolerance Level II—"reacting to beliefs and practices and disapproval but worthy of respect and/or engagement"— is emerging in public political discourse and attitudes. In my interviews and interactions with southern politicians and elites, they willingly state that neither Shari'a nor the Arabic language are central issues any longer. Southern member of parliament Helen Lalyec Oller (National Assembly omduman) expressed to me a common sentiment among southerners that Shari'a and Islam were never the real issues, and that a "live and let live" philosophy is best. The deputy director of Islamic affairs in the government of South Sudan, southern Muslim Fatima Mohamed Abdel Jabber, told me, "The days of Shari'a and politics are finished— there will be no more cutting of the hands of the poor" (January 8, 2008). Other

Southerners whom I interviewed in Juba in 2008 expressed stronger sentiments of forgiveness that "we will never do to them what they did to us."[2]

Little's Tolerance Level I—"reacting with disapproval or disagreement but without incitement to discrimination or violent acts"—is still present wherever the remnants of extremist Islamism are still evident. This is present in the continued harassment of both southern women beer and alcohol brewers and male consumers and sellers of the brew, especially in the IDP camps where the CPA exists more in theory than practice. This continued harassment is viewed by non-Muslims as blatantly discriminatory and illegal after the signing of the CPA. It is also viewed as unfair by many Muslims who increasingly embrace a peace-with-reconciliation formula for solving Sudan's history of chronic conflict.

Key variables involving religion that would improve levels of tolerance among all Sudanese include (1) decisive Sudan government movement away from religious extremism, realistically but not amounting to full separation of religion from the state; (2) a national program of reconciliation and practical trust-building using indigenous concepts of Sufi spirituality and animist respect for life; (3) acknowledgment by Muslims that Islam is not Sudan's sole legitimate religion, and that respect for other religions includes indigenous African beliefs and extends beyond rhetorical recognition of its Christian minority; and (4) acknowledgment by non-Muslims that Shari'a is the religious law for the Muslim majority population in Sudan, and that reinstating Shari'a was a decolonization move that remains a popular demand whose installation was met with little resistance by Sudanese Muslims.

Naturally, religious healing is only one part of any potential postconflict program, but it is one that has been neglected in favor of emphasis on more basic economic and infrastructure development that, in the case of Sudan, is needed to begin to reverse the drain of resources from the peripheries to the center.

RELIGIOUS LEADERS

The role of religious leaders in deeply divided societies is precarious. Weak leaders devolve to opportunism, which permits their survival, while strong leaders gain their position and voice within authoritarian and increasingly illegitimate circles of power. Individual religious leaders have distinguished themselves as voices for peace, but there has never been a religiously based peace movement in Sudan. Under these extreme circumstances, we may ask under what conditions do religious leaders act as a stimulus to violence? Hassan al-Turabi is perhaps the chief catalytic agent for outbreak of violence and the years of civil war from 1983 to 2005. His Muslim Brotherhood organization—later the NIF—policies of a relentless program of Islamization of people and culture are directly responsible for this chronic conflict. The conditions involving the role of the NIF and religion that are necessary but not sufficient to explain this recent history include (1) engineering policies from the strong center (Khartoum) yet claiming legitimacy from the weak periphery (Darfur and East Sudan); (2) projecting a "new" nonhereditary religious legitimacy with personal claim of being "Imam"; (3) international recognition from Islamist states, especially Saudi Arabia and Iran; and (4) development of a security state using fear, intimidation, and torture of indigenous opposition as well as belligerence against rival states, with Egypt as a special target.

Turabi, isolated since 1999 when he challenged al-Bashir's preeminent power, has nonetheless continued his legendary chameleon-like political transformations to remain a force to be reckoned with. He is widely believed to be behind the Darfur rebel JEM that launched an attack on Omdurman, across the river from Khartoum, in May 2008, the first such assault on the center from a movement in the periphery. His opportunistic Islamic reform program now includes advocating that women be elevated to the status of imams and that Muslim women can marry Christian and Jewish men, thus equalizing the law for women. His reforms have piqued the state religious establishment to the extent that he was declared "apart" from the movement—a virtual apostate—for his radical stands aimed at creating a new base for his Popular Congress Party created after the movement split in 2000 (Majmua' Fiqhī 2006). In the end, Turabi has opportunistically distanced himself from his own projects, revealing the oldest aphrodisiac—power—to be at the center of his ambition, not religion.

But when are religious leaders a catalyst for peace? Perhaps the greatest disappointment is the lack of public Muslim leaders as voices for peace. This role has been cast for Sudanese Muslims in the diaspora and includes notable figures such as Islamic reformer Abdullahi al-Na'im, and the founder of the Sudan Human Rights Organization, Mahgoub al-Tigani Mahmoud, both of whom express the essential message of peace inherent in Islam, literally "the peace," from submission to God by the Muslim and the core Sufi base of Sudanese Islam.

Under the intensity of both political and religious repression, Christian public figures have been cast in the role of vocal peacemakers because they are allowed to comment publicly and thus retain their credibility as critical but loyal subjects of the government. Significant international religious support opposing the Islamization moves by various regimes since 1983 has been in the form of Christian-based humanitarian and relief groups, such as Save the Children, the Sudan Interior Mission, and various projects of the National Association of Evangelicals. The Roman Catholic Church, which has a Sudanese cardinal, Gabriel Zubeir Wako, canonized Mother Josephine Bakhita during the height of the Bashir jihadist push for a final solution to the Southern conflict. Saint Josephine Bakhita, originally from south Darfur and beloved by Southern Catholics as one of their own, was an enslaved woman who became a Catholic nun and settled in Italy where she became known to the Verona and Comboni missionary orders, which have deep roots in Sudan.

Continued religious repression against Christians was referenced at the Lambeth conference in 2008 by Sudanese archbishop Dr. Daniel Deng, who led a movement of 150 bishops of the global south to protest the church's seemingly equivocal position on homosexuality, which, Dr. Deng said, puts Anglicans in his country at risk of persecution by extremist Muslims.[3] Recall that the Anglican movement in Sudan, as elsewhere in Africa, was a central part of the colonial mission, thus its decolonization has legitimacy. That era symbolically ended when al-Bashir turned the main Anglican cathedral in Khartoum, next to the Republican Palace, into the new Museum of National Independence.

Identifiable religious groups who could act as "spoilers" to the fragile peace between the North and South are the Salafist Islamic movements to the right of al-Bashir and Turabi's Islamism. The Ansār al-Sūnna, based in the heart of the regime's global geographical core, is a continuing threat from the extreme right to the official government line of peace and shared governance with the Southern movement, the SPLM. They are historically skeptical toward the Islamist project, which they view as fabricated for politics, and not based in the true Islam that transforms the person and society (Ali 2004; Salomon 2008a). Salomon (2008b) quotes Turabi's newfound self-criticism reflecting on past practice: "People became obsessed with politics. . . . We forgot culture, we forgot, education, we forgot society and the mosques. There was no one from among us who went to the mosques—instead we went to the government offices."

FINDINGS FROM SUDAN

Sudan, one of the world's most recognized "deeply divided societies," makes an important case for theoretical analysis. Based upon the foregoing, it can be asserted that religion has been a major issue in the post-independence history of national conflict, coupled with the conflation of Muslim religious identity with the ruling elite's ethnicity. Moreover, according to David Little's analysis "illiberal authoritarian" nations—those lacking constitutional democracy and with high levels of majority/minority intolerance—are the nations most likely to have high levels of violence. Sudan could be a textbook case for this insight. Among the root causes of war and conflict cited in this chapter, religious factors—if not primary, such as the causes of uneven wealth and power sharing—are certainly secondary. While any analysis focusing on a single cause of conflict must be avoided, religion (its beliefs, practitioners, leaders, and power to mobilize for both good and ill) cannot be ignored, as Appleby (1999) has noted in his analysis of "the ambivalence of the sacred." Paul Collier (2007) has analyzed the characteristics of fifty failed states where corrupt leaders dominate a chronic system of bad governance, civil wars are common, and dependence on export of extractive resources drives the local economy. These features fit the Sudanese case.

Another underrepresented factor gaining attention, but still little analyzed, is the role of race in Sudan's conflicts. Sudan's manifold complexities of race, ethnicity, region, and religion (which has mistakenly been conflated with race) demand critical analysis. It is imperative that ethnicity and race be distinguished where relevant, and that religion be added to race as a racial-ethnic marker in the politics of Islamism and resistance to it. The ways in which "race" has been deployed to encourage violence are better documented than are the shared genetics and culture of Sudan's antiquity in the Nile Valley and environs (Keita 2007). Common bonds of kinship that extend deeply into historically shared use of space and resources may yet be a source of reconciliation, but so far this effort has appeared mainly in the novels of Francis Deng, *Seed of Redemption* (1986) and *Cry of the Owl* (1989). It is often remarked that the Sudanese are lovely, hospitable people who have become expert at killing one another. A theory of violence beyond the scope of religion and the state is needed to explore and explain how traditions of hospitality, openness to the other, and generosity of the material and spiritual can be turned into their opposite.

CONCLUSION: INTERRELIGIOUS DIALOGUE AND PEACE BUILDING

If there was ever a need for interfaith dialogue and a truth and reconciliation process, it is in deeply divided Sudan. In large measure, the success of the CPA and the maintenance of national unity were vested in "trust-building" by the Sudan government in order to "make unity attractive." Lack of trust and the lack of any significant government effort to devise a trust-building process since the CPA was signed have resulted in an overwhelming Southern sentiment for separation. Sudan's bitter experience along the religious divide is a major contributing factor to this sad state of affairs. With independence near in 2011—if the Sudan government meets its promise to respect a referendum on separation or unity—southern voices of compassion and forgiveness can be heard along with the practical realization that an independent South will need to cooperate with the North. "With independence forgiveness will surely come."[4]

While interfaith dialogue is promising for a long-term benefit in education and the validation of one's experience ("letting off of steam"), it rarely addresses the root causes of conflict and can represent an added frustration to victims and sympathetic individuals from the other side who are willing to engage in the process of dialogue. One such example is the Sudan Inter-Religious Council under the direction of Tayeb Zein Abdin, a former Muslim Brother who is now critical of the al-Bashir regime and affiliated with the US Institute of Peace. Their logo combines the crescent and the cross. In a 2007 conference hosted by this group in Khartoum titled "Role of Religious Groups in Peace Building," they made the following observations and recommendations: (1) Continuous dialogue is needed among the urban poor; (2) new ways and means of representing non-Muslim and non-Christian religious groups must be found; (3) women religious leaders must be included in the dialogue process; and (4) the Sudanese are remarkable, flexible, and forgiving people.

Their list of the ingredients necessary for forgiveness relating to religion includes the defense of animist religions and the development of a national curriculum on Christianity involving the ministries of education and religious guidance. True to the criticism of such interfaith dialogue groups, greater emphasis is placed on the victims to forgive than on the government to ask for forgiveness of its long-suffering people. Greater effort to include grassroots Muslim leaders in truth, reconciliation, and apology would yield a high return in peacebuilding.

Among the hundreds of new indigenous NGOs are some groups devoted to nonviolence and democracy who employ the deep and reflective spirituality inherent in Sudanese cultures, monotheist and animist alike. One such NGO is an intercultural youth group SONAD, Sudanese Organization for Non-Violence and Democracy, which draws upon the spiritual approach of Gandhi and Martin Luther King Jr. for peace training primarily directed toward youth along the North–South, political–religious divide. Other NGOs emphasize the role of women in peacebuilding, such as SUWEP, the Sudanese Women's Empowerment for Peace, who have specialized in outreach to women at the margins. External funding for these initiatives is the norm, coming heavily from European Union countries, but the leadership is indigenous and the vision is shared that there will eventually be a genuine postconflict Sudan and is now independent South Sudan.

Whatever the outcome of separation or unity of the Sudan, the role of religion has been key. Religion, well known for its ability to mobilize for division, was part of the genesis of civil war. And religion also has the potential to provide the vision as well as the leadership for a more peaceful future. Unlike the politicians who have lost legitimacy with the masses, religious leaders across the spectrum of belief and custom have yet to locate and fulfill the role they might play with the mass of Sudanese spiritually depleted by decades of war and conflict. While no Muslim or Christian Desmond Tutu–like figure has emerged as a unifying moral voice, accountability for wrongdoing cannot be left solely to secular international bodies such as the International Criminal Court. Repentance, revival, and especially forgiveness as vehicles for healing are parts of Muslim and Christian traditions as well as southern animist belief. Without this neglected point of intervention, Sudan will continue its well-worn cycle of war-peace-war.

NOTES

1. I have visited the IDP camps around Khartoum, many of which are becoming permanent urban shantytowns. I interviewed their leaders, whose greatest desire is to return home but who realistically expect to remain in Khartoum for years to come. Some youth even express the desire to remain even as secondary or tertiary citizens in their own country for the economic and educational opportunities the capital city affords.
2. Interview with Hoth Chan, UNDP Rule of Law, Customary Law Project; and Stephen W. Bichiok, January 2008, Juba, South Sudan.
3. "Sudanese Anglicans Demand Gay Bishop Gene Robinson Resign." *Times Online*. July 22, 2008. Available at www.timesonline.co.uk.
4. Interview with Hoth Chan and Steven Bichiok, Juba, January 2008.

REFERENCES

Ali, Osman, Osman Mohamed. 2004. "The Dynamics of Interpretation of Textual Islam in Northern Sudan: Case Study among the Rural and Urban Population of Shendi." Doctoral Thesis, University of Khartoum.

An-Na'im, Abdullahi Ahmed. 2006. *African Constitutionalism and the Role of Islam.* Philadelphia: University of Pennsylvania Press.

Appleby, Scott. 1999. *The Ambivalence of the Sacred.* Lanham, MD: Rowman & Littlefield.

Collier, Paul. 2007. *The Bottom Billion.* Cambridge: Oxford University Press.

Cooper, Barbara M. 2006. *Evangelical Christians in the Muslim Sahel.* Bloomington: Indiana University Press.

Deng, Francis Mading. 1986. *Seed of Redemption: A Political Novel.* New York: Lilian Barber Press.

———. 1989. *The Cry of the Owl.* New York: Lilian Barber Press.

deWaal, Alex, and Julie Flint. 2008. *A Short History of a Long War*, 2nd edition. London: Zed Books.

Fluehr-Lobban, Carolyn. 2004. "A Critical Anthropological Review of Race in the Nile Valley." In *Race and Identity in the Nile Valley: Ancient and Contemporary Perspectives*, edited by Carolyn Fluehr-Lobban and Kharyssa Rhodes, 133–54. Metuchen, NJ: Red Sea Press.

Hanlon, Joseph. 1996. *Peace without Profit.* Oxford: Oxford University Press.

Ibrahim, Haydar Ali. 2003. *Al-Suqqut al-mashrū' al-hādarī* (*The Collapse of the Civilization Project*). Cairo: Center for Sudanese Studies.

Johnston, Douglas H. 2003. *The Root Causes of Sudan's Civil Wars.* Bloomington: Indiana University Press.

Jopson, Barney. 2008. "Dust and Duplicity: Bashir's 'Brutal Pragmatism' Binds Fragmented Sudan." *Financial Times*, July 30.

Keita, S. O. Y. 2007. "Review Essay of *Race and Identity in the Nile Valley*." *Bulletin of the Sudan Studies Association* 25, no. 4: 24–33.

Lobban, Richard. 2006. "Relations between Islamic Egypt and Christian Nubia: The Case of the Baqt." *Sudan Studies Association Newsletter* 24, no. 2: 12–20.

Lobban, Richard, Robert Kramer, and Carolyn Fluehr-Lobban. 2002. *Historical Dictionary of the Sudan*. Metuchen, NJ: Scarecrow Press.

Mahmoud, Mahgoub al-Tigani. 1993–present. *Sudan Human Rights Quarterlies*.

Majmua' Fiqhī al-Islāmī (Islamic Fiqh Group). 2006. *Rīsāla al-fasl al-aqūl fi al-rid'ali min kharuj'an alasil* ("Note on the Remarks of Apostasy [and] Departure from Fundamental Principle"). Sudan Government.

al-Mubarak, Khalid. 2001. *Turabi's Islamist Venture, Failures and Implications*. Cairo: Dār al-Thaqafia.

Powell, Eve M. Troutt. 2003. *A Different Shade of Colonialism: Egypt, Great Britain and the Mastery of the Sudan*. Berkeley: University of California Press.

Salomon, Noah. 2008a. "The Salafi Critique of Islamism: Doctrine, Difference and the Problem of Islamic Political Action in Contemporary Sudan." Paper presented at the 27th annual conference of the Sudan Studies Association, Florida State University, Tallahassee, May 16–18.

———. 2008b. "Post-Islamism, Questioning the Question." Social Sciences Research Council blog, Making Sense of Sudan. http://blogs.ssrc.org/sudan/.

Sisk, Timothy. 1992. *Islam and Democracy, Religion, Politics and Power in the Middle East*. Washington, DC: US Institute of Peace.

Sudan Organization Against Torture (SOAT). 2004. "Annual Report Sudanese Organization against Torture: Executive Summary from Report," February. "The Status of the Judiciary," 4–7. London.

Wani, Abdalla Keri. 2006. *Islam in Southern Sudan, Its Impact: Past, Present and Future*. Khartoum: Khartoum University Press.

CHAPTER 7

NIGERIA'S RELIGIOUS LEADERS IN AN AGE OF RADICALISM AND NEOLIBERALISM

༄

ROSALIND I. J. HACKETT

At one level, Nigeria's religious leaders are not unlike their counterparts across the continent in having to sustain and represent their organizations, speak out on matters of moral import, and decide how they are going to work with, around, or against Africa's often autocratic political leaders and influential economic elites. But viewed in terms of demographics and strategic importance, the stakes are much higher for those exercising religious leadership in Africa's most populous nation. Nigeria ranks as one of the world's largest oil producers; it has developed a reputation as a regional peacekeeper, yet its internal political order is unstable, corruption is endemic, and its report card on development after fifty years of independence is a cause for concern (see Campbell 2010; Dickson 2005; and Denselow 2010). However, the fact that Nigeria is made up of nearly equal numbers of Muslims and Christians helps to keep it in the world spotlight. Nigeria's population of between 130 and 140 million makes it the largest country in the world that is approximately half-Christian, half-Muslim.[1] For political scientist John Paden, this makes Nigeria a test case as to whether the state stands or implodes in the face of these divisions, and "pivotal" for the Muslim world in terms of Muslim-Christian political accommodation (Paden 2008).

Following independence in 1960, ethnic and regional issues first caused fragmentation and violence (Suberu 2001; Kukah 1993). Beginning in the 1970s, religiously motivated conflict (whether inter- or intrareligious) entered the mix (Falola 1998). This spike in violence is linked to a rise in religious revivalism (at times verging on militancy and radicalism) on both the Christian and Muslim sides—often spearheaded by youth groups (Ojo 2007; Hackett 1999; Igwara

1995).[2] Even though this is clearly tied to concerns of marginalization and resource distribution (and, thus, outbreaks of violence are mainly confined to the northern and central regions of the country), these new expressions of religious activism have served to elevate religious issues from the communal to the national level. Those in religious authority are more compelled than ever to address these challenges, whether their own denomination is implicated or not.

Nigeria is never short of scholarly, policy, and press analysis. This chapter seeks to offer, in light of the volume's core concept, some insights into the changing power relations of Nigeria's twenty-first century religious landscape (or what prominent analyst of Nigerian affairs Rev. Dr. Matthew Kukah terms its "dynamic religious economy").[3] The focus is not so much on the contribution of these leaders to the political process, nor is it about their ecumenical initiatives per se. Rather, the chapter is structured around those areas that are proving conducive to cooperation and conflict management, contrasting them with those that generate disagreement, if not outright hostility. In keeping with emergent scholarship on these issues, it is important to not overemphasize Nigeria's religious polarities and to be attentive to what church historian Frieder Ludwig calls the "other levels and layers" (2008, 606) and "creative responses to the tensions of religious co-existence" (603).

Without ignoring relevant historical roots, notably the colonial reinforcement of religious and ethnic divisions (Ojo and Lateju 2010), I shall focus on the last decade for two reasons. First, the paradoxes of neoliberalism in Africa, so well captured by Jean Comaroff and John Comaroff (1999, 2001) and Francis Nyamnjoh (2005), have provided a fertile environment these last few years for those religious groups offering survival strategies and all forms of empowerment and enrichment, spiritual or otherwise (cf. Ellis and Haar 2004). The flourishing of various revivalist (in some cases more extremist) options—the majority of conservative moral bent—needs to be seen in this context. Second, for a host of reasons ranging from political opportunism to economic frustration as well as global movements for Islamic reform and the new discourses of rights attendant upon the current phase of democratization that began in 1999, a number of northern Nigerian states opted to expand Shari'a or Islamic law to include criminal matters. This sparked a number of crises within the Muslim community, but especially among Christians. There were ugly clashes between Muslims and Christians over the issue, such as in Kaduna in 2000 (Yusuf 2007) and in Jos in 2001 (Danfulani 2005). In sum, the last ten years offer a critical time frame for examining the role played by Nigeria's religious leadership in promoting national attitudes of tolerance or intolerance, which—as argued by David Little in chapter 1—can be constitutive of liberal or illiberal forms of nationalism.

As discussed in the conclusion to this volume, deciding who qualifies as a religious leader can present challenges. This is particularly the case in Nigeria, where the boundaries between religious, ethnic, economic, and political leadership can be blurred, as with traditional Muslim leaders or emirs in the north of the country and with the former president, Olusegun Obasanjo, who by virtue of his "born-again" Christian status was looked up to by many Christians as a "defender of the faith." This chapter focuses on some of the most recognizable and "official" religious leaders (predominantly Christian and Muslim; traditionalists tend to get overlooked) because they often prove to be the most vocal and influential. Where relevant, the voices and actions of those claiming religious authority but who may hold secular office will be included.

AREAS OF ACCORD: HEALTH AND SOCIAL WELFARE

In identifying those areas where Nigeria's religious leaders speak or act publicly with some measure of agreement, it would be naïve to assume that they always adopt the same positive stance when addressing their respective communities. In other words, decades of mistrust and interreligious tensions, plus the need to promote one's own religious organization in a highly competitive religious environment, undermine the need to work together in the national interest. That notwithstanding, there are a number of pressing social issues that have occasioned statements and actions of shared concern, either via joint religious councils or via individual leaders.

One of the most likely areas where religious leaders can be counted on to speak out is regarding the suffering of the masses. Nigeria has been plagued by persistent corruption, poor governance, lack of rule of law, failed development policies, and crumbling infrastructures in the postcolonial period since 1960 due to a major civil war, long periods of military rule, and patrimonialist politics. Quotidian existence for the majority of Nigerians involves a struggle for survival and security. Religious leaders continue to exert their moral authority and criticize the state for its failure to improve the plight of the poor and underprivileged members of society (Falola 1998, 103–4, 129–36).

A more specific challenge to social welfare reared its head in the 1990s in the form of the HIV/AIDS pandemic. Religious authorities were initially slow to acknowledge the reality and the enormity of the problem, preferring to advocate sexual abstinence (cf. Bongmba 2007; Bryant 2004). With more convincing research data as well as an influx of foreign agencies targeting the issue, religious leaders have begun to take action (Virtue 2000; Josephine, Agapit, and Komla 2001). In addition to the National Faith-Based Advisory Committee on HIV/AIDS, which brings together Christian and Muslim representatives (Christian Association of Nigeria [CAN] and National Supreme Council on Islamic Affairs[4]), there is also the interfaith Nigerian network of religious leaders living with or personally affected by HIV/AIDS, which seeks to reduce stigma against HIV/AIDS patients. Embracing the same cause, the Interfaith Coalition of Nigeria mobilizes and engages both churches and mosques (Seele, Perry, and Karugu n.d.).

Religious leaders have also proved useful in sanctioning and promoting other health initiatives, such as maternal mortality and polio eradication in cooperation with US government organizations, as their well-established networks facilitate what one report terms "positive social mobilization" (CSIS 2007, 30, 36). The resistance in 2003 by some northern Muslim leaders to the polio vaccine originating in the West (because it was believed to be tainted and intended to reduce their fertility or to infect them with HIV/AIDS) and the subsequent rise in cases of polio should also be noted (IRIN 2004).

While outside agencies may be keen to promote the rights of women and children, notably in terms of education reform, these can also prove controversial and divide religious leaders, as in the cases of the two Muslim women (Safiya Hussaini and Amina Lawal) condemned to death by stoning on the grounds of alleged adultery under Shari'a law in 2002 (overturned in 2003) (Nasir 2005, n163).[5] Even the education of children may be a source of contention, with girls sometimes kept from school in more traditional Muslim homes in the north of the country, and often subjected to child marriage (Olaleye 2009). There would seem to be more agreement on the topic of indecent dressing, especially in the workplace and on university campuses (except where Islamic-style dress is imposed [Ludwig 2008, 622, 628]). This has been a matter of great social debate, with religious leaders weighing in on the issue and placing it in the context of general moral degradation. The former Anglican Archbishop of Lagos, the Right Reverend Peter Akinola, wrote in a pastoral letter in September 2006: "We remind our churches to maintain the emphasis on the war against indecent dressing." Anglican women leaders, also, have staged rallies to declare a "War against Nakedness" and organized cultural events under the rubric of "Operation Cover-Up."[6] Women's dressing has been a subject of regulation and even legislation in some of the Shari'a states (Nasir 2007). There is even an indecent dressing bill currently before the National Assembly, spearheaded by a Christian woman senator. The new Christian and Muslim universities springing up around the country have dress codes and social contracts (and, in some cases, health checks) to ensure propriety.

As will be discussed in the following, the initial reactions to the expansion of Shari'a in several northern states in the early 1990s provoked a strong, at times violent, reaction from the Christian community. But as Christians saw that their status as a minority religious community in several of these states was not seriously compromised, they began to appreciate the social benefits, namely the drop in crime, alcohol consumption, and the sex trade (Ludwig 2008, 615–16). Some Christian leaders began to voice their support for the legal reforms; one bishop even looked forward to Muslims converting to Christianity because of their likely inability to live with the demands of Shari'a (Danfulani 2005, 44).

CONFLICT-REDUCTION INITIATIVES

Nigerians have come to expect their religious leaders to deliver messages of peace and tolerance, whether at festival time or following outbreaks of violence. For some, these can be reassuring; for others, they are more empty rhetoric, given the role played by religious actors (and sometimes leaders) in fanning the flames of communal conflict. But the high death tolls (figures range from twelve thousand to sixty thousand) and extensive property damage since the return to civilian rule in 1999 have spawned a number of initiatives aimed at conflict reduction. The most prominent of these is the revival of the Nigerian Inter-Religious Council (NIREC), cochaired by the sultan of Sokoto and the president of CAN, which was originally established by President Olusegun Obasanjo in 1999 as a forum for high-level dialogue between Muslim and Christian leaders.[7] NIREC meets on a quarterly basis in different parts of the country. The current incarnation of the council seems much more proactive in tackling some of the root causes of communal conflict in Nigeria and their detrimental effects on the nation as a whole. For example, addressing a meeting of fifty Muslim and Christian leaders in Abuja in October 2007, the cochair, Sultan of Sokoto Alhaji Muhammadu Sa'ad, linked conflict to underdevelopment: "The issue of peace and religious harmony constitutes one of the cardinal principles which underlie the essence of our collective existence. Peaceful co-existence remains one of the key ingredients of nation-building and socio-economic development" (Shaibu 2007). In addition to holding meetings and conferences to generate mutual respect, the council has been speaking out through its communiqués on a range of problems that foster a "culture of violence," whether the scourge of HIV/AIDS, the proliferation of small arms, food insecurity, or "reckless religious preachers" (Dambatta 2008). Respect for these bridge-building organizations seems to be on the increase,[8] although some lament their elitist composition and lack of (grassroots) "preventive capacity" (Ojo and Lateju 2010, 36). The absence of African traditional religious leaders from many interreligious peacebuilding initiatives is also viewed as problematic, given their mediatory skills (ibid., 37; Blench et al. 2006; cf. Higazi 2008, 125).

Nigeria has a vibrant civil society, so it might be expected that a number of organizations and programs (some faith-based) aimed at peacebuilding and conflict transformation have sprung up in recent years (see Paden 2008, 64–65n18–19). Some of these initiatives may involve religious leaders; at very least, they help nurture a culture of peace and naturalize peace talk in civil discourse. The Society for Peace Studies and Practice would be a good illustration of this trend.[9] Headquartered in Abuja, it "seeks to integrate peace scholarship and practice as a way of advancing the development of the culture of peace." Not unsurprisingly, its June 2009 conference was titled "Trends and Tensions in Managing Ethnic and Religious Conflicts," and asked why previous efforts had failed. It is housed in the building of the government-run Institute for Peace and Conflict Resolution in the federal capital territory of Abuja.[10] While Paden commends the development of umbrella organizations at the national level, he emphasizes the importance of grassroots initiatives that are better equipped to develop capacity using local cultural strategies (2008, 64–65, 225–26; 2005, 222).

This is well evidenced in the case of Kaduna State, with its modern capital, Kaduna, known for its interethnic and interreligious interactions. This area has suffered some of the worst religious riots in 2000 and 2002. It is also the home of two religious leaders—one Muslim, the other a Pentecostal Christian—who have worked valiantly in the areas of religious conflict mediation and peace education, especially for the youth. In fact, their original grassroots organization was known as the Muslim-Christian Dialogue Forum, launched in 1995 after Imam Muhammad Ashafa and Pastor James Wuye decided to forego their religious militancy and, instead of seeking revenge against the other's religion, work for tolerance and peace (Ashafa and Wuye 2006; 2007). They developed a popular television program where they answered religious questions on social issues, and before long they were receiving international support for their successful mediation model.[11] Despite their regional Nigerian focus, they now travel to various parts of Africa and even further afield, leading workshops in interreligious dialogue and peacemaking.[12] Through their Interfaith Mediation Centre based in Kaduna, they have developed peace clubs and curricula for schools to reverse what they call a "theology of hate." With the support of the state governor, Alhaji Ahmed Mohammed Makarfi, who went out of his way to accommodate the various constituencies in the expansion of Shari'a and foster good Muslim-Christian relations in his jurisdiction (Ludwig 2008, 624–27), they were instrumental in creating a Kaduna Peace Committee, which led to the adoption of the Kaduna Peace Declaration signed by religious leaders in August 2002.[13]

Ashafa and Wuye have received numerous international awards and been featured in magazine articles (Griswold 2008), television documentaries, and an award-winning film/DVD "The Imam and the Pastor."[14] They have also coauthored a book on their own life-changing encounter (Ashafa and Wuye 1999). One of the particular merits of this peacemaking team is their sensitivity to the positive and negative uses of media. In 2006, at the height of rising tensions over the Danish cartoon controversy, they urged leaders of the various branches of the Christian Association of Nigeria to appear on radio and television to condemn the negative representations of the Prophet Muhammad.[15] During the clashes over the Miss World contest in 2002 (Muslims became angry over a newspaper journalist who suggested that the Prophet Muhammad would have enjoyed taking a wife from among the contestants), they drove religious leaders around affected neighborhoods on a bus and arranged to have them appear on television to appeal for calm (Crawley 2003). Another reason for their embrace is their focus on youth—many of whom feel alienated from the influential traditional elites (CSIS 2007, 35). John Paden attributes these intergenerational tensions to educational differences (2008, 63; 2005, 132–34). However, a recent study of the role of traditional rulers in conflict prevention and mediation in Nigeria highlights successful efforts by some of these leaders to ensure religious harmony in their emirates and chiefdoms (Blench et al. 2006).

The city of Jos, the capital of Plateau State, has seen some of the worst violence in recent times (2001, 2008, and 2010) in clashes between indigenes and settlers (the former being predominantly Christian and the latter Muslim) (Ostien 2009; Higazi 2008; Tertsakian 2005; Danfulani and Fwatshak 2002). The violence is described by journalist Hajiya Bilkisu as "the reference point for intractable communal, value based conflicts in Nigeria" (Bilkisu 2009). The major disturbances have occasioned interreligious (Christian-Muslim) peacebuilding talks around the city (Danfulani 2005). The Jos crisis also triggered a national interreligious youth summit, organized by NIREC in Minna, the Niger State capital in January 2009. It aimed to provide skills for promoting peace and interreligious harmony in each of the thirty-six states of the federation as well as in the federal capital territory, Abuja (ibid.).

AREAS OF DISACCORD: RELIGIOUS BALANCING

The question of religious balancing in terms of political and military appointments at the federal and state levels and in terms of funding for religious activities has proved to be a major source of tension between the Christian and Muslim communities over the years. Accusations of bias in the case of state funding of religious pilgrimage or religious structures have flown back and forth for years. It is sometimes hard to sort out fact from fiction, and serious communiqués from conspiracy theories. As I was working on this chapter in 2009, a Nigerian Catholic leader and acquaintance sent me a breaking news story on a purported plot to Islamize the federal government. It concerned a letter leaked to the press, written to the Federal Character Commission by a pro-Islamic group, the Supreme Council for Shari'a in Nigeria (Gobert 2009). The letter complained about the "deliberate marginalization of Muslims," notably in terms of federal appointments, and the urgent need to redress this to avoid a Rwandan genocide scenario.

This recalls CAN's massive protests in the 1990s over Muslim domination in executive appointments at the state and federal levels (Falola 1998, 111–12; Christian Association of Nigeria 1988). They have also fought discrimination against Christians in Muslim-dominated areas, whether in terms of permits for building churches, missionary activity, or media access (Falola 1998, 113). One of their more recent battles with the Obasanjo government was over the inclusion of religious data in the national census. In 2005–6 CAN threatened to boycott the census if religion was not included in the forms. Many Christians have refused to accept past census results that indicate they are in a slight minority compared with Muslims. In the end, questions on both religion and ethnicity were left out because of their sensitivity.

While this is not the place to evaluate claims of marginalization, it can be affirmed that all sorts of ambiguities abound with regard to the role of religion in the Nigerian constitution (Ilesanmi 1995, 2001; Ostien 2006). As cogently demonstrated by comparative law scholar W. Cole Durham, although Nigeria's constitution contains a "no state religion" clause (Article 10), it does not specify that the state should be secular or that religious associations should be separated from the state (Durham 2005). He considers that the provisions call for an interpretation situated between cooperation and benign neutrality (159–61). Ebenezer Obadare considers that under President Obasanjo only lip service was paid to the secularity of the state (2006). He attributes this to what he calls the Pentecostalization of governance and the rise of a "theocratic class" that has been instrumental in constituting a discursive Muslim "other." This echoes Iheanyi Enwerem's earlier fears about a rising "fundamentalism" in mainstream Christian churches and his criticism of Christian hypocrisy in condemning state sponsorship of the hajj while welcoming government financing of Christian pilgrimages and the establishing of Christian Pilgrim Boards (Enwerem 1996, 99–100). Ogbu Kalu further links the demonization of Islam in Pentecostal rhetoric and practice to Christian Zionist ideas about Hebraic sources and the glory of Israel (Kalu 2008, 244).

In fact, many analysts of the Nigerian religious and political scene attribute the rise of Islamization discourse to the Christian Association of Nigeria. This multidenominational organization that overlooks most theological differences to promote a united Christian front began picking up steam in the 1980s as it broadened its constituency (Falola 1998, 108). It became increasingly politicized and militant under various leaders as it sought to combat the feared Muslim "other" in the wake of the Iranian revolution and stepped up Muslim activism and militancy in Nigeria. For example, the former president, Archbishop Peter Akinola, declared in the wake of the violent Muslim responses to the Danish cartoon controversy in Nigeria in 2006 that they were part of a plot to make Nigeria an Islamic country. "It is no longer a hidden fact that a long-standing agenda to make this Nigeria an Islamic nation is being surreptitiously pursued," he said (quoted in Meldrum 2006). Akinola is famous for his extensively circulated February 2006 statement, written when serving as president of the Christian Association of Nigeria, in response to Muslim riots ignited by the printing in Danish newspapers of cartoons depicting the Prophet Muhammad:

> From all indications, it is very clear now that the sacrifices of the Christians
> in this country for peaceful co-existence with people of other faiths has been

sadly misunderstood to be weakness.... May we at this stage remind our Muslim brothers that they do not have the monopoly of violence in this nation.... CAN may no longer be able to contain our restive youths should this ugly trend continue.[16]

Many attribute the revenge attacks on Muslims in several cities by Christian youths to Akinola's "call to arms" (see Meldrum 2006). Despite the violence unleashed by the cartoon controversy in 2006 (more people lost their lives in Nigeria [more than 150] than in any other country), some Christian leaders expressed their sympathy to their fellow monotheists for the defamation of their religion. Some of these leaders, such as Matthew Hassan Kukah, are critical of the naïve politics that engender theories of Muslim takeover plans (Kukah 1995, 226–27). Christian fears of Muslim hegemony began with the Organization of the Islamic Conference (OIC) crisis in the late 1986, when the government secretly joined the OIC (an international organization of Islamic states promoting Muslim solidarity in economic, social, and political affairs) before reaching a peak with the moves by several northern states to implement full Shari'a from 1999 onward.

Archbishop Akinola is perhaps more widely known for the massive campaign he has spearheaded to condemn same-sex unions and homosexuality in general.[17] His strong belief that "homosexuality is nothing short of sinning against God" has led him to be vehemently critical of the ordination of gays in Western Christian churches.[18] Some argue that his conflict is more with international Anglicans (he has threatened schism) than with the Nigerian church; he repeatedly justifies his position as a defense of Christianity in the face of what he describes as Nigeria's own brand of "militant" Islam (cf. Ludwig 2008, 632).[19] He also taps into more general (Christian) fears of Islamization through higher birth rates and new patterns of immigration in Europe (Griswold 2010, 53).

It is noteworthy that CAN is dominated by evangelicals, especially from the northern region, who are more concerned about propagating their religion and possible restrictions thereon (Imo 2008). Yet the former CAN president, Roman Catholic Archbishop of Lagos Anthony Okogie, was so renowned for his political outspokenness that Muslims accused him of acting like a head of state (ibid., 51). CAN's confrontational approach to protecting its interests has been criticized, not least by Muslim organizations such as the Jama'atu Nasril Islam and the Muslim Students Society (Falola 1998, 114). However, as rightly noted by Falola, their criticisms "tend to read like condemnations of Christianity, furthering the tension that defines contemporary relations between Islam and Christianity in Nigeria" (ibid.).

In his study of the contest between evangelicals and Islamic revivalists, notably in relation to the expansion of Shari'a in the northern states, religion scholar Cyril Imo notes the growing politicization of evangelical theology (2008, 60f.; see

Kalu 2008, 244, on equivalent Pentecostal responses). This has led to a new "theology of retaliation," moving beyond the notion of turning the other cheek to the necessity of self-defense. It has been spearheaded by those who live in the cities most affected by the Shari'a crisis, such as Kano, Jos, and Kaduna. The Anglican Bishop of Kano encouraged his members to defend themselves when attacked by Muslims, and the pastor of the Good News ECWA Church in Jos, Rev. David Laje, quoting Luke 22:36, preached to his congregation that "those who do not have a sword should sell what they have to buy one" (Imo 2008, 62–63). In an interview, he further stated: "There is no way one can fold his hands and allow the Muslims to come and destroy our property and kill our church or family members" (ibid., 62). In similar vein, Paul Freston suggests that "there is no way that [Nigerian] Christians can avoid the gauntlet thrown down by Islamist politics" (Freston 2001, 190). Such is the tone of some of the Christian leaders affected by or involved in the violent killings in Yelwa in 2002 and 2004. Some believe that Africa is a new (or renewed) battleground for the proxy war between Islam and the West while others find meaning for their suffering in premillenialist, apocalyptic teachings in the Bible (Griswold 2010, 45–53).

While this new emphasis on retaliation may appear to be a contraindication to democratic processes, evangelical leaders argue that it has helped keep Muslim militancy in check and brought a "modicum of stability" to conflict-prone areas (Imo 2008, 63). They also claim that it has led them to question their civic obedience to (ungodly) political leaders (ibid., 64). Imo notes the potential ambiguities of this new spirit of resistance, which could lead to reneging on civic responsibilities. Overall, though, he believes that evangelical activism has contributed to the relaxation of certain aspects of Shari'a law that were enforced in the early stages of implementation (ibid., 66).

PROSELYTIZATION

Another important area of contention relates to proselytization. Many clashes in the past resulted from public expressions of Christianity in the North (Ludwig 2008, 613). While older religious leaders from the mainline churches may look askance at some of the aggressive proselytic strategies of the newer (evangelical and Pentecostal) groups, for younger leaders these new tactics and mass-mediated messages are par for the course in a religiously competitive environment (Hackett 1999, 2008). The stakes are high in terms of gaining members, public recognition, patronage, and resources from the state or private sector. The newer "home-grown" movements, whether Muslim or Christian, are less beholden to tradition, territory, or centralized authority.[20] The means can justify the end, especially if there is an apocalyptic tinge to the religious ideology (Hackett 2011a; Griswold 2010, 47–48). This can be seen in the recruitment practices of the extremist Boko

Haram group that purportedly abducted children to serve in its ranks (Ujah et al. 2009). In its campaign to have Islamic law implemented throughout the country and to reject Western education, members of Boko Haram have been involved in violent clashes with security forces and public officials, with serious loss of life in July 2010. They also killed an outspoken Wahabi cleric, who had criticized their actions, in October 2010 in Maiduguri.

New alliances are being formed between mainline and Pentecostal churches to strengthen evangelization campaigns (see Yakubu 2009). The former have tended to view the newer generation churches as a threat to their authority and as a departure from time-honored Christian beliefs and practices. But the new united, proactive Christian front nurtured by CAN in the face of perceived Islamization campaigns, especially in the north and middle belt of the country, provides a platform for more cooperation between the churches (see Ojo 2007, 186–87). The historic churches have to acknowledge that successful church-planting techniques, such as those developed by Pastor E. A. Adeboye and his Redeemed Christian Church of God (one of Nigeria's largest and most successful Pentecostal churches) in their quest to develop parishes within five minutes walking distance of every African (and five minutes driving distance of everyone in the developed world), result in rapid growth and international renown (Ukah 2008).

As a keen analyst of Nigerian Pentecostal politics, Ruth Marshall underscores the risks of Pentecostal intentions to colonize the public sphere for national unity (Marshall 1995, 2009; see also Hackett 1999). This new "theology of engagement," according to Ogbu Kalu, that emphasizes uniqueness and urgency, is inimical to "the development of an interfaith theology of dialogue" (2008, 246). Muslims in turn become frustrated with this new Christian radicalism as they have over secularism—which they interpret as a pretext for promoting Western Christian values (ibid., 245). Kalu proposes that Nigerian Pentecostals overcome their fear of pluralism and "develop a concept of dialogue for the sake of a stable public space" (ibid.). That same concern for dialogue led the Centre for Law and Social Action to initiate a series of meetings between civil society and Pentecostal leaders in Nigeria in 2004–5 to explore avenues of cooperation in order to "promote peace, social justice and accountable governance."[21] The report contains important exchanges over the need for the burgeoning Pentecostal movement to develop more social awareness, internal accountability, and personal responsibility so its leaders could be more publicly involved in the processes of democratization and conflict resolution. In his lucid study of corruption in Nigeria, Daniel Jordan Smith contends that the prosperity brand of Pentecostalism has compromised its earlier moral critique of corruption (Smith 2007, 210–19). The new "domestication of Pentecostal moralism," with more attention to personal behavior in the realm of sexuality, marriage, and family, has enabled, in his view, "the prosperous to live piously even as they loot the state and society" (214).

SHARI'A

If Nigeria's membership in the OIC was the flashpoint of the late 1980s (Christian leaders were incensed at not being consulted and believed it was part of a secret plan to Islamize the country; Ibrahim 1991), then the recent revival of Shari'a law in northern Nigeria has been the major controversy of the last decade (Kogelmann 2006). In fact, a political leader, Governor Ahmed Sani Yeriman Bakura, set the ball rolling by declaring a full implementation of Shari'a law in Zamfara State in October 1999. He became a popular hero overnight and before long was being talked of as a reformer, as a God-guided one who removes evil from society (Danfulani 2005, 13). This then led political and religious leaders to begin mobilizing in other states in response to the growing agitation from the masses for a society organized along Islamic lines (17). In Kaduna State the pro-Shari'a and anti-Shari'a rallies and demonstrations in February 2000 turned violent. Following sermons against the evils of Shari'a, Christians marched to Government House to deliver a letter to (Christian) Deputy Governor Stephen Shekari protesting the proposed legal changes. As they returned through the central market, clashes occurred between Christian and Muslim youths that then spiraled into three days of carnage and destruction. Following a meeting some days later with religious and political leaders, and after surveying the devastation in the city, President Olusegun Obasanjo declared: "The people who did this could not have done it for any religion" (quoted in Danfulani 2005, 24). Such discursive moves are common and understandable under the circumstances, but they fail to recognize the entanglements of political, socioeconomic, or religious interests (Lincoln 2003) and the dynamics of religious activism (Juergensmeyer 2008).

In the days that followed the Kaduna crisis, the federal government equivocated over whether to force states to drop the proposed adoption of Shari'a law, accusations flew back and forth over actions and inactions of key players, and heated opinions were exchanged over the constitutionality of an expanded Shari'a and the social consequences for non-Muslims. Some of the harshest criticisms came from Christian leaders (Danfulani 2005, 30–35). The Catholic Archbishop of Lagos (now cardinal) and a former CAN president, Dr. Anthony Okogie, was very critical of the government's plan in 2000 to merely suspend the Shari'a implementation because it would not, in his view, put an end to the activities of religious fanatics. In the end, Shari'a state governors denied that they had reached such a decision with federal government officials and Shari'a implementation went ahead.

The Pentecostal Fellowship of Nigeria was even more vehement in its criticism. In a full-page newspaper advertisement, it denounced the "medieval, crude, stone age laws, in the public square for zina adultery, for women to be discriminated against and separated from men in public places, including markets, schools, public transport, etc" (quoted in Danfulani 2005, 33). In addition, several prominent Christian leaders and governors of predominantly Christian states in the southeast and midwest threatened to introduce canon (biblical) law in their jurisdictions (Danfulani 2005, 44). The generally negative response from Christians at the time was informed by the (manufactured) memories of the oppressive imposition of Muslim (Hausa-Fulani) rulers under the old emirate system on minority ethnic groups (many of whom were traditionalists or Christians) during the colonial period (ibid.; see also Yusuf 2007). This sparked what was termed the Tafawa-Balewa crisis in the 1990s, and recent unrest in the middle belt region (Ostien 2009; Danfulani 2005, 42–43). Christians feared a diminished social status and restrictions on their activities (Ludwig 2008, 613). In addition to their qualms about initiatives to capture the North for Islam, Christians also recall the famous claim by one of Nigeria's most well-known Muslim leaders, Abubakar Gumi (d. 1992) that neither Christians nor women could ever rule Nigeria (Danfulani 2005, 60).

Philip Ostien, who taught for several years at the Faculty of Law, University of Jos, links the recent revival of Islamic Law of 1999 to the constitution-making processes of the late 1970s. He contends that by waging war on the proposed federal Shari'a Court of Appeal during the drafting of the constitution in 1979, Christians "missed a golden opportunity to make a lasting peace with their Muslim compatriots on honorable terms and to eliminate or at least partly reduce the matter of religion as a national political issue" (Ostien 2006, 252). He identifies three contributory factors: first, the failure by Christians to appreciate the importance Muslims attach to their sacred law and to making an honorable place for it in Nigeria's constitutional order; second, the overestimation by Christians of Muslim ambitions for the actual implementation of Shari'a in Nigeria; and, third, the overestimation by Christians of Muslim political strength. Ostien believes that Christians should "grant Muslims their just demands, which have, after all, been extremely modest, so that religion as a political problem can be put aside and everyone's attention can turn to other things" (253–55). He accuses both Christians and Muslims of exploiting religious controversy to serve their own interests (cf. Last 2007).

Franz Kogelmann wishes that the debates over the "Shari'a factor" would become less emotionalized and focus more on the compatibility of religious systems (whether Muslim or Pentecostal, for example) and human rights norms (Kogelmann 2006). Sanusi Lamido Sanusi, a leading Muslim intellectual, now governor of the Central Bank of Nigeria, urges Muslim critics of Shari'a to consider internal reform rather than wholesale rejection of Islamic law as proposed by the predatory West (Sanusi 2005). He aspires to a synthesis of Islamic laws and teachings with those "modern values that satisfy the yearnings of the modern Muslim for emancipation, justice and equity" (271–72). Moreover, by encouraging "free and unfettered conversation" among Muslims and between the Muslim community and others on the place of Shari'a in Nigeria—and, by extension, the law in general, citizenship and human rights—he believes that the reality of the world we live in, the demands of women for greater freedom, the requirements of good governance, and the increased awareness of the capacity of religious demagogues for mischief will all push the debate toward more secular areas and reduce the religious tension (Sanusi 2007, 186).

CONCLUSION

This has been a critical decade for Nigeria's much publicized experiment in federalism and pluralism. Religion has assumed a greater salience on the national scene than in previous decades. Flashpoints and communal violence reflect changing configurations of international and local identities. This is counterbalanced by a corresponding upsurge in initiatives—proactive, not just reactive—to manage religious tensions. The peace rhetoric from religious leaders has become conjoined with talk about national integration and communal development. Students can now join peace clubs in their schools and religious officials may be invited to interreligious meetings to monitor and mediate religious conflict. All these developments have occurred in a changing, and arguably more challenging, international environment—one marked by new global insecurities, heightened religious activism, economic decline, and the wide-ranging effects of neoliberal market forces and deregulated media.

As Philip Ostien has sagaciously noted in his most recent article on ethnoreligious conflict in Jos, "the causes of the problems are in fact quite well understood. The difficulty is how to overcome them" (2009, 2). In exploring the sustainable management of religiously related conflict in the highly charged Nigerian context, the following points have emerged from this chapter:

- First, more than ever before, modern media have the capacity to make or break a flashpoint situation: they can amplify unguarded statements of religious leaders and broadcast images of corpses and burned churches and mosques to audiences of millions, just as they can transmit messages of peace and unity. Considering that a number of violent incidents in Nigeria's litany of religiously related conflict were sparked by media insensitivities, this remains a neglected dimension of research and professional training (Hackett 2011b, 2003).

- Second, multilateral and multilevel efforts to address grievances, whether between religious communities or between religious communities, government, and civil society organizations, appear to be more effective than unilateral, top-down action.
- Third, a "deficit of dialogue" in conflict-ridden contexts is a recipe for the manipulation of "fault lines" and historical memory, at times leading to violence (Kwaja and Kew 2010). Religious leaders have the capacity and authority to set the tone for (and mediate) reconciliation.
- Fourth, when the lives and livelihoods of minority religious and ethnic communities are adversely affected by new legislation, new patterns of marginalization (perceived or real), and acts of violence, their leaders may give higher priority to the survival of the group over national unity.

In his study of Nigerian Muslim civic cultures, political scientist John Paden holds to the view that the Muslim commitment to national unity since independence in 1960 will continue to prevail, especially if sustained by a stable democratic federalism (2005, 226). Although the furor over Shari'a has died down, it remains, in his view, a "symbol of division" both within and outside Nigeria (2008, 59). He recommends that the United States "appear evenhanded" in its relations with Muslim and Christian leaders, so it does not fuel a "clash of civilizations" scenario (2005, 223). Conerly Casey, in her studies of Muslim Hausa youths in the ancient city of Kano in northern Nigeria, argues that their sense of victimhood and potential radicalization is fueled by "media portrayals of violence against Muslims within and outside Nigeria's national borders" (Casey 2009, 277). Thus, language and framing assume increasing significance in a media-saturated world, especially for the younger generation. Murray Last suggests that the "clash-of-civilizations" analysis of the Nigerian scene that is so much in vogue these days is fueled by political and economic interests both at home and abroad (Last 2007). He refers to this as "an economy of political panic." For at least the last century, Muslims and Christians have for the most part coexisted peacefully, and it is only because of certain local factors—new political and residential arrangements, and politico-economic competition—that "hotspots" of religiously related violence have developed.

Whether one subscribes to the inclusion of Nigeria on a list of deeply divided societies, few would disagree with it being designated as "deeply paradoxical," with abundant evidence of—what Scott Appleby aptly terms—the "ambivalence of the sacred" (2000). Both old and new sources of conflict have arisen in the course of the last decade to challenge the religious leaders of this "powerful" state that still fails so many of its people. As this chapter has shown, those with religious authority have a mixed record to date on managing inter- and intrareligious tensions and the potential for violence.

NOTES

My thanks go to Benjamin Soares and Philip Ostien for their insightful suggestions and critical reading of this chapter.

1. Statistics on religious affiliation are hard to come by in Nigeria (they were excluded from the last census), but there are sizeable minority communities of those who adhere to traditional/indigenous/ancestral forms of belief and practice, as well as practitioners of Eastern religions, spiritual science organizations, and syncretistic sects.

2. In a 2007 Pew survey, 91 percent of Muslims and 76 percent of Christians said that religion is more important than their identity as Africans, Nigerians, or members of an ethnic group.

3. For helpful historical overviews of the imbrications of religion and politics in Nigeria, see Adogame (2005) and Ojo and Lateju (2010). For a range of perspectives on more current developments, consult CFR (2007).

4. For their 2007 communiqué, see http://data.unaids.org/pub/Report/2007 /communique_3rd_interfaith_forum_28-29_august_07_en.pdf.

5. For an extremely helpful overview of some of the responses to the effects of Shari'a on women, see the introduction to the second edition of Ezeilo, Ladan, and Afolabi-Akiyode (2004).

6. "Anglican Women at It Again: 'War against Nakedness': Mothers Pledge Their Commitment to Eradicate Indecent Dressing." May 8, 2006. *The Church of Nigeria*. www.anglican-nig.org/waragnst_nakedness2.htm.

7. The US government has promoted Muslim-Christian reconciliation by organizing *Iftar* dinners in Abuja, Lagos, and Kwara State. See US Department of State (2005).

8. "Nigeria: Agenda for NIREC." Editorial, *Daily Trust*, October 27, 2010 http://allafrica.com/stories/201010270349.html.

9. See the society's website: www.spspng.org/index.php.

10. See the institute's website: www.ipcr.gov.ng.

11. For example, their 2006 DVD, "The Imam and the Pastor," was supported by the US Institute of Peace; http://beta.usip.org/events/imam-and-pastor-healing -conflict-nigeria.

12. Their recent film, "An African Answer," was produced in the wake of Kenyan postelection violence. www.anafricananswer.org/.

13. A detailed account of the various conflict management initiatives in Kaduna State can be found in Yusuf (2007, 247f.). The absence of women from these initiatives as well as their own efforts to organize for peace are discussed in McGarvey (2009, 264f.).

14. www.fltfilms.org.uk.

15. "Mohammad Ashafa," *Ashoka International*, http://fellows.ashoka.org/fellow /3874.

16. "Rev. Peter Akinola Speaks out Against Cartoon Violence in Nigeria." See *Christianity Today*, February 22, 2006, www.christianitytoday.com. He reiterated the

comment about Muslims not having the monopoly on violence in Griswold (2010, 52).

17. See Rudy Gaudio's new book, *Allah Made Us* (2009), for insightful comments about Akinola and the antihomosexual rhetoric/agenda in relation to the West and the Muslim north.

18. "An African Archbishop Finds Common Ground in Virginia," interview in *The Christian Science Monitor*, January 8, 2007. www.csmonitor.com/2007/0108/p01s 03-woaf.html.

19. Ibid.

20. For an example of criticism of their tactics, notably with regard to noise pollution, see "Nigeria: Agenda for NIREC." Editorial, *Daily Trust*, October 27, 2010. http://allafrica.com/stories/201010270349.html.

21. *Pentecostalism and Public Life in Nigeria: Perspectives and Dialogue*, Centre for Law and Social Action with the support of the Heinrich Böll Foundation. Lagos, 2007.

REFERENCES

Adogame, Afe. 2005. "Politicization of Religion and Religionization of Politics in Nigeria." In *Religion, History, and Politics in Nigeria: Essays in Honor of Ogbu U. Kalu*, edited by Chima J. Korieh and G. Ugo Nwokeji. Lanham, MD: University Press of America.

Appleby, R. Scott. 2000. *The Ambivalence of the Sacred: Religion, Violence, and Reconciliation*. Lanham, MD: Rowman and Littlefield.

Ashafa, Muhammad, and James Wuye. 1999. *The Pastor and the Imam—Responding to Conflict*. Lagos: Ibrash Press.

———. 2006. "Training Peacemakers: Religious Youth Leaders in Nigeria." In *Training Peacemakers: Religious Youth Leaders in Nigeria*, edited by D. R. Smock. Washington, DC: US Institute of Peace.

———. 2007. "Warriors and Brothers." In *Peacemakers in Action: Profiles of Religion in Conflict Resolution*, edited by D. Little. New York: Cambridge University Press.

Bilkisu, Hajija. 2009. "Nigeria: Beyond Jos—Youth for Peace." *Daily Trust*, January 29. http://allafrica.com/stories/200901290345.html.

Blench, Roger, Selbut Longtau, Umar Hassan, and Martin Walsh. 2006. "The Role of Traditional Rulers in Conflict Prevention and Mediation in Nigeria." Report prepared for the Department for International Development, London. www .rogerblench.info/Development/Nigeria/Conflict%20resolution/Final%20 Report%20TRs%20September%2006.pdf.

Bongmba, Elias K. 2007. *Facing a Pandemic: The African Church and the Crisis of AIDS*. Waco, TX: Baylor University Press.

Bryant, Elizabeth. 2004. "Nigerian Anglicans Leading Resistance to Gays in the Church." *Toronto Star*, February 1. Available on Sodomy Laws website, www .glapn.org/sodomylaws/world/nigeria/ninews009.htm.

Campbell, John. 2010. *Nigeria: Dancing on the Brink*. Lanham, MD: Rowman & Littlefield.

Casey, Conerly. 2009. "Mediated Hostility: Generation, and Victimhood in Northern Nigeria." In *Regional and Ethnic Conflicts: Perspectives from the Front Lines*, edited by J. Carter, G. E. Irani, and V. D. Volkan, 274–91. Upper Saddle River, NJ: Pearson Education.

Center for Strategic and International Studies (CSIS). 2007. "Mixed Blessings: US Government Engagement with Religion in Conflict-Prone Settings." A Report of the Post-Conflict Reconstruction Project. Washington, DC: CSIS.

Christian Association of Nigeria. 1988. "Leadership in Nigeria (to Date): An Analysis." Kaduna: CAN Publicity, Northern Zone.

Comaroff, Jean, and John Comaroff. 1999. "Occult Economies and the Violence of Abstraction: Notes from the South African Postcolony." *American Ethnologist* 26, no. 2: 279–303.

———, eds. 2001. *Millennial Capitalism and the Culture of Neoliberalism*. Raleigh-Durham, NC: Duke University Press.

Council on Foreign Relations (CFR). 2007. "Symposium on Religious Conflict in Nigeria: Session 2: Contemporary Religious Dynamics in Nigeria," May 8. www .cfr.org/publication/13314/symposium_on_religious_conflict_in_nigeria.html.

Crawley, Mike. 2003. "Two Men Create Bridge over Nigeria's Troubled Waters." *Christian Science Monitor*, February 28. www.csmonitor.com/2003/0228/p07s01 -woaf.html.

Dambatta, Salisu Na'inna. 2008. "Nigeria: Nirec Calms Religious Frayed Nerves." *Daily Trust*, June 22. http://allafrica.com/stories/200806230739.html

Danfulani, Umar H. D. 2005. *The Shari'a Issue and Christian-Muslim Relations in Contemporary Nigeria*. Stockholm: Almqvist & Wiksell International.

Danfulani, Umar, and S. Fwatshak. 2002. "Briefing: The September 2001 Events in Jos, Nigeria." *African Affairs* 101:243–55.

Denselow, Robin. 2010. "Nigeria at 50: 'Nothing to Celebrate." *BBC News Africa*, September 24. www.bbc.co.uk/news/world-africa-11398020.

Dickson, David. 2005. "Political Islam in Sub-Saharan Africa: The Need for a New Research and Diplomatic Agenda." Washington, DC: US Institute of Peace.

Durham, W. Cole. 2005. "Nigeria's 'State Religion' Question in Comparative Perspective." In *Comparative Perspectives on Shari'ah in Nigeria*, edited by P. Ostien, J. M. Nasir, and F. Kogelmann. Ibadan: Spectrum Books.

Ellis, Stephen, and Gerrie ter Haar. 2004. *Worlds of Power: Religious Thought and Political Practice in Africa*. New York: Oxford University Press.

Enwerem, Iheanyi. 1996. "Religious Leaders and Their Role in the Political Process: The Nigerian Experience." *Orita: Ibadan Journal of Religious Studies* 28, no. 1–2: 85–105.

Ezeilo, Joy Ngozi, Muhammed Tawfiq Ladan, and Abiola Afolabi-Akiyode, eds. 2004. *Sharia and Women's Human Rights in Nigeria*. 2nd ed. Lagos/Abuja: Women Advocates Research and Documentation Centre/Women's Aid Collective.

Falola, Toyin. 1998. *Violence in Nigeria: The Crisis of Religious Politics and Secular Ideologies*. Rochester, NY: University of Rochester Press.

Freston, Paul. 2001. *Evangelicals and Politics in Asia, Africa, and Latin America*. New York: Cambridge University Press.

Gaudio, Rudolf Pell. 2009. *Allah Made Us: Sexual Outlaws in an Islamic African City*. New York: Wiley-Blackwell.

Gobert, Emerson, Jr. 2009. "Plot to Islamize Govt: Islamic Group's Letter to Federal Character Commission Leaks." *Saturday Sun*, August 8, www.sunnewsonline .com/webpages/news/national/2009/aug/08/national-08-08-2009-01.htm.

Griswold, Eliza. 2008. "God's Country." *The Atlantic*, March. www.theatlantic.com /magazine/archive/2008/03/god-8217-s-country/6652/.

———. 2010. *The Tenth Parallel: Dispatches from the Fault Line between Christianity and Islam*. New York: Farrar, Straus and Giroux.

Hackett, Rosalind I. J. 1999. "Radical Christian Revivalism in Nigeria and Ghana: Recent Patterns of Conflict and Intolerance." In *Proselytization and Communal Self-Determination in Africa*, edited by A. A. An-Na'im. Maryknoll, NY: Orbis.

———, ed. 2008. *Proselytization Revisited: Rights Talk, Free Markets, and Culture Wars*. London: Equinox Publishers.

———. 2011a. "Millennial and Apocalyptic Movements in Africa." In *Oxford Handbook of Millennialism*, edited by C. Wessinger. New York: Oxford University Press.

———. 2011b. "Devil Bustin' Satellites: How Media Liberalization in Africa Generates Religious Intolerance and Conflict." In *Religious Dimensions of Conflict and Peace in Neoliberal Africa*, edited by Rosalind I. J. Hackett and James H. Smith. Notre Dame, IN: University of Notre Dame Press.

Higazi, A. 2008. "Social Mobilization and Collective Violence: Vigilantes and Militias in the Lowlands of Plateau State, Central Nigeria." *Africa* 78, no. 1: 107–35.

Ibrahim, Jibrin. 1991. "Religion and Political Turbulence in Nigeria." *Journal of Modern African Studies* 29, no. 1: 115–36.

Igwara, Obi. 1995. "Holy Nigerian Nationalisms and Apocalyptic Visions of the Nation." *Nations and Nationalism* 1, no. 3: 327–55.

Ilesanmi, Simeon O. 1995. "The Myth of a Secular State: A Study of Religious Politics with Historical Illustrations." *Islam and Christian-Muslim Relations* 6, no. 1:105–17.

———. 2001. "Constitutional Treatment of Religion and the Politics of Human Rights in Nigeria." *African Affairs* 100:529–54.

Imo, Cyril. 2008. "Evangelicals, Muslims and Democracy: With Particular Reference to the Declaration of Sharia in Northern Nigeria." In *Evangelical Christianity and Democracy in Africa*, edited by T. O. Ranger. New York: Oxford University Press.

IRIN. 2004. "Nigeria: Muslim Suspicion of Polio Vaccine Lingers On." *IRIN* (UN Office for the Coordination of Humanitarian Affairs). February 19. www .irinnews.org/Report.aspx?ReportId=48667.

Josephine, Sanvee Kokoe, Akolatse Yao Agapit, and Tatagan-Agbi Komla. 2001. "Churches and the HIV/AIDS Pandemic: Analysis of the Situation in 10 West/ Central African Countries." Paper presented to the World Council of Churches and World Alliance of YMCAs, March. http://wcc-coe.org/wcc/what/mission /ehaia-pdf/aids-study-e.pdf.

Juergensmeyer, Mark. 2008. *Global Rebellion: Religious Challenges to the Secular State, from Christian Militias to al Qaeda*. Vol. 16, *Comparative Studies in Religion and Society*. Berkeley: University of California Press.

Kalu, Ogbu. 2008. *African Pentecostalism: An Introduction*. New York: Oxford University Press.

Kogelmann, Franz. 2006. "The 'Sharia Factor' in Nigeria's 2003 Elections." In *Muslim-Christian Encounters in Africa*, edited by B. Soares. Leiden: Brill.

Kukah, Matthew Hassan. 1993. *Religion, Politics and Power in Northern Nigeria*. Ibadan, Nigeria: Spectrum.

———. 1995. "Christians and Nigeria's Aborted Transition." In *The Christian Churches and the Democratisation of Africa*, edited by P. Gifford. Leiden: E. J. Brill.

Kwaja, Chris, and Darren Kew. 2010. "Analysis: Nigeria's Smoldering Crisis in Jos." *GlobalPost*, April 10. www.globalpost.com/dispatch/africa/100407/nigerias-jos -violence.

Last, Murray. 2007. "Muslims and Christians in Nigeria: An Economy of Political Panic." *The Round Table* 96, no. 392: 605–16.

Lincoln, Bruce. 2003. *Holy Terrors: Thinking about Religion after September 11*. Chicago: University of Chicago Press.

Ludwig, Frieder. 2008. "Christian-Muslim Relations in Northern Nigeria since the Introduction of Shari'ah in 1999." *Journal of the American Academy of Religion* 76, no. 3: 602–37.

Marshall, Ruth. 1995. "'God Is Not a Democrat': Pentecostalism and Democratisation in Nigeria." In *The Christian Churches and the Democratisation of Africa*, edited by P. Gifford. Leiden: E. J. Brill.

———. 2009. *Political Spiritualities: The Pentecostal Revolution in Nigeria*. Chicago: University of Chicago Press.

McGarvey, Kathleen. 2009. *Muslim and Christian Women in Dialogue: The Case of Northern Nigeria*. New York: Peter Lang.

Meldrum, Andrew. 2006. "Revenge Attacks Kill 20 Nigerian Muslims." *Guardian*, February 23. www.guardian.co.uk/world/2006/feb/23/andrewmeldrum.mainsection.

Nasir, Jamila M. 2005. "Sharia Implementation and Female Muslims in Nigeria's Sharia States." In *Comparative Perspectives on Shari'ah in Nigeria*, edited by P. Ostien, J. M. Nasir, and F. Kogelmann. Ibadan: Spectrum Books.

———. 2007. "Sharia Implementation and Female Muslims in Nigeria's Sharia States." In *Sharia Implementation in Northern Nigeria 1999–2006: A Sourcebook*, edited by P. Ostien, J. M. Nasir, and F. Kogelmann. Ibadan: Spectrum Books.

Nyamnjoh, Francis B. 2005. *Africa's Media: Democracy and the Politics of Belonging*. London: Zed Books.

Obadare, Ebenezer. 2006. "Pentecostal Presidency? The Lagos-Ibadan 'Theocratic' Class and the Muslim 'Other.'" *Review of African Political Economy* 110:665–78.

Ojo, Matthews A. 2007. "Pentecostal Movements, Islam and the Contest for Public Space in Northern Nigeria." *Islam and Christian-Muslim Relations* 17, no. 2: 175–88.

Ojo, Matthews A., and Folaranmi T. Lateju. 2010. "Christian-Muslim Conflicts and Interfaith Bridge-Building Efforts in Nigeria." *Review of Faith and International Affairs* 8, no. 1: (April): 31–38.

Olaleye, Mufutau Adewole. 2009. "Child Brides in Nigeria." *IslamOnline.net.* March 2. www.islamonline.net/servlet/Satellite?c=Article_C&cid=12356287657 86&pagename=Zone-English-Family%2FFYELayout.

Ostien, Philip. 2006. "An Opportunity Missed by Nigeria's Christians: The Shari'ah Debate of 1976–78 Revisited." In *Muslim-Christian Relations in Africa*, edited by B. Soares. Boston: Brill.

———. 2009. "Jonah Jang and the Jasawa: Ethno-Religious Conflict in Jos, Nigeria." *Muslim-Christian Relations in Africa*, www.sharia-in-africa.net/pages /publications/jonah-jang-and-the-jasawa-ethno-religious-conflict-in-jos-nigeria.php.

Paden, John N. 2005. *Muslim Civic Cultures and Conflict Resolution: The Challenge of Democratic Federalism in Nigeria.* Washington, DC: Brookings Institution Press.

———. 2008. *Faith and Politics in Nigeria: Nigeria as a Pivotal State in the Muslim World.* Washington, DC: US Institute of Peace Press.

Ruby, Robert, and Timothy Samuel Shah. 2007. "Nigeria's Presidential Election: The Christian-Muslim Divide." *Pew Forum on Religion & Public Life*, March 21.

Sanusi, Lamido. 2005. "The West and the Rest: Reflections on the Intercultural Dialogue about Shari'ah." In *Comparative Perspectives on Shari'ah in Nigeria*, edited by P. Ostien, J. M. Nasir, and F. Kogelmann. Ibadan: Spectrum Books.

———. 2007. "Politics and Sharia in Northern Nigeria." In *Islam and Muslim Politics in Africa*, edited by B. F. Soares and R. Otayek. New York: Palgrave Macmillan.

Seele, Pernessa, Tonya Perry, and Nguru Karugu. n.d. "Hope for Africa: The Balm in Gilead Forges Cross-National, Cross-Faith Partnerships with Five African Nations to Mount a Formidable Response to HIV/AIDs." *Global Health Council.* www.globalhealth.org/reports/report.php3?id=194.

Shaibu, Mohammed Lawal. 2007. "Nigeria: 50 Religious Leaders Meet in Abuja." *Daily Trust*, October 27. http://allafrica.com/stories/200710180440.html.

Smith, Daniel Jordan. 2007. *A Culture of Corruption: Everyday Deception and Popular Discontent in Nigeria.* Princeton, NJ: Princeton University Press.

Suberu, Rotimi. 2001. *Federalism and Ethnic Conflict in Nigeria.* Washington, DC: US Institute of Peace.

Tertsakian, Carina. 2005. "Revenge in the Name of Religion: The Cycle of Violence in Plateau and Kano States." *Human Rights Watch*, May 25. www.hrw.org/en /node/11755/section/1.

Ujah, Emma, Emeka Mamah, Kingsley Omonobi, Chioma Obinna, and Daniel Idonor. 2009. "Yar'Adua Orders Probe of Boko Haram Leaders' Killing." *Vanguard*, August 4. www.vanguardngr.com/2009/08/04/yaradua-orders-probe-of-boko -haram-leaders-killing/comment-page-7/.

Ukah, Asonzeh F. K. 2008. *A New Paradigm of Pentecostal Power: A Study of the Redeemed Christian Church of God in Nigeria.* Trenton, NJ: Africa World Press.

US Department of State. 2005. "Nigeria: International Religious Freedom Report 2005," November 8, Bureau of Democracy, Human Rights, and Labor, International Religious Freedom Office, www.state.gov/g/drl/rls/irf/2005/51489.htm.

Virtue, David. 2000. "Nigerian Primate Adds New Title: AIDS Workshop Calls for Behavioral Change." *Virtue Online* blog. http://listserv.virtueonline.org/pipermail /virtueonline_listserv.virtueonline.org/2003-November/006222.html.

Yakubu, Abubakar. 2009. "Nigeria: Arch-Bishop Calls for Harmony among Christians." *Daily Trust,* June 22.

Yusuf, Hajiya Bilkisu. 2007. "Managing Muslim-Christian Conflicts in Northern Nigeria: A Case Study of Kaduna State." *Islam and Christian-Muslim Relations* 18, no. 2: 237–56.

CHAPTER 8

JUST ENOUGH TO HATE—
NOT ENOUGH TO LOVE

༄

Religious Leaders in Northern Ireland

MARI FITZDUFF

We have just enough religion to make us hate,
and not enough to make us love one another.

JONATHAN SWIFT (QUOTED IN MCCREARY 1975)

Ireland, both North and South, remains one of the most religious countries in Western Europe (Mitchell 2006, 25). When civil war broke out in Northern Ireland in 1968, 95 percent of Catholics went to mass every week, and 45 percent of Protestants attended weekly church—figures far higher than the rest of the mostly Protestant United Kingdom. The figure for Catholic attendance in the Republic of Ireland in the same year was 94 percent. Even today, a survey in 2007 revealed that there are significantly more current regular churchgoers than average in Northern Ireland—the highest at 45 percent than anywhere else in the United Kingdom, with 81 percent professing to be Christians and only 0.4 percent belong to other religions.[1]

Religious membership in Northern Ireland is almost synonymous with political persuasion, particularly on the part of Protestants. In a survey carried out in 1995 by the Northern Ireland Social Attitudes Survey, 90 percent of Protestants opted to remain part of the United Kingdom, compared to just 24 percent of Catholics, while 60 percent of Catholics were in favor of the reunification of North and South Ireland.

Such division is part of the heritage of the island of Ireland, whose divisions reflect the history of Christendom itself. Following the arrival of Saint Patrick and other Christian missionaries in the early to mid-fifth century AD, Christianity became the major religion and by the sixth century had completely subsumed the indigenous pagan religion. The Norman/English invasions and settlements in Ireland began in 1169, and millions of acres of land were given to English soldiers who had served in wars against Ireland. These earlier occupier-settlers integrated relatively easily into the native population—becoming "more Irish than the Irish themselves" (*Níos Gaelaí ná na Gaeil iad féin*). They located themselves within Irish social and cultural society, spoke the Irish language, and intermarried with the Irish. They integrated so well that the British decided that the later settlements, which happened mainly in the northern part of the island, needed to be designed to ensure the separation of settlers and the natives to maintain orderly governance by the British. This separation tactic was assisted by the religious divisions of the sixteenth-century Reformation, which meant that most of the settlers were Protestant while most of the indigenous remained Catholic and loyal to Rome. Unlike the earlier plantations, therefore, the later influxes of the seventeenth- and eighteenth-century settlers led to an extremely divided society in Northern Ireland. Many of those divisions have remained in place until today.

RELIGION, THE STATE, AND CIVIL SOCIETY

In the post-Reformation northern part of the island, Catholics were almost completely excluded from the political structures. Many had been deprived of their land and livelihood by the settlers, and they came to be seen as second-class citizens, poor, priest-ridden, and, above all, lacking in loyalty to the British government.[2] Inevitably, the native Irish harbored great resentment toward the settlers, and the settlers in turn felt continually under threat from the Irish. In land settlement terms, the colonization of Ulster was particularly successful. In 1703 only 14 percent of the land if the island remained in the hands of the Irish, and in Ulster, only 5 percent of the land remained indigenous (Darby 1997, 20). By 1921 only ten percent of the southern part of the island was Protestant, in contrast to the 70 percent of the northern part of the island who were Protestant.

Throughout the centuries since colonization began in 1169, there had been frequent attempts (many violent) by the Irish people to achieve independence from Britain. In the earlier part of the twentieth century, the pressure on the British government to grant some form of limited independence to the island continued to increase, and in 1920 Britain eventually agreed. Northern Protestants, however, feared such independence because they were afraid that their faith would suffer in a mainly Catholic Ireland, where they believed their religious freedom would be restricted. They also feared the poorer economic state of the rest of the island, compared to their own relatively prosperous and more industrialized region. The Protestants (usually referred to as "unionists" because of their desire to retain union with Britain) therefore threatened to use force if they were coerced into a united Ireland and began to mobilize private armies against such an eventuality.

In 1921, in an effort at compromise, Lloyd George, then prime minister of Britain, insisted that the island be divided into two sections, the northeastern six counties, and the rest of the island, each with its own parliament. Irish Catholic leaders were divided over this suggestion, but the offer was eventually accepted, under significant pressure, by those leaders who were sent to conduct treaty negotiations with the British in London. These leaders were anxious to avoid a return to what could become an increasingly bloody conflict in Ireland. The suggestion of a division of the island was also accepted by the unionists, although reluctantly, as their first wish was for the whole of the island to remain within the United Kingdom of Britain and Ireland.

The decision to partition the island led to bitter and violent civil conflict between those nationalists who accepted partition and those who rejected it. Eventually, in 1923, those who accepted partition achieved a victory. The Irish Free State was formally created and set out to create a Catholic state for its people. The "special position" of the Catholic Church was recognized in the new Irish constitution.[3] In 1938 the Irish Free State adopted the status of a republic under the official name of Eire, although it is known internationally as the Republic of Ireland.

In Northern Ireland, the divisions between settlers and natives continued as they had since the seventeenth century. These divisions successfully combined to create what LeVine and Campbell (1972) have termed a "pyramid-segmentary" structure in Northern Ireland—that is, a structure in which segregation became the norm and in which different categories of a religious, political, social, economic, and cultural nature supplemented and consolidated each other. Religion and politics remained almost completely coterminous in the new region of Northern Ireland; that is, Catholics overwhelmingly saw themselves as "Nationalists" who would have preferred to see a united Ireland formed in 1921 when Britain began to break its colonialist ties, and Protestants overwhelmingly saw themselves as "Unionists," in other words, those who sought to retain the link with Britain in 1921 and threatened violence if such link was broken.

Such political loyalties remain basically the same until today, notwithstanding the signing and implementation of the Belfast agreement of 1998.[4] A survey in 1994 showed the churches to be the largest nongovernmental institutions in Northern Ireland and the largest organizations with voluntary membership in Northern Ireland (Morrow et al. 1991). They were also a significant part of the Northern Ireland economy with much volunteer work undertaken under their auspices, and their management of many of the community employment schemes was an important part of livelihood for many in depressed areas. Their churches played a significant part in people's social life with many dances, social nights, and other activities being held in church halls. They held significant authority over many of the primary schools (almost all, in the case of Catholics) and ran many of the youth clubs. They also remained an important source of "moral order" in many areas, particularly rural ones. Priests and pastors were widely respected, much more so than in nearby secular Britain. Their very coherence around issues of religion, nationalism, and intolerance, as outlined by David Little in chapter 1 of this book, which provided for so many needs within individual and communities' lives, was also a huge factor in the ghettoization of societies.

Nowhere is this segregation more evident than in settlement patterns. In rural areas, many of the smaller villages are completely "owned" by one tradition or the other; ownership is easily recognized from the churches and Orange and Hibernian Halls in the area, and through the presence of the organizations that flourish in these areas that are also generally segregated.[5] Farmers generally belong to the credit unions, a Catholic tradition in Northern Ireland, which usually meet on church premises. The Women's Institute, a rural women's organization, usually meets in Protestant church halls, which are often decorated with political symbols.

The education system in Northern Ireland is almost totally segregated. Catholics rarely attend the public schools, which in theory are open to all denominations and religions; the Catholic Church frowns upon their attendance at such schools.[6] While integrated schools have recently begun to flourish, they as yet only cater to about 6 percent of the school-age population. Training for higher education is also segregated, and suggestions about a possible merger of such training over the last few decades have been met with adamant opposition, particularly by the Catholic Church.[7] Youth clubs are also usually separate, and organizations such as the Scouts and Girl Guides have different organizations for Catholic and Protestant youth.

Sports in Northern Ireland also generally reflect the denominational split and are often played on church grounds. Catholics generally play Gaelic football, camogie, and hurling, games indigenous to Ireland. Protestants generally play rugby, hockey, and cricket at school, games usually associated with Britain. While both communities play soccer football, support for teams is mainly given on a denominational basis, and the game has on occasion given rise to violent expressions of sectarianism by both players and spectators alike.[8] Even where communities enjoy the same sport—for example, boxing, bowling, or athletics—these tend to be organized around churches and played on church playing fields or at youth clubs, which are mostly denominational and thus prevent mixing. Even political canvassing is known to happen within church grounds—reflecting the bias of each church; that is, Catholics toward nationalist political organizations and Protestant toward the various unionist parties.

Within this divided context, the police have usually been seen as not only consolidating the divisions but also largely representing and supporting the unionist, Protestant hegemony. In 1922 a new police force for the state was established, the Royal Ulster Constabulary, and it was recommended that one-third of its recruits should be drawn from the Catholic population. In the end, political pressures and threats, both from unionists and from Catholics themselves who were suspicious and rejecting of the new state, ensured that the quota of Catholics was never filled. By 2000 the proportion of Catholics in the police force had dropped to just over 7 percent.[9]

Given the ubiquitous nature of church and people involvement, and the overlapping nature of church and identity politics in Northern Ireland, it is not perhaps surprising that the role of the churches in Northern Ireland has been either profoundly ambivalent toward communities that are not their own or, in some cases, deeply reinforcing of divisions and community violence. As Morrow has said, "The churches are not simple institutions with members whose members change their hats in other parts of life. They are also communities of people whose whole lives are lived in the light of their church experiences and knowing. Thus when they are in the workplace, in pubs, bringing up children, or whatever they may remain partly in church. This makes the designation of simple lines, divisions between the secular and the religious completely misleading" (Morrow et al. 1991).

A THEOLOGY OF EXCLUSION

In the early 1980s in Northern Ireland, the conflict that had started in 1969 had been going on for more than a decade. The area where I lived in rural Ireland was called "the killing fields" because of the high rate of murders that had killed Protestant, Catholic, and British security forces. Almost all of the lives of the people who lived in the mainly Protestant Coagh and the neighboring Catholic Ardboe were segregated in schooling, support for the security forces, political party support, social lives, and so on, but there was at least one crosscutting connection, and that was the local doctor. A Protestant, his waiting room was one of the few places where the communities met. He served all equally—even on the darkest and most violent of nights, he never hesitated to go where he was needed, and all sides respected him. Then tragedy struck. His two-year-old son had wandered out through an unlocked door on the side of the house that faced the river that ran beside his house, and the child drowned. The funeral for the child was held in the local Presbyterian church and was attended by hundreds from all sides who came to pay their respects to the grief of a good man who had served them well. For once they were united with their other-believing brethren. Until, after paying their respects to the grieving parents, the crowd began to move toward the church. The

Catholics fell back—murmuring to each other "are we not forbidden to enter any church other than our own?" I remember one person asking my husband if it was still a sin to enter into the church and participate in the funeral service. For the most part, the Catholics stayed outside, curtailed by the lack of trust their church had in their ability to withstand any possible influence from any unholy contact with those who were of something other than the true faith.

Although many scholars have suggested that religion functioned merely as a badge of ethnic difference (McGarry and O'Leary 1995) within the divisions in Northern Ireland, religious and theological energy has been a potent factor in fueling the conflict. Memories are long in Northern Ireland—with events of centuries ago serving to adrenalize the divisions. Catholics' distrust of Protestants has been in place since the Reformation, when Protestants were denounced by the Roman Catholic Church as heretics and destined for damnation. A tenet taught to every Catholic child in Catholic schools was the superiority of the Roman Catholic Church over other faiths, the "one true church." Ecumenism was often seen as the process that would enable the "return of the separated brethren" to the one true church.[10] Such a belief was and is behind the insistence of the Catholic Church that children in mixed marriages must be brought up as Catholics.[11]

For their part, Protestants have also been imbued with distrust, at least in part fueled by their theology. In particular, the Confession of Faith drawn up by the 1646 Westminster Assembly became and remains the doctrine in the Church of England and the Church of Scotland and has been influential within Presbyterian churches worldwide. This doctrine states: "There is no other head of the Church but the Lord Jesus Christ: nor can the Pope of Rome in any sense be head thereof; but is that Antichrist, that man of sin and son of perdition, that exalts himself in the Church against Christ, and all that is called God" (Westminster Confession of Faith, XXV: VI).[12] This article of faith has been widely challenged by many Catholics, but it remains to this day, to the embarrassment of more ecumenically minded Protestants. Its tenets are often used in conjunction with cherry-picked quotations from the Bible by the evangelical sections of the Presbyterian Church led by Ian Paisley, called the Free Presbyterians. This church is free from any ecumenical leanings and consistently attacks the pope as an Antichrist, and the Catholic Church as the whore of Babylon prophesied in the book of Revelation. In 1966 Ian Paisley set up his own newspaper, the *Protestant Telegraph*, specifically to challenge Catholicism. In it he wrote extravagantly about the sins of the Catholic Church; for example, he wrote: "Through Popery the Devil has shut up the way to our inheritance. Priestcraft, superstition and papalism with all their attendant vices of murder, theft, immorality, lust and incest blocked the way to the land of gospel liberty" (*Protestant Telegraph*), January 1967, quoted in Coogan 1995, 49).[13]

The association between the Orange Order and the churches has also helped to fuel divisions. The order was founded in 1795 and is evangelically committed to

Protestantism, to challenging biblical error, and to opposing the Catholic Church. It forbids its members to marry a Catholic or to attend a Catholic service. On July 12, 1996, Robert Saulters, who was later elected Grand Master of the Orange Order on December 11, told the Orange Order that British prime minister Tony Blair, whose wife is a Catholic, "has already sold his birthright by marrying a Romanist. He would sell his soul to the devil himself. He is not loyal to his religion. He is a turncoat."[14] The Orange Order also has many strong connections to all aspects of political Unionism, but particularly to that of the Democratic Unionist Party (DUP), the political party led by Ian Paisley. Although not synonymous, there is a clear overlap between the two organizations (Bruce 1986). From 1972 to 1980, 64 percent of DUP Party members belonged to the Free Presbyterian Church (Bruce 1994, 23). Thirty-six of the current members of the Northern Ireland Legislative Assembly are from the DUP, and they remain the largest political party in Northern Ireland and a potent power in politics.[15]

Although the details of theology are rarely grist for public debate, they often imbue the political ideas of many in Northern Ireland. Certain paramilitary loyalist groups have seen themselves as the lost Tribe of Israel. Such a belief has validated their murdering and bombing of Catholics, believing as they do that Northern Ireland was given to them by God to retain their Protestant faith.[16] The fact that the succession of the British monarchy is governed by several enactments, the most important being the *Bill of Rights 1689* and *Act of Settlement 1701*, is also interesting to note. These enactments include religious restrictions against Roman Catholics, which were imposed because of the English people's mistrust of Catholicism that had grown during the Reformation. Only individuals who are Protestants at the time of their succeeding to the throne can become king or queen. In addition, anyone who has at any time been a Roman Catholic or married to a Roman Catholic cannot succeed to the throne. While there have been some efforts in recent years to remove these clauses, all such efforts have so far failed.

The struggle to gain and hold onto souls is nowhere as evident as within the sphere of education, where young hearts, minds, and souls are so evidently at stake. In the first years of the new British province, Lord Londonderry was the minister in charge of education in 1923. He courageously suggested integrated education for Protestants and Catholics at primary school level, and he also abolished religious instruction in schools in order to introduce a nonaligned form of education. Both religious communities opposed it and organized to change it. The Catholic Church felt it would destroy the "ethos" of Catholic schooling. Protestants wanted religious instruction reinstated, and they disliked the idea of Catholic teachers being able to work in state-funded schools. They demanded the power to appoint only Protestants, and to have Protestant clergy on appointment boards. "'Protestant teachers for Protestant schools' was the theme at protest rallies. People were told that the Act threw 'the door open for a Roman Catholic to become a teacher in a Protestant school,' and when the Orange Order complained and a general election loomed, the Act was amended in 1925. Lord Londonderry resigned" (Brewer and Higgins 1998, ch. 3). With the departure of Lord Londonderry, the education system subsequently moved in a more sectarian direction. The Education Act of 1930 established a completely separated system, with Protestant clergy assisting in teacher appointments in state schools to which Protestants were appointed. The Education Act was described by the prime minister at that time as making the state-funded schools "safe for Protestant children" (Somerset Fry and Somerset Fry, 328). The Catholic Church agreed to partly fund its own schools.[17] Within these schools, each school taught its own version of history, which was often overtly political, taking into account only the perceptions of one side.

The churches' insistence on the continuance of Catholic schools is also due to the belief of the church that only Catholic education can guarantee the development of a Catholic spirituality. The establishment of integrated schooling did not begin to happen until 1981, when the first integrated school, Lagan College, was established; it received huge criticism from all churches, but particularly from the Catholic Church. Although there are now more than sixty such schools, the Catholic Church has consistently refused to encourage its priests to connect with the Catholic children at these schools, often making it difficult for such children to receive the Catholic sacraments. In 2006 a BBC investigatory program said that local priests would not enter the buildings of more than one-third of integrated primary schools (Taggart 2006). Such insistence combined with the perceived unity and power of the church continues to inspire great distrust of the Catholic Church by many within the Protestant community.

Obviously, given the nature of the history of Northern Ireland, another hugely significant division that separated the churches was the proactivity of many Catholic Church officials to challenge what they saw as ubiquitous discrimination toward their Catholic constituents.[18] Many priests were keen supporters of the civil rights movement that arose in 1969 seeking civil rights for Catholics (votes for everyone on an equal basis, equal access to public housing, nondiscrimination in employment, etc.). Many Unionists saw such activity as going far beyond that of seeking civil rights, and as a desire to end the Northern Ireland entity itself. Both groups found themselves in a double-minority situation—the Catholics as a minority in Northern Ireland, and the Protestants as a minority in the island of Ireland that was almost totally Catholic in nature. What one side saw as justice, the other side saw as the desire to destroy the very entity within which they were a majority. As Morrow points out, in such a situation, "theology and politics come to be one. For Catholics this may be a theology of popular justice, for example liberation theology, which seeks to justify Catholic outrage as that of the people of God (the Poor?). For Protestants this may be a theology of siege which seeks to justify Protestant experience as that of the people of God (the Israelites?). Both give support, intellectual backing and faith to others whose theology may be weak but whose knowledge of violence and fear is strong" (Morrow et al. 1991). Sustained separation, allied with fear of retributive justice being directed toward the Protestant settlers by the Catholics whose lands they had appropriated, and anger by Catholics at the second-class nature of their citizenship of Northern Ireland have left little space within the psyche of either community for any understanding of religious crosscutting principles.

Given the inseparable connection between religion and politics in Northern Ireland, and the pervasive influence of religious identity on the cultural economic, social, and educational lives of almost all of the people in Northern Ireland, it is not surprising that the churches found it difficult to wholeheartedly involve themselves in theological boundary crossing. Quite literally, at the time of the breakout of the civil war, each side thought the other was damned and headed for eternal fire—or at least the equivalent of "limbo" on the Catholic part.[19] The ecumenical movement only began in Northern Ireland in the late 1960s, and it took many years for its effects to be felt. It is not surprising, therefore, that Morrow and colleagues (1991) found in their survey that anti-Catholicism in theological terms was fairly widespread among Protestant clergy, especially Presbyterians. They stated: "From our research, it is clear that theological reflection by many clergy is focused on defense of clear doctrine rather than on repentance and change.... 'The problem' is usually located in the doctrines, attitudes and actions of the others, whoever they may be. The corollary of this is that the speaker is always unable to act, because the other has to change first.... The churches remain identified with particular sides and there are few consistent indications that this has radically changed in the last twenty years" (ibid.). The churches therefore are by no means "neutral" actors in Northern Ireland; they are organizations that are primarily interested in their own power and their own theological perspective. By and large, each side fell into what Appleby (2000) has labeled as enclave builders, that is, exclusivists who insist there is only one way of understanding reality and interpreting the sacred. Because the church leaders obviously mostly shared such exclusionary doctrines, it was inevitable that their roles in helping people reach out to each other would be limited.

LEADERS OR FOLLOWERS?

In 1984 a colleague and I were asked by the British government to address the field of community relations, that is, work that is done to specifically address the issue of promoting positive community relationships across the sectarian divide. We discovered that fifteen years after the latest phase of the conflict had broken out in 1969, there were forty-five groups undertaking community relations work, of which nine were specifically allied with the churches. However, most people we talked to believed that the churches had not done enough to actively encourage reconciliation and that church initiatives in the field of community relations tended to depend on the work of a few committed individuals (Frazer and Fitzduff 1994).

Field studies (see, e.g., Morrow et al. 1991) that were undertaken on the churches' involvement in intercommunity relations work from 1988–1989 also questioned the limited nature of church involvement in such work, suggesting that the churches had seldom developed or undertaken community relations initiatives, and had seldom even attempted to foster dialogue on the part of their constituents with or about the other church and its congregations. The report furthermore pointed out that the churches remained identified with particular political sides, and there were few indications that this had radically changed in twenty years since the first of the civil rights marches took place in 1969. The involvement of the churches has since increased somewhat, mainly due to the work of the Community Relations Council (CRC), set up in 1990, which helped to multiply and fund community and institutional work on issues of equality, diversity, and dialogue.[20] A tally of those organizations now pursuing community relations work listed on the website in 2008 is 129. Of those, 20 are listed as having a church foundation or affiliation.

Appleby has referred to religious actors as falling into three subsets: the churches and their official leaders, the faith-based reconciliation groups and organizations, and the religiously motivated individuals acting as intermediaries and mediators (2000, 181). Examples of such subsets and their activities in Northern Ireland are described in the following.

CHURCHES AND THEIR OFFICIAL LEADERS

Cahal Brendan Cardinal Daly, archbishop/cardinal during the last two decades of the conflict, was frequently heard to denounce the use of violence to solve political problems, as was Archbishop Robin Eames, the Church of Ireland Bishop Archbishop since 1976.[21] They engaged in public denunciations of political violence, and engaged in ecumenical handshakes, both separately and together. Some of the Presbyterian leaders—such as John Dunlop, moderator of the General Assembly of the Presbyterian Church in Ireland in 1992–93—were very involved in efforts to further better relations between Protestants and Roman Catholics. Such activities were assisted by such church bodies as the Irish Council of Churches, set up in 1922 to network among the more liberal of the Protestant churches. This council was joined in 1973 by the Catholic Church to found the Irish Inter-Church

Meeting, which has had twenty-one plenary meetings since its foundation and has published a number of reports and papers.

Such activities appeared limited and seemed to have little effect on changing the perceptions of many in their churches. In some cases, their congregations have deliberately blocked such work. In the mid-eighties, a Presbyterian clergyman was forced out of office by his congregation because he crossed the road one Christmas Eve to shake hands with the local Catholic priest in a very minor gesture of reconciliation. A decade later, he still received threatening letters about his action. In 1996 Protestants gathered outside a Catholic church in the middle of a mainly Protestant area called Harryville to protest; they said that if the Protestant Loyal Orders were not permitted to march through the nearby village of Dunloy, which was 97 percent Catholic, the Catholic parishioners would be stopped from getting to their church.[22] The protest lasted for twenty months. Every Saturday evening a crowd of loyalists ranging in size from thirty to three hundred attempted to prevent the Catholic parishioners from attending Mass and forced the shutdown of many Catholic services.[23] For the most part, from 1969 to the cease-fires of 1994, the dominant or mainstream churches, with a few honorable exceptions, had by and large not used the power and opportunity of their influence in any significant way to address the extensive divisions between the churches. In many cases they have denied that addressing the conflict was their business, and in some cases they have given a religious endorsement to political and cultural allegiances.

Faith-Based Reconciliation Groups and Organizations

Faith-based reconciliation groups and organizations were generally made up of people who, while part of a traditional faith group, nevertheless sought to acknowledge their respect for differing ways of believing in God and were willing to enter into dialogue with other faith groups that had a willingness to listen. Such groups obviously varied in their capacity for openness. It is perhaps helpful to think of the predispositions of such faith groups along the line suggested by Diana Eck (2001), who has suggested three fundamental ways of reacting to religious diversity. One is the traditional exclusivist approach, which maintains that a person's particular religion is the true one, and everyone else is wrong. Many who believed thus in Northern Ireland belonged to the more traditional official faith groups and vehemently eschewed any work that involved meeting those they perceived a heretics. Eck suggested that others adopt an inclusivist view, which suggests that although there are many religions worthy of respect, a person's particular one is somewhat superior to the others; damnation for others has been shelved. One's own superiority is usually believed in rather quietly and rarely stated publicly. Much of modern ecumenism is of this mode, which is characterized as polite tolerance.

The pluralist approach acknowledges the existence and the validity of a variety of perspectives on religion and assumes that each person is capable of learning something from dialogue with others, and that each person will be changed for the better by such a process. The faith-based reconciliation groups and organizations were mostly inclusivist, and the people who belonged to them generally continued to practice their own faith. They did, however, provide for a great deal of the social and community porosity that helped to ease the fiercely divisive theological and political perspectives that maintained the historical ghettoization of the communities of Northern Ireland.

Faith-based groups dedicated to intercommunal dialogue were surprisingly few, given the churches' influence and membership in Northern Ireland, but those that did exist provided a valuable space for people who wanted to move beyond the narrow confines of their own faith and church communities. The oldest of these, which preceded the outbreak of the conflict in 1995, was Corrymeela, set up in 1965 by a Presbyterian minister named Ray Davey. Set on the beautiful northern coast, it has provided a welcome space, retreat, and meeting house for those who are Christians and who want to testify to the possibility of a uniting fellowship between the Christian churches.

Since 1990, aided by the large influx of funding money provided by the CRC, there has been an increase in the number of church-based organizations that concentrate on community relations. Projects such as the Cornerstone Community, situated in a sectarian interface in West Belfast; the Christian Renewal Center, situated at the foot of the Mourne Mountains; and the Columba Community, situated in Derry/Londonderry, all worked extremely hard at witnessing to the possible power of religion to connect rather than to divide.[24] These were joined in the 1990s by organizations such as the YMCA, which began to address issues of sectarianism among its members, and by the Evangelical Conference on Northern Ireland, which specialized in working with evangelical groups to broaden their religious horizons and increase their tolerance. This group was one of the first Protestant organizations to involve Sinn Féin publicly in dialogue.[25] Youthlink, an organization whose purpose is to foster youth work across the community divide, was set up by all the main churches in 1991.

In addition to these faith-based groups were many members of the Quaker community, whose outreach to prisoners' families and whose work on mediation earned them the trust of almost all communities in Northern Ireland. Inspirational as they were, the people involved in such faith groups were numbered only in the thousands. The majority of believers just attended their church services, where issues of ecumenism were rarely discussed, where services were often conducted as if the societal context of violence did not exist, and where, in extreme cases, societal and faith divisions were defended or applauded.

Religiously Motivated Individuals

There are a variety of individuals among the churches who see it as their business, and God's business, to involve themselves in efforts at reconciliation between the communities. A few of these deliberately have attempted to mainstream such work into their official church or parish work, witnessing, as they see it, the healing power of Christianity. Such individuals include, for example, Ken Newell, a minister at the Fitzroy Presbyterian Church in Belfast who has been closely in dialogue between Protestants and Catholics in Northern Ireland since 1981, when he initiated a formal fellowship between himself and Fr. Gerry Reynolds, who was the pastor of a Catholic church in nationalist West Belfast (Wells 2005). Their work includes visiting the families of people in Belfast who had been murdered. Another clergyman noted for his work in intercommunity relationships is Brian Lennon, a Jesuit priest who lived in the heart of a community involved in a bitterly sectarian dispute over issues of marching.[26] Based on his experience, he set up a group called Community Dialogue, which helped people of all religious persuasions to talk together about the most difficult constitutional and political issues facing their communities.

There are many thousands of people from the whole of the voluntary and community sector who are involved in developing cross-community work in Northern Ireland. Some of them have found themselves at times involved in either shuttle mediation or face-to-face mediation with many of the contentious parties such as the political parties, the British or Irish government, or the paramilitaries. There appears to be some evidence that such work was extremely important in bringing an end to the conflict (Williams and Fitzduff 2008). Among such "mediators" are three people who are officially attached to a church and whose work and words are seen to be seminal in a very direct way in bringing about an agreement in Northern Ireland.

The first mediator is a Catholic priest, Denis Faul, who became actively involved in the Northern Ireland civil rights movement in 1968, participating in many of their marches. He first came to prominence in 1969 when he spoke out against the judiciary, claiming that Catholics felt judges were biased against them. For many years he protested vigorously against civil rights abuses by the British army and Royal Ulster Constabulary, the police force in Northern Ireland, an activity that was not unusual among many other priests. He campaigned against the ill treatment of political prisoners, and he campaigned for the release of the Birmingham Six and the Guildford Four, Republican groups who had been wrongly convicted by the British government and who spent many years in jail.[27] Denis Faul was also one of the most vehement protesters against the killings perpetrated by the Provisional Irish Republican Army. And in 1981, when he was Catholic chaplain of the Maze prison, he played an important role in ending a hunger strike started by Republican prisoners to achieve "political" status within the prisons. After ten men had died from hunger, he persuaded the families of the others that their strike would not change the mind of Margaret Thatcher, then the British prime minister, and nothing could be gained by more deaths. The families eventually persuaded the remaining hunger strikers to desist from their fast. Although castigated by the IRA for his actions, Denis Faul was undeterred, and it helped that he also fearlessly condemned what he saw as the human rights abuses of both the British Army and the Northern Ireland police force.

The second mediator is Fr. Alec Reid, an Irish priest who is noted for his facilitator role in the Northern Ireland peace process. He was a priest of the Clonard monastery in Belfast, which stands on the interface between the Nationalist Catholic Community and the Protestant Shankill Road. In the late 1980s Reid facilitated a series of meetings between Sinn Féin president Gerry Adams and the leader of the Social Democratic and Labour Party, John Hume, in an effort to establish a "Pan-Nationalist front" to enable a move toward a political agreement. Reid also acted as their contact person with the Irish government in Dublin, meeting with the Irish prime minister and various members of the ruling Fianna Fáil party. All of these meetings were critical to the eventual development of the peace agreement.

The third mediator is Rev. Roy Magee, a Presbyterian pastor who kept the lines of communication open to the secretive Protestant paramilitary groups during the course of the conflict, and who helped to deliver the cease-fire in 1994 of Northern Ireland's main loyalist paramilitary organizations under the umbrella of the Combined Loyalist Military Command. The cease-fire, which followed the IRA's cessation of violence, was crucial in paving the way for the peace process that led to the signing of the 1998 Good Friday Agreement on which Northern Ireland's devolved government is now based. He was frequently used as a mediator in community conflicts, and he also assisted at the talks involving Drumcree, a rural Church of Ireland parish in County Armagh, which had become the catalyst for sectarian unrest between the Protestant marchers and the Catholic residents of the area in 1998 and continued as a flashpoint for many years.

While all of these activities by the mediators were essential to the success of the peace process, there were others who were undertaking similar work with the governments, the paramilitaries, and political parties (Williams and Fitzduff 2008). What was different, however, was the fact that these priests and pastors belonged to a faith group that gave them freedom, status, and motivation in a context where, even until the end of the conflict, these things mattered. Respect for the churches was still strong when they began their work. Sinn Féin had continually found themselves at odds with the Catholic Church because of their support for violence, which was often critiqued by the head of the Church in Ireland, Cardinal Daly. For many of the years since the conflict began again in 1969, they had tried to engage the open support of the Catholic Church in their endeavor. The Clonard monastery, where Fr. Alec Reid lived and worked, was very much part of the fabric of the Sinn Féin community. For many decades Sinn Féin parishioners had benefited from the ministry of Clonard. The combination of Catholic authority and insider status proved to be invaluable for the final part of the peace process. Also, the confidentiality that was part of a Catholic priest's repertoire was also significant in assisting the dialogues. Sinn Féin/IRA was extremely cautious about with whom they worked, and confidentiality was a prime quality that they needed.

The pronouncements of Fr. Denis Faul were all the more effective because he too was a priest. He lived in a rural area that was also home to many of the IRA militants. He was in many ways a "true" Catholic priest—that is, he remained adamantly in favor of segregated education. Accusations that the Catholic Church brainwashed children were true, he said—and he said it was perfectly proper to do so because Catholic education was dictated by canon law. He was completely in tune with the canon law's hard line on issues such as abortion, divorce, and contraception. He continued to find succor in his clerical collar. He received numerous death threats, some from his own community, and he believed firmly that it was only his clerical collar that prevented them from being carried out—he thought that the outrage generated by the murder of a priest would be too much even for the IRA. He also maintained that his celibacy was a positive advantage in this regard; he had no family who could be threatened or harmed. "It would be very stupid to kill a clergyman, and I think that my celibacy, the fact that I don't have a wife and children to be bullied, intimidated or threatened puts me in a privileged position," he used to say (McHardy 2006). There is little doubt that it was his clerical collar that kept him safe—but it also enabled him to become a respected adjudicator and campaigner on human rights abuses occurring on all sides of the conflict. There were few others in Northern Ireland who were willing or able to carry this role, which was probably only effective because of his church base and connections.

The role of Rev. Roy Magee and his work with the loyalists were somewhat different from the role played by the Catholic priests mentioned earlier. Roy Magee was very explicit about his work being part of his role as a minister. In an interview he said: "As a minister of the gospel I see myself as a spiritual policeman, encouraging people to live in accordance with the Law of God . . . what I do is nothing more and nothing less than an extension of my pastoral work" (Bardon 2000). There is, however, little evidence of his work being successful because of his Christian faith per se. There were no converts to the Christian faith among the groups that he worked with, and no evidence that he used Christian morality in any way to persuade the paramilitaries to stop their violence. (There were many known cases of loyalists who were "saved" while in prison and thus saw the error of their ways of violence—but Roy Magee never saw himself in that business.) What he did, in fact, was to lend them the respectability of conversations with a minister, which still had sway in both Protestant and Catholic communities. By involving himself with the loyalist groups—often fractured and disorganized but even more dangerous because of this—he actually created a cloak of capacity and representativeness around them. He was able to do this because of the seriousness with which clerics were viewed. Achieving such respected visibility for both himself and the loyalist groups would have been difficult outside of his pastor role.

In all of the cases mentioned earlier, the work of mediation and of consensus building among fractured groups was much more successfully achieved because of the pastoral roles of these individuals. There is no evidence to show that they in any way "converted" men of violence to more peaceful ways because of their gospel or faith exhortation. Evidence of their effectiveness points rather to the fact that what they achieved in furthering both the cease-fires and the political agreement was more easily done because of the respect in which the churches and their priest and pastors were still held for most of the decades of the conflict. Within the context within which they were working, they were endowed with leadership roles because of the value placed on the status of the church during the times in which they were operating.

RELIGIOUS LEADERS AS RECONCILERS?

Despite the valiant efforts noted earlier, the responsibility of faith leaders to assume the mantle of reconcilers in Northern Ireland was confined to the few. Ken Newell estimated that only 10 percent of the clergy of either confession were and are actively involved in peacebuilding efforts (see Williams and Fitzduff 2007, 51). Among the laity, only a tiny percentage was involved in the work of the faith-based reconciliation groups. And there is little evidence that their work achieved major changes in the pattern of church relationships during the time of the conflict, despite the ecumenical movement, which started in the early 1970s and paralleled the conflict in time.

Why did the formal churches find it so difficult to lead their people from their often bitter and sometimes violent sectarianism onto the more productive paths of dialogue and tolerance? Why did most of these ministers and priests reject the opportunity of using their Sunday sermons—and a guaranteed audience of almost the whole population of Northern Ireland—to speak of the need for a society that was shared and peaceful? Why did it take two decades of violence before the churches began to try to mainstream clergy training in reconciliation work among their ministers and priests?

I was thinking of these questions when, in 1999, I was invited to facilitate a dialogue in Galilee in Israel hosted by the Interreligious Co-coordinating Council of Israel and sponsored by the Jubilennium Foundation. The conference was titled the "First Annual Interfaith Conference for World Peace" and the objective of the conference was to understand the role of religion in pursuing conflict resolution and peace. It was attended by, among others, Archbishop Nduruso H. Ngada, president of the Federation of African Churches; Michael Fitzgerald, an official representative of the Vatican; Wallace Dean Muhammad, leader of a Black Islam group (2.5 million strong) in the United States; Sheik Nazim El Hakani, world leader of the "Nakshabandi Sufi Order"; Nichiko Niwano, head of a Japanese Buddhist organization; and the Dalai Lama, the leader of Tibetan Buddhists; along with senior representatives of the Jewish faith and the Eastern Orthodox church. The conference took place over two days, and as it moved toward its end, it became obvious that for many of the church leaders, adopting leadership that went against the grain of the emotions and the directions of their people, their flocks, was extremely difficult. Their fear, like that of many political parties, was that they would find themselves too far ahead of their people and thus decrease their constituency—and ultimately their power. Some of them tried to exercise what is called "elastic-band" leadership—that is, leadership that attempts to "stretch" its constituents in the interests of peace while remembering that, if the elastic is stretched just a little too far, there is always the danger of the elastic snapping (Gormley-Heenan 2001).

Leaders are extremely sensitive to such a danger—if the band snaps, they will be left without a mandate, and they will not get reelected or chosen as leader. Cahal Daly, the Irish Catholic cardinal, and Robin Eames, the Church of Ireland archbishop mentioned earlier, had consistently faced strong opposition from hard-liners within their respective faith communities, as had John Dunlop, the ecumenically minded Presbyterian who had involved himself in intercommunity work. All had privately spoken about the pressures they had to contend with from within their own communities. Few of them were afraid of what they might face from the apparently opposing communities. What they mostly feared was the sometimes-severe castigation from some of their own members who paid them visits whenever they seemed to be "going soft" on the other side in the conflict. This meant that, except for the few mavericks, their main interest during the years of the conflict appeared to be to locate themselves in the political mainstream of their respective communities (Mitchell 2005).

In addition, the tension for many of the leaders was the tension between being a "transactional" or a "transformational" leader. In situations of conflict, leaders and followers are often locked into what is called a transactional (as opposed to transformational) process whereby leaders will usually act with a high awareness of what their followers want, and followers, for their part, often give their leaders little leeway in terms of what decisions should be taken into account in conflict situations (MacGregor Burns 1978). In such situations, an individual's need to both categorize and belong can easily be harnessed to serve the purposes of leaders.

Individuals and groups are particularly vulnerable to succumbing to simplification about who bears responsibility for the problems they are facing, and at the same time desirous of such simplification by their leaders at times of crisis, particularly when they feel under threat. At moments of fear and crisis, individuals often come to feel overwhelmed, in need of a strong leader, and willing to all too easily follow their leaders in assaulting their enemies.

Those who exercise power by heightening the claims of one group as opposed to another; shoring up competing group claims of a theological, cultural, or other nature; and thereby weakening any collective sense of common humanity can be a source of violence. They often consciously or unconsciously exercise divisive leadership, as opposed to transformational moral leadership whose values inspire people to seek and to satisfy the higher needs of all of their communities, attempting to transform a situation of conflict by a promotion of collective well-being that is above and beyond their own particular local or even national belonging. Such leadership occurs when one or more persons engage with others in such a way that leaders and followers raise one another to higher levels of motivation and morality. Their purposes—which might have started out as separate but related, as in the case of transactional leadership—become fused. Power bases are linked not as counterweights but as mutual support for common purpose. Nelson Mandela, Gandhi, Martin Luther King Jr., even in the most difficult of circumstances, all sought to find an inclusive approach to leadership in their time.

Unfortunately, such "transformational" leadership can be hard to find (Peake, Gormley-Heenan, and Fitzduff 2004). For the most part, the churches in Northern Ireland failed to provide such leadership. They were held too tightly within their elastic bands, and stretched them only rarely—in many cases, not at all. While on an individual basis, some church leaders did attempt to cross symbolic and other barriers, their people were generally left untouched by much of their gestures, and there were few attempts to ensure that they engaged in dialogue or cooperative activities with their brethren of a different persuasion. In doing so, church leaders failed to provide the kind of leadership that could have defined how the conflicts were played out in Northern Ireland. By failing to provide such leadership, the churches failed to take account of how significant leadership can be in situations of conflict. Inequality by itself rarely causes conflict. Grievances about exclusion often begin to publicly emerge to the fore only when people are mobilized around a particular identity that can be ethnic, racial, religious, or cultural. Such mobilization itself can be either negative or positive, depending upon the kind of leadership that emerges to assist or control the efforts that are made by a group to achieve their goal. Some leaders, such as Martin Luther King Jr., Mahatma Gandhi, and Nelson Mandela, all took the high road in terms of nonviolence and in terms of the inclusion of their perceived oppressors in future societal decisions. The decisions of leaders in such mobilizations are critical. The leaders who are powerful are those who have the respect of their societies—whether they are secular or religious. In situations of conflict, and particularly where issues of justice are concerned, it is not only important to get as many people as possible involved in pursuing their ends through methods that respect the lives and needs of others, but also to get key people involved in such work (Anderson and Olson 2003).

When the latest phase of the conflict began in Northern Ireland in 1969, among the most important of people who could have helped address it were those who had the respect and ear of the vast majority of the people of Northern Ireland—the religious leaders of all persuasions. While there were some individuals of some denominations who rose to the moral, theological, and societal challenge posed by the conflict, they were often lone voices in a sea of avoidance by the many. While some leaders, such as Ian Paisley, were a large and obvious part of the problem in terms of the hate and exclusion they evidenced toward their Catholic neighbors, the majority of church leaders failed to find ways to assist their flocks in moving toward any kind of just reconciliation with their neighbors because of their fear of losing their power and their people. They rarely moved beyond the confines of the transactional nature of their relationship to their people, and failed to encourage them into the possibilities of transformative relationships that could have changed the course of the conflict. If the opportunities offered by the Sunday morning sermons and the ubiquitous church halls that are to be found in every part of the region had been used more productively toward this end, the conflict might not have taken nearly four decades to grind to a halt.

THE FUTURE—WHERE TO FOR RELIGIOUS LEADERS?

As the conflict comes slowly to an end, so too does the capacity of the churches to exert much influence anymore over the futures of their flocks. All churches face the waning of their influence, as Ireland goes the way of Europe, and as the Republic of Ireland moves into increasing secularism. Acute problems with recruiting and maintaining clergy are being experienced by almost all churches, many of whom have had to give up their traditional roles in the hospitals or in the teaching institutions. There has been a huge collapse in church authority—particularly within the Catholic Church, whose reputation has been significantly damaged by the child abuse and sex scandals of the last years. Church attendance is rapidly dropping, particularly among the young. The majority of Catholics are now "a la carte Catholics" who pay little attention to the church's directives on, for example, contraception or the sacraments or church attendance.

Protestants, for their part, now see that the once-feared Republic of Ireland, which they saw as poor and priest-ridden, had by 2007 now become the fifth-richest country (in terms of gross domestic product per capita) in the world and the second-richest in the European Union, with the consequent confusion of their stereotypes. There are an increasing number of mixed marriages—1 in every 4 has been cited in West Belfast, and few of the couples are asking the church about which faith they should bestow upon their children. The increasingly low birth rate, from what was once the highest in Europe, means that many schools, particularly the rural schools, are having to consider "transformation"—a form of somewhat minimal integrated schooling that is now being undertaken by many schools to survive. There is now a vibrant, secular community that exists outside of the churches' authority and influence, with more than 4,500 nongovernmental organizations in Northern Ireland (Northern Ireland Office 2005), the vast majority of which are now increasingly secular. Although ethnic minorities in Northern Ireland are still less than 1 percent, between them they speak more than fifty languages and add to Northern Ireland's diversity mix in very constructive ways, helping to break down the binational thinking that has informed the last one thousand years of Irish history.[28]

As a much more equal opportunity society, given the success of the many equality and diversity programs of the last thirty years, there is now much less need for in-group identification. Many structures now provide for cultural diversity and have removed the dominance of the churches and the Catholic and Protestant institutions. Even the Orange Order is now involved in community relations work, and is moving toward having its marching activities reframed as culture called "Orangefest."[29]

The old days of reverence for churches and their representatives appear to be fast disappearing. In many communities, clergy are treated with a respect that is only equal to that which is accorded to others, particularly by the young, and they are having to articulate the whys and hows of their belief in a way that they have never before had to do. Perhaps this challenge to their traditional ways, and the loss of much of the traditional respect that has usually been accorded to them will in itself free them from the bonds of constituents who would keep them in thrall to their conventional frameworks of belonging, and will energize them to think beyond their immediate, singular theologies to frameworks that embrace rather than exclude those who would be Christian. Or perhaps the opposite will happen. Perhaps some will just draw up their particular Christian drawbridges and continue to find familiarity and solace behind them. Given the developing peace that now exists in Northern Ireland, what they do may not really matter.

The opportunity for the formal churches to make a real difference through a Christian message of dialogue and respect was sadly missed by many of them over the last forty years and can never be regained. The inability of the major churches to produce significant leadership among their ranks that was theologically and socially transformative and inclusive raises questions about the ability of large institutions to move at a pace that is significantly beyond that of their many followers, given that their power and influence is dependent upon the retention of such followers. In Northern Ireland, it was the smaller institutions, such as the Quakers, and the mavericks among the many faiths and connecting faith groups who managed to raise their horizons to what was possible beyond the violence. Through their actions, many of them exemplified what transformations could take place when theologies and sourcebooks were mined for connections rather than for divisions. It was they who held out the promise of a charitable and inclusive gospel message that possibly could have, if used constructively by their mother faiths, altered the course of the centuries of bitter history in which competing ideas of their relationship to their god/s had divided rather than united the churchgoing communities of Northern Ireland.

NOTES

1. The demographic proportions of the two communities have changed throughout the last forty years of the conflict. While Catholics constituted 34 percent of the population in 1969, today it is estimated that 44 percent of the Northern Irish population is Roman Catholic and 53 percent is Protestant (Northern Ireland Census, December 2002), and those not wishing to state a denomination comprise the rest of the population. The number of Catholic children in schools today is estimated to be 55 percent.

2. Post-Reformation Northern Ireland not only discriminated against the native Irish Catholics but also against some of the new Protestant immigrants. While the Anglican Church became the established church of Britain and possessed all political rights, the Scottish Presbyterian settlers—the main settlers of the seventeenth and eighteenth centuries to the northern part of the island of Ireland and dissenters from the established church—came to the island of Ireland seeking religious freedom. They were barred from public positions until 1780 and remained politically unequal until well into the nineteenth century.

3. This was changed by referendum in 1973.

4. See NILT (Northern Ireland Life and Times) Survey 2004. www.ark.ac.uk /nilt/2004.

5. Orange Halls belong to the Protestant Orange Order and Hibernian to the Catholic Hibernian Association. Both orders are church-linked and restricted to male membership.

6. Catholics make up fewer than 5 percent of the pupils in public schools.

7. In 2008 the Protestant teacher training college, Stranmillis, was merged with Queen's University, but the Catholic Training College of St. Mary's tenaciously refuses to participate in such a merger.

8. This has begun to subside with a number of programs that address such soccer sectarianism.

9. This is now being addressed as a result of the Belfast Agreement, signed in 1998, which placed great emphasis on the reform of the police.

10. Indeed, the primacy of the Roman Catholic Church was recently reaffirmed by the current pope, Pope Benedict.

11. In many places the Catholic Church still insists on a "verbal" promise from the Catholic partner that he or she will bring up the children of the marriage as Catholics.

12. "American Revisions to the Westminster Confession of Faith," Orthodox Presbyterian Church, www.opc.org/documents/WCF_orig.html.

13. Paisley also saw the Jews as being in cahoots with the Roman Catholics: "Watch the Jews ... watch the papist Rome rising to a grand crescendo with the communists. . . . They are heading for an alliance against the return of the Lord Jesus Christ" (*Protestant Telegraph*, June 1972).

14. In December 2007, after he had ceased being the British prime minister, Tony Blair did in fact convert to Catholicism.

15. "Northern Ireland Assembly Election, 2007," *Wikipedia*, http://en.wikipedia.org /wiki/Northern_Ireland_Assembly_election%2C_2007.

16. "Lost Tribes of Israel," *BibleProbe*, http://bibleprobe.com/lost.htm.

17. This was subsequently changed in the early 1990s; the state now funds all Catholic education.

18. Such discrimination has been well documented in Rose et al. (1971) and Fitzduff (2002).

19. Limbo is "the abode of unbaptized but innocent or righteous souls, as those of infants or virtuous individuals who lived before the coming of Christ." *Free Dictionary*, www.thefreedictionary.com/limbo.

20. The CRC was set up in 1990 to facilitate the multiplication of community relations work throughout Northern Ireland, www.nicrc.org.uk. I was its first founding director.

21. More than 3,500 people were killed during the course of the conflict—this is equivalent to 650,000 fatalities in the United States as a percent of total population.

22. Loyal Orders are overtly male and Protestant societies. Their "loyalty" is to the British Queen.

23. In 2005 Protestants again threatened the church with another siege, and it was paint-bombed as late as 2006.

24. Catholics call the city Derry, and Protestants call it Londonderry.

25. Sinn Féin is the political wing of the Irish Republican Army, the illegal militia who were responsible for the majority of the murders in Northern Ireland from 1971–2008.

26. There are more than three thousand marches a year in Northern Ireland, the majority by members of the Protestant Loyal orders. Many neighborhoods are now Catholic, but these orders want to retain the right to march through their old neighborhoods.

27. The term "Republican" generally referred to those groups who wanted a united Ireland and were prepared to use violence to achieve it.

28. National Literacy Trust, 2008. www.literacytrust.org.uk/Database/STATS /EALstats.html#UK.

29. "Northern Ireland: Orange Order Marches On, but Now It's a Festival." *Independent*, UK, July 8, 2007. www.independent.co.uk/news/uk/this-britain/northern -ireland-orange-order-marches-on-but-now-its-a-festival-456435.html.

REFERENCES

Anderson, Mary, and Lara Olson. 2003. *Confronting War: Critical Lessons for Peace Practitioners*. Cambridge, MA: Collaborative for Development Action. www .usaid.gov/our_work/cross-cutting_programs/private_voluntary_cooperation /conf_anderson_doughty_olson.pdf.

Appleby, Scott. 2000. *The Ambivalence of the Sacred: Religion, Violence, and Reconciliation*. Lanham, MD: Rowman and Littlefield.

Bardon, Jane. 2000. "The Minister Who Offers to Mediate." *BBC News*, August 22. http://news.bbc.co.uk/2/hi/uk_news/northern_ireland/891412.stm.

Brewer, John D., and Gareth I. Higgins. 1998. "Northern Ireland: 1921–1998," In *Anti-Catholicism in Northern Ireland: The Mote and the Beam*, edited by John Brewer. Hampshire, UK: MacMillan Press. www.cain.ulst.ac.uk/issues/sectarian /brewer.htm.

Bruce, Steve. 1986. *God Save Ulster! The Religion and Politics of Paisleyism*. Oxford: Clarendon Press.

———. 1994. *The Edge of the Union: The Ulster Loyalist Political Vision*. Oxford: Oxford University Press.

Coogan, Tim Pat. 2005. *The Troubles: Ireland's Ordeal 1966–1995 and the Search for Peace*. London: Hutchison.

Darby, John. 1997. *Scorpions in a Bottle*. London: Minority Rights Group Publication.

Eck, Diana L. 2001. *A New Religious America: How a "Christian Country" Has Become the World's Most Religiously Diverse Nation*. San Francisco: Harper San Francisco.

Fitzduff, Mari. 2002. *Beyond Violence: Conflict Resolution in Northern Ireland*. Tokyo: United Nations University Press.

Frazer, Hugh, and Mari Fitzduff. 1994. "Improving Community Relations: A Paper Prepared for the Standing Advisory Commission on Human Rights." Belfast: Community Relations Council. www.cain.ulst.ac.uk/issues/community/frazer.htm.

Gormley-Heenan, Cathy. 2001. "From Protagonist to Pragmatist: Political Leadership in Societies in Transition." INCORE Research Summary, February. www.incore .ulst.ac.uk/publications/pdf/ptpressumm.pdf UNU/INCORE.

LeVine, Robert, and Donald Campbell. 1972. *Ethnocentrism: Theories of Conflict, Ethnic Attitudes and Group Behaviour*. New York: Wiley.

MacGregor Burns, James. 1978. *Leadership*. New York: Harper Torchbooks.

McGarry, John, and Brendan O'Leary. 1995. *Explaining Northern Ireland*. Oxford: Blackwell.

McHardy, Anne. 2006. "Monsignor Denis Faul: Turbulent Priest Who Stood against Injustice and Liberalisation in Ireland." *Guardian*, June 22. www.guardian.co.uk /news/2006/jun/22/guardianobituaries.mainsection1.

Mitchell, Claire. 2005. "Behind the Ethnic Marker: Religion and Social Identification in Northern Ireland." *Sociology of Religion* 66:3–21.

———. 2006. *Religion, Identity and Politics in Northern Ireland.* London: Ashgate.

Morrow, Duncan, Derek Birrell, John Greer, and Terry O'Keeffe. 1991. *The Churches and Inter-Community Relationships.* Coleraine: University of Ulster, Centre for the Study of Conflict. http://cain.ulst.ac.uk/csc/reports/churches.htm.

Northern Ireland Office. 2005. "Voluntary and Community Sector at Heart of Northern Ireland Life: Hain." Press release, October 13. www.nio.gov.uk/voluntary -and-community-sector-at-heart-of-northern-ireland-life-hain/media-detail .htm?newsID=12377.

Peake, Gordon, Cathy Gormley-Heenan, and Mari Fitzduff. 2004. *From Warlords to Peace Lords: Local Leadership Capacity in Peace Processes.* Tokyo: United Nations University Press/INCORE.

Rose, Richard. 1971. *Governing without Consensus: An Irish Perspective.* Faber: London.

Somerset Fry, Peter, and Somerset Fry, Fiona, 1991. *A History of Ireland.* Routledge, London.

Taggart, Maggie. 2006. "Why Do Priests Not Enter Integrated Schools?" *BBC News*, October 10. http://news.bbc.co.uk/2/hi/uk_news/northern_ireland/6038306.stm.

Wells, Ronald. 2005. *Friendship towards Peace: The Journey of Ken Newell and Gerry Reynolds.* Dublin: Columbia Press.

Williams, Sue, and Naill Fitzduff. 2007. "How Did Northern Ireland Move toward Peace?" Cumulative Impact Case Study, June. www.cdainc.com/cdawww/pdf /casestudy/rpp_cumulative_case_northern_ireland_final_Pdf.pdf.

CHAPTER 9

RELIGION, WAR, AND PEACE IN TAJIKISTAN

༈

KARINA KOROSTELINA

S ocial identities do not arise as a result of conflict between groups, but they do have the potential to become more salient and evolve into mobilized form. They do not cause or initiate conflict, but they become a powerful tool of social mobilization provoked by leaders. As David Little argues in chapter 1 of this book, social identity becomes a tool for the groups "claiming the 'right to rule' within a given territory based upon competing conceptions of nationhood." Thus, social identities should be understood neither as sources nor as consequences of conflict but instead as a form of consciousness that entirely changes the dynamics and structures of conflict. Once social identity becomes involved in interest-based or instrumental conflict, then it changes the nature of political or economic conflict in particular ways, making conflict protracted. Because religious identity is one of the most important and salient of social identities, it is invariably a critical factor in the dynamics of violence. The moral and sacred dimensions of religion can facilitate an even more profound transformation of interest-based conflicts into acts of extreme violence but can also make reconciliation more possible. The "Four-C" model of the dynamics of identity conflicts illustrates the specific role of religious identity in the dynamic of conflict and formation of violent behavior (Korostelina 2007a). This model includes four stages: comparison, competition, confrontation, and counteraction.

The Four-C model of identity-based conflict provides a basis for the systemic analysis of the role of religious identity in conflict dynamics. Religious groups living in multicultural communities develop intergroup stereotypes and biases. These biases can be formed through historical experience and are the result of biased comparisons, prejudice, and attribution errors. In situations of competition for power or resources, group leaders use these stereotypes and beliefs as well as loyalties to a religious group as a tool of group mobilization. Perceived external threats, especially when there is a lack or manipulation of information, strengthens these feelings of insecurity among in-group members. The religious identity becomes more salient and mobilized, and finally dominant, influencing the development of the dual "positive we/negative they" perception and specific collective axiology. Because of the strong moral dimension of religious identity, an out-group is easily devalued, dehumanized, and turned into a homogenous evil. It becomes moral and honorable to take actions against the other group and totally destroy it. These actions are in turn perceived by the out-group as threatening, resulting in the development of counteractions and causing a new turn in the spiral of conflict and violence. To resolve such religious conflict, it is important to address each of the stages reversibly, beginning from the last stage of moral perception and evaluation.

THE CIVIL WAR IN TAJIKISTAN

The example of Tajikistan shows how in Little's continuum shown in figure 1 (this volume), illiberal nationalism was reflected in a high degree of Soviet intolerance toward religion combined with authoritarian regime, develop a foundation for a high violence potential score. Tajikistan, one of five countries in Central Asia, lies between Afghanistan, China, Kyrgyz Republic, and Uzbekistan. Before the twentieth century, diverse communities lived interdependently in this region and shared a common Turko-Persian Islamic culture. Two major regional powers existed here: the emirate of Bukhara in the west and the Khanate of Kokand in the Ferghana Valley. By the end of the nineteenth century Tajikistan became part of the growing Russian empire and the emirate of Bukhara retained nominal autonomy over its central and southern zones. In 1924–25, based on a "National Delimitation" plan (*natsional'no-gosudarstvennoe razmezhevanie*), Soviet authorities created five "national" republics, each given a national language and national symbols. This process was impeded by the Basmachi Rebellion, which sought to restore the Bukharan emirate. The fighting between Red Army and Basmachi was brutal and violent: more than ten thousand Tajiks and Uzbeks were killed, and many people fled to Afghanistan. After the fall of the Soviet Union, these republics gained independence but were left with a legacy including political oppression, social disorder, economic security, and ecological catastrophe (Denison 2003). The countries' leaders faced the dilemma of either following the path of pan-Islamism or developing as secular states. Political elites accepted the second option and began to develop new national identities within the boundaries created by Soviet cartographers.

Despite the predictions that the quest for ethnonational identity would increase the salience of an ethnonational Tajik identity, strong regionalism impeded the formation of these identities. Thus, in 1999, only 34.3 percent of Tajiks strongly identify themselves ethnically, and only 18.4 percent mentioned national identity as the most important form of identity (Olimova 1999). From the first days of independence, salient regional identities have prevailed in Tajikistan. According to Akiner and Barnes (2001), "one distinction has been between the peoples of the plains in the north, who in ancient times were a part of the rich urban-based culture of Transoxiana, and the people of the mountains in the centre, east and south-west, who were comparatively isolated and developed strong localized identities. There was relatively little interaction between the peoples of these regions until the Soviet era." Regional identities were most salient in the north (Fergana Valley) and south of Tajikistan (Hatlon region) where people define themselves through regional identity and tend to have a well-developed religious identity (Olimova 1999). In 1991 the economic and political interests of regions fueled a civil war, which lasted six years until the establishment of Peace and National Accord in the 1997. Islamic leaders had been profoundly involved in the processes of escalating conflict and in peace negotiation. Their role in both catalyzing violence and ameliorating social tensions will be analyzed through the stages of Four-C model presented earlier.

THE RISE OF ISLAMIC RENAISSANCE PARTY

The Islamic identity has always been one of the most widespread identities in Tajikistan: nearly 98 percent of people mentioned that it is important for them to be Muslim (Roy 1996). During the Soviet era, the state controlled the religious institutions and repressed expressions of religious fervor. These policies led to the expression of Muslim identity in daily practice and as a way of life (Korostelina 2007a).[1] This form has been presented in two groups of Tajik society. The first group consists of people with predominant advanced Russian language skills, a good knowledge of Western culture, and negative attitudes toward the politicization of Islam. Nevertheless, this group follows many Muslim cultural traditions including observation of holidays, similar cuisine and dress, and the internalization of some Islamic values and beliefs. The second group consists of "traditionalists" who preserve traditional culture, Islamic tradition, and heritage. The so-called popular Islam reflects narratives about local religious figures in history and preserves rather than develops the expression of Muslim identity (Dodkhoudoeva 2003). Some people, including local religious leaders, have had a reflected form of Muslim identity.[2] They attend legal and illegal mosques and religious schools. A minority of people have had a mobilized form of Muslim identity.[3] This group includes Sufi *pirs* and some Islamic leaders.

Islamic identity has several modes of meaning (Korostelina 2007b). In northern Tajikistan, characterized by the prevalence of secular authoritarianism with a subordinate position for clerics, Muslim identity has a depictive mode with perception of Islam predominantly as traditions and culture.[4] In Khatlon and Gorno-Badakhshan, where the Sufi *pirs* promote Ismai'lism as an ethnopolitical movement rather than a faith, Muslim identity has an ideological mode of meaning with the emphasis on political Islam and Islam's future in general (Olimova 1999).[5] Nevertheless, the leaders are cautious of the possible use of Islam by the state and, therefore, push for more moderate forms of politicization of Islam.

The first open conflict between the Islamic movement and secular powers in what is currently known as Tajikistan occurred during the 1920s. The Soviet regime challenged the power of religious leaders: it enforced the nationalization of land, including land belonging to clerics, and initiated antireligious legislation, banning Koran schools and Shari'a courts (Olcott 1981). In 1918, following the brutal massacre of Tajiks by Bolsheviks near Kokand, the Basmachi movement was established. The leader of the resistance, a former chief of militia in Kokand, was able to get support of local leaders and landowners. The first fighting began in Fergana Valley and then rose into a civil war that involved different territories. By 1919 the Basmachi rebel movement consisted of twenty thousand people.

The leaders of the movement sought to regain power and land; nevertheless, Islamic ideas were used to justify the fighting and were essential sources of loyalty among Basmachi. The subgroups within the movement were diverse on their acceptance of radical Islam. Several attempts were made to unify all fractions under the control of radical groups, such as the Ulema faction (Olcott 1981). By 1920 the war with the Soviet regime was orchestrated from Afghanistan by the emir of the former Khanate of Bockhara. He succeeded in unifying the different groups under the idea of fighting against the new secular regime and defending the fate of Islam. The majority of local Muslim leaders joined the movement. Enver Pasha, who was sent by Bolsheviks to fight the rebels, jointed the Basmachi movement and strengthened the idea of fighting for an Islamic state (Ritter 1985).

The Bolsheviks addressed the rebellion through military and ideological means. They offered land to all Basmachi who surrendered, returned Islamic valuables taken by Czarist Russia, restored Shari'a courts, and opened some mosques. In 1922 the gradualistic approach to Islam was adopted to show Soviet tolerance to Muslim religion (Olcott 1981). By 1924 the majority of Basmachi were captured or killed; others fled to Afghanistan or surrendered. In 1927 the Soviets restored their strict antireligious policy, banning Koran schools, mosques, and Shari'a courts and prohibiting participation of clerics in local government.

During the 1970s a network for underground Islamic worshipers developed and became popular among marginalized youth and those who were forcibly relocated from Pamir. On June 1990, at the Congress of Muslims of the USSR, the Islamic Renaissance Party (IRP) was officially established as an opposition to the prevailing communist ideology. The party was illegal until Tajikistani independence and was officially registered on December 4, 1991 (Sharipov 2004). Only about 10 percent of the population supported the idea of a religious state and approximately another 10 percent of population considered the participation of religious leaders in government as necessary for the country (Olimova 2003). The majority of people with a salient Islamic identity had high confidence in the imams of local mosques while few people trusted the new Islamic leaders.

COMPARISON, COMPETITION, AND CONFRONTATION

During the late 1980s Tajikistan society was suffering from a growing economic and social crisis. After the dissolution of the Soviet Union in 1991, political competition and conflict over the allocation of state resources began to escalate. During this period, several new political movements organized frequent public demonstrations in the capital, Dushanbe. During the first multiparty elections, nine candidates competed for the position of president. Nevertheless, the former Communist leader managed to preserve his power. His victory had provoked questions over the legitimacy of his presidency and led to tension between supporters of the government and the opposition parties. The opposition parties differentiated themselves by ideologies, including democratization and revival of the Tajik nation, but also had strong region-based attachment and represented interests of particular regional clans. All these parties competed for the control over the state and its resources using secular, or Islamic, and "democratic" ideas as tools to gain more loyal supporters. As David Little mentions in chapter 1 of this volume, "nationalist conflicts are contests over which national ideal will prevail in a given nation-state."

The IRP was the largest among the opposition parties. After independence, it began to operate legally and participated in the national elections. Most of its supporters were concentrated in the southwest and included families forcibly relocated during the Soviet period to the cotton fields of the Vakhsh Valley from the mountainous Qarateghin region (Akiner and Barnes 2001). The IRP united diverse and even contradictory groups ranging from radicals led by Said Abdullo Nuri to official religious "establishment" led by Khoji Akbar Turajonzoda. The party leaders hoped to win the support of the majority of Tajiks who considered themselves Muslim, but, as discussed earlier, people with a cultural form of Muslim identity did not support the extremist movement. Most local religious leaders did not endorse the IRP either (Akiner and Barnes, 2001).

In 1991–92 the IRP organized mass demonstrations, hunger strikes, and rallies in direct confrontation to the state. It initiated an ideological war against Soviet values and provoked discussions in local communities about the role of religion and culture in Tajikistan (Usmonov 2004). It also joined the Government of National Reconciliation (GNR), a coalition of eight representatives from opposition groups that managed to take power in May 1992. In December 1992 the existing Tajik government defeated the GNR and banned oppositional parties. Most IRP leaders and Islamist activists went into exile. The IRP became one of the leading parties in the United Tajik Opposition (UTO). According to Olimova and Olimov (2001), "its unlikely alliance with the 'democratic' parties was based partly on shared interests (a coalition of regional elites opposing the Communist status quo) and partly on the tradition of egalitarianism and communal democracy in the Islamic culture of mountainous Tajikistan. Any remaining ideological contradictions were soon overshadowed by the logic of political and, later, military struggle."

COUNTERACTION: THE TURN TO VIOLENCE

The aim of some Islamist leaders was to destroy the existing regime. IRP leaders played an important role in the development of a civil war. To justify their military actions, they portrayed the Communist regime as evil and its actions as hostile and brutal (Olimova and Olimov 2001). They used the slogan "down with Islam," shown by some pro-Communists in their rallies, as an example of the aggressive and antagonistic nature of the government. The mythic narratives, which described the ruling regime as atrocious and vicious with the intention of rapidly destroying Islam in Tajikistan, were created. A jihad (holy war) was presented as the only means with which to defend virtuous Islamic ideas and the lives of Muslims.

In the fall of 1991 IRP leaders initiated the transformation of the opposition alliance into a military-political organization and formed the military movement Najot-i Vatan (Salvation of the Motherland). Distributing weapons among supporters of the ruling regime in the spring of 1992 strengthened the willingness for an armed struggle among Islamic militants. In early 1993 the opposition started the armed insurgency, in particular from across the Tajik-Afghan border. To coordinate military and political actions, the IRP formed a united front, the Movement for Islamic Revival in Tajikistan, in Taloqan, Afghanistan. In 1994 the IRP became the leading force in the military opposition movement.

Neighboring countries, including Afghanistan, Iran, Pakistan, Russia, the Central Asian republics, and particularly Uzbekistan, provided significant support to the parties in the war. Russia and other Central Asian countries supported the progovernment non-Islamist forces and sent peacekeeping troops to guard the Tajik-Afghan border. Islamist leaders from Afghanistan, Pakistan, and Saudi Arabia helped the IRP (Akiner and Barnes 2001). According to the UN High Commissioner for Refugees (UNHCR), between twenty thousand and forty thousand people are believed to have been killed in this civil war. Insurgents murdered thousands of unarmed civilians, forcing them to flee their homes. Nearly a half million people were displaced. "Some 60,000 persons sought asylum in northern

Afghanistan where they were assisted by UNHCR. An additional 80,000 were left massed along the border with Afghanistan unable to cross the icy waters of the Amu Darya River" (UNHCR 1994).

ISLAMIC LEADERS AND THE PEACE PROCESS

The process of peace negotiations began under the initiative of foreign powers that saw a growing threat in changes to the regional geopolitical context. According to Akiner and Barnes (2001), "fears that the Taliban might threaten Tajikistan encouraged foreign governments to pressure their Tajik allies to negotiate a settlement to the war. They subsequently provided practical support to the peace process." The United Nations played an important role in the peace process: "UN staff conducted more than a year of preparatory consultations and then facilitated three years of difficult negotiations between the delegations of the government of Tajikistan and the United Tajik Opposition (UTO)" (Hay 2001). In December 1996 the foreign facilitators organized a meeting between Emomalii Rakhmonov, president of Tajikistan, and Nuri, the IRP leader, in Khos Deh, Afghanistan. This meeting became the starting point for the long process of reconciliation.

Religious leaders decided to participate in the peace process for several reasons. The first group of motives is connected with the assessment of the opportunity to reach the main goal of the movement, the creation of an independent Islamic state. First of all, they were afraid that the rise of the Taliban movement could lead to the loss of Tajikistani independence. They understood that a continuation of the war and support of radical Islamists from Afghanistan could result in the diminishing of their control: "a power-sharing compromise to govern a unified country was preferable by far to losing the country entirely" (Akiner and Barnes 2001). Second, the goal of unifying Tajikistan under Islam and Islamic law was impeded by the growing conflict between ethnoregional groups. IRP leaders realized that the idea of unification would not be realized as war continued. Third, they considered the possibility for the isolation of Tajikistan by the Commonwealth of Independent States, justified by a perceived "Islamic threat" (Olimova and Olimov 2001). This isolation could lead to the further decline of an already poor economic situation (between 1992 and 1996, gross domestic product decreased by more than half) and further loss of independence.

The second group of reasons is connected with the ability of the party to win the war by military means. First of all, the opposition was exhausted by the war and lacked supplies and financial resources. Second, UTO militants began to lose their important operational bases in Afghanistan. "Although UTO leaders had contacts with Taliban officials, the Taliban were suspicious of the UTO's close links with Iran and its affiliation with the predominantly ethnic Tajik and Uzbek political and military leaders in northern Afghanistan. . . . In addition, Afghan President

Rabbani and Commander Masoud became dependent on cooperation with the Tajik government and Russia for arms, administration, fuel, food and routes of re-supply and consequently ceased their alliance with the UTO" (Hay 2001). IRP leaders understood that they could preserve power over the central government by using military tactics. They also did not want to repeat the example of the defeat of Basmachi movement that forced many people to flee to Afghanistan and live in exile.

The third group of reasons is connected with the recognition that the IRP was losing supporters. Thus, IRP leaders had acknowledged that the majority of Tajiks would not join the IRP and preferred secular political ideologies. "This became especially obvious in 1994, when many young people from 'rebel' regions migrated to other CIS countries in search of work, thus reducing the pool of new recruits" (Olimova and Olimov 2001). Nevertheless, Islamic leaders continued to use military means during the peace negotiations to increase their stakes in the final resolution. For example, to strengthen their positions, the IRP leaders and progovernment forces used military operations seven to ten days before the next round of talks. The IRP leaders also used bombing and hostage-taking. However, as Olimova and Olimov (2001) point out, "in the end, these tactics failed. As the peace process progressed, the warring parties demonstrated greater flexibility and shifted from military pressure to political strategies."

What strategies did Islamic leaders use in the peace process? How they were able to terminate the military struggle and begin to negotiate with former enemies? First, the IRP and UTO leader, Said Abdullo Nuri, made important concessions during the December 1996 meeting with Rakhmonov in Afghanistan. These concessions, according Olimova and Olimov (2001), opened the door for the process of reconciliation but also created conflict within the UTO leadership and deep frustration among many IRP members. For them, this move by the leaders was treasonous to the main goals of the movement and a betrayal of the idea of an Islamic state. Many IRP members and leaders did not understand the actions of Nuri and did not follow his orders. But finally, respect for and faith in religious leaders allowed them to overcome their suspicions and mistrust.

In addition, during the peace process, the IRP showed the ability to compromise to avoid a possible collapse of the peace negotiations. During the first stage of the talks, Islamic leaders avoided any discussions of an Islamic state. Instead, "the future legal status of the Islamic Renaissance Party (IRP) was made conditional on its implementation of the Protocol on Military Issues and its adherence to the [secular] laws of the country. The notion of an Islamic state was not disputed directly or addressed explicitly in the documents adopted by the negotiating teams. It was instead tacitly postponed and became a central feature of the work of the Commission on National Reconciliation between 1997 and 1999" (Asadullaev 2001). The importance of the readiness of the IRP for compromise is hard to overestimate: both sides had contradictory goals and opposing views on the future of Tajikistan (Smith 1999).

The IRP's commitment to reconciliation impacted the government's position in negotiations and made it more ready to compromise. During the next six months, both parties increasingly cooperated in the discussion of military, political, and legal issues, and in June 1997 signed a General Agreement in the Kremlin. It was witnessed by Russian president Boris Yeltsin, eight foreign ministers from observer countries, and the secretaries-general of the Organization for Security and Cooperation in Europe and the Organization of the Islamic Conference. The IRP's ability to compromise and be flexible in discussing issues helped religious leaders reach an agreement that granted them legal status in the secular state of Tajikistan. This agreement gave the representatives of UTO 30 percent of the executive positions in the presidential republic.

By 2000 the IRP had become one of the most powerful political parties in Tajikistan. The IRP has had a unique position in the region: it was the only political party based on religious ideas to legally operate in a secular state. The Islamist movement that previously used military tactics against the government was peacefully incorporated into the constitutional political process. Representatives of IPR received the majority of the government positions allocated to the UTO by the peace agreement. As a parliamentary party, the IPR has been using peaceful and legal political methods. It has addressed major socioeconomic issues, including issues of women and children. The IPR also has actively collaborated with the government on the formation of a national identity and the development of national security (Rahnamo 2004). Thus, IPR went beyond a position of being a political party based on religious ideas and principles: it evolved over time to become a party that had a much more nationally inclusive, wider agenda than simply addressing religious agendas such as creating a religious state.

Nevertheless, the IRP was not able to totally overcome the difficulties of its position (Olimova and Olimov 2001). First of all, the influence of the party was limited because if its commitment to a particular region. Thus, the representative of IRP, Usmonov, could not collect the 5 percent of electoral signatures necessary for the registration of a presidential candidate (Sharipov 2004). Second, some party members considered the idea of an Islamic state to be incompatible with the IRP position as a limited political party, and they left the IPR. Other party members have conducted political activities in mosques and madrasas, which are prohibited by the state law.

BETWEEN ACCOMMODATION AND REESCALATION

Tajiks who lived though this period of violent conflict (1992–97) generally had an excessive willingness for compromise and even submission to the president to avoid any tensions. There is a strong common agreement that "a bad peace is better than a good war" and that discord should be avoided by any means. The ideas of national unity and the importance of compromise were used by President Rahmonov to suppress differences in opinions and approaches to the future of Tajikistan. He has stressed that the opposition threatens peaceful coexistence and unity of the country. The government reshuffled after the election of 2006 broke the 1997 agreement; most government representatives from the opposition parties were dismissed. The president justified these changes by declaring the end of the postconflict restoration period that required compromises and the beginning of a new era in Tajikistani development. As a result, the IRP has lost positions in the government and has proclaimed the beginning of active opposition. As party leader Dr. Muhiddin Kaberi mentioned during a roundtable discussion at the Institute for Conflict Analysis and Resolution in 2006, if national unity is no longer the main goal in Tajikistani society, the IRP is ready to become a strong opponent of the government. However, recent developments show that current IRP has fractured leadership, including Kaberi, who tends to prioritize stability over pushing back against government injustices. The growing level of corruption and, thus, inability to confront the government decreased political involvement of the general population in IRP.

The current government of Tajikistan emphasizes Islamic radicalism as a major threat to the country. However, radical groups that appeared in Central Asia have found only limited support among population. In May 2005 seven people accused of belonging to an outlawed Islamic group, Hizb ut-Tahrir, were sentenced to prison for three to nine years. The government continues to stress the threat of Islamic radical movements to stability in Tajikistan, and uses the US-led "war on terror" to increase control over religious institutions and suppress Islamic opposition. The heads of numerous mosques have been asked to swear loyalty to the current leadership. The IRP of Tajikistan has been accused of spreading extremist ideologies designed to divide the state. The government has made a series of unofficial decrees regarding women wearing hijabs and regarding signs of "radicalization." For example, there have been cases in Khatlon of women being detained in the bazaar if they are wearing their hijabs, and young men detained for "looking wahhabi" by wearing beards.

The internal security dilemma rests on a growing distrust between the government and opposition parties as well as on apprehensions based on the belief that the winning side would deny the other party the right to participate in governance. Secular leaders fear that if the IRP comes to power through democratic elections, it would begin to establish a theocratic state. Their fears are supported by the fact that IRP is widening its agenda and becoming very popular among youth in Khatlon (along the Afghan border) and to some extent among youth in Khujand (Sugd region). In addition, public dissention regarding the president's policies is growing among the youth generation who are unemployed, have limited opportunities, and thus are getting more restless and aggressive. Islamic leaders fear that their party could be banned or lose the right of participation in the government. The government realizes that even a disorganized opposition such as the IRP still has an influence over the population despite their limited capacity to challenge the state. Unemployed youth could easily be persuaded to follow the lead of more radicalized elements that could follow the most radical members of the IRP. This mutual mistrust, together with the absence of a clear understanding about the future of the Tajik state, leads to competitive actions against the other group.

CONCLUSION

The case of the Tajik civil war and peace process provides an opportunity to assess the role of religious leaders in catalyzing violence along identity lines and in developing foundations for peace processes. Muslim identity is the most salient identity in Tajikistan; however, few people have had a mobilized form of this religious identity and have been ready to fight with the government for the ideas of Islamic state. The IRP, which was formed as an opposition to Soviet ideology in 1990, gained supporters during the social instability of the early years of Tajikistan's independence. Similar to other parties that fought for economic and political power in 1991–92, it was based on the interests of regional elites. The majority of people in southwest Tajikistan, the regional base for the IRP, had a salient Muslim identity and memories of the pan-Islamic Basmachi Rebellion of 1920s.

To achieve economic and political power in Tajikistan, the leaders of the IRP employed the idea of an Islamic state. The sentiments toward radicalism have been reshaped by a lack of democratic reforms and economic deprivation. Thus, religious leaders used salient religious identity, existing prejudices, and biases as well as memories of success and defeat to promote loyalty among their supporters and gain the control over the country. The next step was to deepen the intergroup divide and intensify tensions through the employment of the moral dimension of conflict.

The IRP leaders used narratives in profound ways that portrayed the progovernment coalition as a brutal force intent on destroying Islam in Tajikistan and presented military tactics as the only means of survival. Thus, religious identity was used to justify the violence against progovernment forces as well as against unarmed civilians. Both parties in the war perceived each other as an evil enemy that could not be trusted and had to be destroyed. The success of IRP military operations and establishment of Shari'a law in some regions of Tajikistan was based on transnational sponsorship. Leaders and field commanders of northern Afghanistan as well as militant Islamists based in Pakistan and Saudi Arabia provided support (financial, training, and arms). The IRP was able to develop military bases in Afghanistan and conduct operations across the border.

The geopolitical interests and situations in neighboring countries also contributed to the beginning of the peace process. Thus, the military advance of the Taliban posed a threat to the military bases of the IRP in Afghanistan that significantly diminished the party's influence in the region. Russia and Iran, who were interested in decreasing the US influence in the region and in minimizing Taliban, Pakistani, or Saudi involvement in Tajikistan, actively engaged in the promotion of peace in Tajikistan.

The loss of external and internal support as well as the recognition that the main aims of the party could not be reached by military means led IPR leaders to realize the necessity of peace negotiations. First attempts of both sides were unsuccessful and were impeded by the use of military strategies employed to strengthen the positions. The conflict that developed through all four stages of the conceptual framework had to be addressed beginning from the last stage of negative moral perceptions and unbalanced collective axiology. The concessions made by the IRP leader and his call for forgiveness and understanding were the first steps toward conflict resolution and reconciliation. Only through compromises, trust-building, and changes in negative perceptions were the parties able to negotiate economic and political issues and cooperate on the development of a mutual agreement. The religious identity that made the conflict more profound and violent became a powerful source for shifting negative perception and moral judgments of the other toward acceptance and collaboration.

However, as the government decision to cancel the peace agreement shows, the society in Tajikistan did not reach real reconciliation and mutual trust. Tolerance toward others was based on the willingness to preserve a negative peace and prevent further violence and not on the readiness to peacefully coexist and cooperate with the former enemy. The former can help to avoid escalation of conflict by political and legal means. The latter is based on the changes in the perceptions of people and development of common overarching identity. Tajikistan has a long way to go to achieve the second type of tolerance. It is possible only through the open dialogue between all parties in the society.

NOTES

I would like to thank PhD student Kim Toogood for her brilliant comments on the most recent developments in Tajikistan.

1. The cultural form of identity is based on characteristics of the everyday life of a culture that includes cuisine and diet; clothes; typical day routine; songs, music, and dancing; traditions and customs; and even holidays and ways of celebration or mourning. Values, beliefs, attitudes, and norms are also integrated within this

identity, but they are perceived as essential or given and are never questioned. People live "within" their social identity, following all in-group recommendations and instructions but never think deeply about the goals and intentions of their in-group or its status and position within the society.

2. See Korostelina 2007a. The reflected form of identity includes an advanced under-standing of the history of in-group and its relationship to out-groups, awareness of the current status and position of the group, and recognition of future goals and perspectives of the in-group. Such an identity also reflects an appreciation of the values and beliefs of the group and an understanding of their roots and sources as well as the role of a group in society.

3. See Korostelina 2007a. The mobilized form of identity rests on an understanding of in-group identity within the framework of intergroup relations through in-group comparisons of position, power, and status. In this case, the estimation of the in-group and out-group is based on the positions and goals of both in-groups and out-groups; the traditions, customs, and cultural characteristics do not play an important role in this intergroup comparison. Such ideologization of identity results in the perception of competition between the group and the incompatibility of goals.

4. If such components as in-group traditions and values, characteristics of in-group members, and reverberated identity dominate, it can be defined as a depictive mode of identity meaning (for example, Amish people) (Korostelina 2007a).

5. Ideological modes of identity meaning are characterized by the prevalence of an ideology of in-groups and interrelations with out-groups.

REFERENCES

Akiner, Shirin, and Catherine Barnes. 2001. "The Tajik Civil War: Causes and Dynamics." London: Conciliation Resources. www.c-r.org/our-work/accord/tajikistan/causes-dynamics.php.

Asadullaev, Iskander. 2001. "The Tajikistan Government." *Conciliation Resources*, March. www.c-r.org/our-work/accord/tajikistan/tajikistan-government.php.

Denison, Michael. 2003. "Identity Politics in Central Asia." *Asian Affairs* 34:58–64.

Dodkhoudoeva, L. N. 2003. "Some Aspects of the Social Dynamics of Culture in Tajikistan." In *Sotsial'no-duckhovnoe; politicheskoe obrazovanic*, May 11. www.humanities.edu.ru/db/msg/42584.

Hay, Elena Rigacci. 2001. "Methodology of the Inter-Tajik Negotiation Process." *Conciliation Resources*, March. www.c-r.org/our-work/accord/tajikistan/methodology.php.

Korostelina, Karina V. 2007a. *Social Identity and Conflict*. New York: Palgrave Macmillan.

———. 2007b. "The System of Social Identities in Tajikistan: Early Warning and Conflict Prevention." *Communist and Post-Communist Studies* 40, no. 2: 223–38.

Olcott, Martha Brill. 1981. "The Basmachi or Freemen's Revolt in Turkestan 1918–24." *Soviet Studies* 33:352–69.

Olimova, Saodat. 1999. "Political Islam and Conflict in Tajikistan." In *Political Islam and Conflicts in Russia and Central Asia*, edited by Lena Johnson and Murad Esenov. Stockholm: Swedish Institute of International Affairs.

———. 2003. Musulmanskie lideri: sotsialnaya rol i avtoritet. (Muslim leaders: social role and authority). Research Center Sharq and Friedrich Ebert Stiftung, Dushanbe: Divashtich, 2003.

Olimova, Saodat, and Muzzafar Olimov. 2001. "The Islamic Renaissance Party." *Conciliation Resources*, March. www.c-r.org/our-work/accord/tajikistan/islamic -renaissance-party.php.

Rahnamo, A. 2004. "Potrebnosti adaptatsii politicheskogo islama k zadacham postroeniya natsional'nogo gosydarstva v Tajikistane" ("The Needs of Adaptation of Political Islam to the Tasks of the Building of National State in Tajikistan"). In *Postroenie doveria mezdy islamistami I seculyaristami- tajikskii eksperiment (The Confidence Building between Islamists and Secularists- The Experiment of Tajikistan)*, edited by J.-N. Bitter, F. Geran, A.K. Zafert, and D. Rahmanova-Shvarts, 161–83. Dushanbe: Devahtich.

Ritter, William S. 1985. "The Final Phase in the Liquidation of Anti-Soviet Resistance in Tadzhikistan: Ibrahim Bek and the Basmachi, 1924–31." *Soviet Studies* 37:484–93.

Roy, Olivier. 1996. "Islam in Tajikistan." Open Society in Central Asia. Occasional Paper Series 1. Budapest, Hungary: Open Society Institute.

Sharipov, S. 2004. "Regulirovanie otnoshenii mezdy politicheskoi sistemoi I islamom v tajikskom nachional'nom gosudarstve" ("The regulation of relations between political system and Islam in Tajik national state") in *Postroenie doveria mezdy islamistami I seculyaristami- tajikskii eksperiment (The Confidence Building between Islamists and Secularists- The Experiment of Tajikistan)*, edited by J.-N. Bitter, F. Geran, A. K. Zafert, and D. Rahmanova-Shvarts, 122–38. Dushanbe: Devahtich.

Smith, R.Grant. 1999. "Tajikistan: The Rocky Road to Peace." *Central Asian Survey* 18:243–51.

UNHCR. 1994. "Review of UNHCR Activities in Tajikistan," UNHCR Evaluation Reports, September 1. www.unhcr.org/research/RESEARCH/3bd420b54.html.

Usmonov, I. 2004. "Primenenie principa otdeleniya religii ot gosudarstva v usloviyah tajikskogo gosudarstva" ("The Application of the Principle of Separation of Religion and State in the Framework of Tajik State") in *Postroenie doveria mezdy islamistami I seculyaristami- tajikskii eksperiment (The Confidence Building between Islamists and Secularists: The Experiment of Tajikistan)*, edited by J.-N. Bitter, F. Geran, A. K. Zafert, and D. Rahmanova-Shvarts, 54–64. Dushanbe: Devahtich.

CHAPTER 10

THE SPOILER AND THE RECONCILER

⌒

Buddhism and the Peace Process in Sri Lanka

SUSAN HAYWARD

I have occasionally lamented with Sri Lankan Buddhist monks about the manner in which the Sri Lankan *sangha* (the monastic community) has become a global exemplar. When evidence is presented that no religion is immune to becoming a vehicle for violence, Sri Lanka's orange-robed monks are pointed to as an example of a militant form of Buddhism. The images presented as evidence— monks burning former peace facilitator Norway's flag, a monk assassin, throngs of monks disrupting peace rallies—are persuasive. Sri Lanka's *sangha* has earned this reputation due to monks who have drawn on Buddhist scripture to define the "national problem" as a struggle for the sake of the *buddhadharma* (the doctrine or teachings of Buddha), and who have repeatedly mobilized the public in opposition to negotiated agreements or political restructuring to address minority Tamil grievances. They have also, along with opportunist Sinhala politicians and elites, used Buddhism to shape and propel the evolution of a Sinhala nationalism that is the ideological warrant for a highly centralized state structure. The development of religious identity as an element of ethnic Sinhala nationalism and consciousness, the maturation of a quasi–just war Buddhist narrative of the twenty-six-year civil war, and the political mobilization of monks to disrupt or propel conflict-related policies have often complicated the dynamics of the relationship between Sri Lanka's ethnic communities.

Yet Sri Lanka's conflict is not a religious conflict in the sense of a dispute between competing religious beliefs. Rather, it is often described as a conflict over access to political power, economic and social well-being, and minority rights. In fact, daily life illustrates a deep coexistence of Sri Lanka's four major faiths, particularly Buddhism (the primary religion of the ethnic Sinhala majority) and

Hinduism (the primary religion of the ethnic minority Tamil). These manifestations of religious pluralism—Hindu gods in Buddhist temples, Buddhist statues blessed by passing Hindu worshippers, images of the Christian figure of Mary reverently recognized as manifestations of Indian religious goddesses (Christianity is practiced by 8 percent of the population, with roughly equal representation of Sinhala and Tamil), and Muslim soldiers who discreetly seek ritual protection at Hindu festivals (the Sri Lanka Muslim community constitutes the island's third main ethnic group, making up 7 percent of the population)—stand in contrast to the stark ethnic and linguistic differentiation that marks Sri Lanka's politics.[1] While this religious pluralism leads some observers to dismiss the religious divide in Sri Lanka's identity politics as irrelevant, other observers have argued that ethnicity and religion are not so easily disentangled (Little 1994, 42).[2] Many analysts agree that although religion may not be a source for the conflict's eruption, religious dynamics have contributed to its sustenance.[3]

When analysis delves below the surface, a complex picture is revealed that frustrates any reductionist conclusion about the role of the religious realm in Sri Lanka's political quagmire. Despite the historic preponderance of monk opposition to political negotiations or restructuring in attempts to solve the conflict, elements of the *sangha*, including its elite membership, have at times rallied in support of peace processes and called for addressing minority grievances. In some villages, monks work alongside other religious clergy to bring humanitarian relief, dispute resolution, sustainable development, and social reconciliation to local populations. These local prosocial efforts by monks and other clergy, and the affect they have on community life, illustrate the transformative power of religious leaders in a deeply faithful community such as Sri Lanka to shape and strengthen greater social cohesiveness, promote a multireligious national identity, and articulate new religious narratives of the conflict that can counter violent religio-political extremism.

In this chapter I offer a brief background to Sri Lanka's conflict and attempts at its resolution. I then examine how Buddhist narrative, identity, supremacy, and monk mobilization has impacted Sri Lanka's politics, particularly with respect to the conflict, and has contributed to the failure of various peace processes during the period of civil war. Although I allude in passing to how religious minority communities have responded to conflict dynamics, I focus primarily on the Buddhist realm given the space constraints and the relatively more influential role the Buddhist religious community has played in Sri Lanka's conflict and peace negotiations, and that Buddhist ideology has played in shaping Sri Lankan governance and state structure. Finally, I offer examples from the field to illustrate how individual monks and small groups of multireligious actors are working cooperatively in constructive ways to promote social tolerance and inclusive governance, and to illustrate the potential this has to dismantle exclusionary ethnoreligious nationalism and strengthen a more liberal form of democracy in Sri Lanka that can address minority grievance. Although I attempt to answer the question that is at the heart of this larger study, namely, what propels religious actors to mobilize for or against peace, this analysis will not lead to easy answers but rather will demonstrate the complicated manner in which the religious realm interacts with political, social, and economic dynamics.

CONTENDING "REVIVALISMS" IN SRI LANKA

Pinpointing the beginning to Sri Lanka's conflict is an exercise fraught with political implications; actors give an answer shaped by their perspective and experience. The most quoted commencement of Sri Lanka's war, however, is July 1983, when, following the slaughter of several government soldiers in the north of the island by the Tamil insurgency group the Liberation Tigers of Tamil Eelam (LTTE), Sinhala mobs wreaked violence against Tamil civilians, businesses, and neighborhoods across the island. Following these riots, which the security forces were unable or unwilling to stop until thousands had been killed, Tamil minority communities lost faith in the government, the LTTE's militant insurgency gained traction, and a civil war began in earnest.

The paths to this "Black July" emerge out of British colonial rule, when the Sri Lankan minority Tamil community sought educational and employment opportunities in new colonial sectors and thereby profited economically and politically in a manner disproportionate to their population (Rotberg 1999, 5). The rise of Tamil elites and the immigration of Tamils from India into Sinhala-areas revived a sense of the vulnerability of the Sinhala nation, a minority in the larger region, to foreign exploitation.[4] This in turn sparked a Sinhala revival movement and an ethnic rivalry that led to sporadic race riots. The rivalry only grew when Sri Lanka achieved independence in 1948. Sinhala and Tamil communities clashed over how representation should be delineated within government, with Tamils worrying that territorial representation would erode the achievements they had made and Sinhala seeking to establish a representative rule that would reflect their majority status within Sri Lanka.

Postindependence, the Sinhala used their majority in parliament to secure greater economic and political control. Over several decades, they passed laws that stripped Tamils of Indian heritage of citizenship and made Sinhala the national language, thereby ensuring that jobs, particularly university and local government positions, went to Sinhala speakers. Tamils pressed unsuccessfully for the retrieval of their previous positions of influence and the repeal of legislation that disenfranchised them.

Throughout the 1960s and 1970s, the tension between the two ethnic communities mounted. The Tamil Federal Party in parliament was unable to stem a tide of laws and new constitutions that further centralized power, rather than devolving power to the provinces, as many Tamils sought. Eventually Tamil armed rebel groups began to emerge, calling for their own independent homeland. These groups harassed local populations, including the Tamil, and pursued violent acts of insurgency against the "imperialist state." By the late 1970s the LTTE, which sought the establishment of an independent Tamil state named Eelam, had begun to emerge as a predominant group.

Throughout the years of violent civil war, from 1983 until the LTTE's military defeat in May 2009, there were several attempts to broker peace between the government of Sri Lanka and the LTTE. Sri Lanka accepted the mediation assistance in the late 1980s, when India strong-armed the two sides into an agreement for devolution of power to the provinces and sought to enforce the agreement through a peacekeeping force. The results of this effort were disastrous; Indian prime minister Rajiv Gandhi was assassinated by an LTTE cadre in retaliation for the deaths of Sri Lankan Tamils by Indian security forces. In a moment of rare collusion, the government of Sri Lanka and LTTE banded together to force out the Indian military monitoring presence. Devolution of power to the provinces has still not been fully implemented.

The LTTE and the government of Sri Lanka pursued direct bilateral negotiations in the mid-1990s under President Chandrika Kumaratunga, who pursued a two-pronged approach of negotiations coupled with military action that sought to pressure and weaken the LTTE. This process eventually fell apart. Finally, in 2000, the government of Sri Lanka and LTTE announced that Norway had been invited to facilitate peace talks between them, inaugurating a process backed by the European Union, the United States, and Japan, who incorporated economic incentives by making aid conditional on progress toward a peace settlement. The process secured a cease-fire agreement in 2002 that lasted several years before being rendered defunct by a steady increase of violence that led the government to abrogate the agreement in early 2008. The military campaign that followed pushed a weakened LTTE into a narrow strip of land, trapping its leadership and leading to the battlefield death of leader Velupillai Prabhakaran and the proclaimed defeat of the LTTE. With the LTTE defeated, the period of overt civil war came to an end. However, the ethnic conflict that led to war's outbreak is not yet resolved, and minority grievances remain that strain ethnic relationships on the island.

SINHALA BUDDHIST NATIONALISM

The development of a Sinhala nationalist movement in Sri Lanka during the twentieth century drew some of its ideological grounding and legitimacy from Buddhism, the religion of most Sinhala. There are two components of the evolution of this dynamic throughout the twentieth century worthy of exploration in this study. The first is how Sinhala Buddhist nationalism as a political ideology has come to shape state policy and structures. The second phenomenon is the rise of politically mobilized monks. Neither serves as the independent causal factor; both of these phenomena have evolved in parallel and have been mutually reinforcing. They have also both been addressed by many scholars, including by David Little (see Little 1994, 1999). In this section I briefly touch upon overarching themes from the literature on Sinhala Buddhist nationalism as a political ideology. In the following section I look at the rise of politically active monks in the twentieth century, particularly at their mobilization in response to the conflict.

The first theme in the scholarship on Sinhala Buddhist nationalism is how Buddhism defines Sinhala identity and cause. As stewards of one of the last remnants of Theravada Buddhism in South Asia, the Buddhist identity of the Sinhala nation was seen to be a defining element of its special character.[5] This defensive exaltation of Buddhism was in large part a reaction to aggressive forms of Christian missionary work that accompanied colonialism. While indigenous clergy initially welcomed foreign Christian missionaries, their coercive techniques for recruiting converts, their disregard for the integrity of native religions and Buddhist monks, and the favoritism they were afforded from British rulers sparked a Buddhist revivalist movement. This movement is first evidenced in a series of debates that took place in the nineteenth century at which Buddhist monks defended their religion against Christianity, and subsequently in the rise of organizations dedicated to the revitalization and propagation of Buddhism (DeVotta 2007, 14).

Anagarika Dharmapala lived at the turn of the twentieth century and is considered the father of Sinhala Buddhist nationalism. Dharmapala sought to resurrect Buddhism from its marginalized and weakened position. He shamed Sinhala for embracing foreign culture, and encouraged them to resituate themselves within the impressive history and culture of the Sinhala people. Through this revival program, Dharmapala claimed that the former glory of a historical Sinhala nation would be reestablished in which the people were unified, lived according to Buddhist moral precepts, and were self-ruled. His program was thoroughly anticolonial while also seeking to empower a moral consciousness grounded in Buddhist values and a pride within Sinhala who felt affronted after centuries of invasions from foreign powers.

The Sinhala Buddhist revival movement drew upon the sixth-century text, *Mahavamsa*, a religious account of Sinhala Buddhist history in Sri Lanka. Recounting three visits of the Buddha to the southeast, north, and south of the island wherein he tamed or expelled non-Buddhist forces, this narrative lays claim to the entirety of the island as a sanctuary for Buddhism. The text also recounts invasions of the island from foreign powers, often from South India, that sought to destroy the indigenous population. In a crucial chapter the heroic Sinhala king Dutthagamani waged war on Tamils who had usurped portions of Sri Lanka.

Upon his victory that united the island kingdom, King Dutthagamani, overcome by remorse for the carnage wrought by his sword, is visited by eight *arahants*, fully enlightened living symbols of the *dharma*, who assure him that his act has not brought bad merit upon him because the enemy Tamils he killed were non-Buddhists and no more esteemed than animals, and because the victory glorified the *buddhadharma* (Bullis 1999, 109–11). As the *Mahavamsa* frames it, the primary obligation of Sri Lankan Buddhists is to preserve the integrity of Buddhism on the island, protecting it from the invasion of nefarious foreign invaders, even through violence (Little 1999, 43).

Drawing from the *Mahavamsa* account and influenced by the rise in inter-ethnic tensions in the twentieth century, a Buddhist just war mentality took shape, which cast the national problem as a struggle to protect Buddhism from foreign powers in Sri Lanka. In so casting the conflict, short-term violence and whatever Buddhist precepts it broke were justified for the sake of the righteous mission.[6] The LTTE's provocative targeting of sacred Buddhist sites, such as their bombing of the revered Temple of the Tooth in 1998, confirmed the perception of the conflict as an assault on Buddhism. And the LTTE's separatist demands, as well as any form of federalism, were seen as a threat to the unitary integrity of the Sinhala Buddhist country. In all of this, Buddhist narratives of the Sinhala cause became lodged securely alongside political and economic dynamics, all of these elements shaping one another and the conflict.

Another theme in the literature is how Buddhism has been used as a source for legitimation of political policy and structure in Sri Lanka throughout its history and in relation to the current conflict (see, e.g., Smith 1978). The phenomenon of religious legitimation of state power and policy is rooted in ancient Asian Buddhist patronage relationship between state and *sangha*, whereby the king offers material support and military protection to the *sangha* in exchange for spiritual merit and religious legitimation of his rule.[7] These roots find their flowerings in contemporary *sangha*–state relations in Sri Lanka, although the parameters of the relationship have changed over time. Today politicians (even non-Buddhist ones) legitimate their authority through publicly staged ritual patronage acts at the temples of high-ranking Buddhist monks.[8] Policies of the main Sinhala-majority political parties are strengthened when blessed by *sangha* authorities, who serve as formal and informal political advisors (a Supreme Advisory Council of Buddhist monks to the president has existed for periods in Sri Lanka's political history). Overt and subtle claims to whether one party or another is "truly" Buddhist is a political rhetorical weapon waged by party politicians and religious actors as a way to undermine rival parties. During President Junius Jayewardene's tenure (1977–89), for example, debate centered on whether his party was authentically Buddhist and, by contrast, whether monks associated with the rival Janatha Vimukti Peramuna party were true stewards of Buddhism. The debate about which political party was "more Buddhist" was a debate over political legitimacy in claims of authority. This is a debate in which both politicians and monks weigh in, and in which senior monks have particular power. This affords the *sangha*, particularly the highest-ranking leader of each of the *sangha*'s main schools, the *mahanayakas*, significant political influence.

Religious legitimation of power and policy, and Buddhism as a central element of Sinhala identity and cause, took its modern political form with S. W. R. D. Bandarnaike's Sinhala Buddhist nationalist platform, which proved successful in galvanizing the Sinhala masses to elect him in 1956. Central to this platform was a "Sinhala Only" policy to restrict government and civil administrative positions to Sinhala speakers. Underlying this campaign promise was the claim to Sinhala supremacy, enlivened by the celebration that year of Buddha Jayanthi, the 2,500th anniversary of Buddha's death. Subsequent Sinhala politicians have similarly used the mobilizing power of Sinhala Buddhist nationalist's ideology to get elected or to garner support for various policies. The power of this rhetoric and ideology to rally and unify the Southern Sinhala masses is the third theme in the literature on Sinhala Buddhist nationalism. This phenomenon was seen most recently in the presidential campaigns of Mahinda Rajapaksa, who won and secured his post and policies by unifying disparate Sinhala parties and forces, ensuring them that he was an appropriate and pure representative of the common Sinhala man, thereby signaling that Sinhala interests would be met in his administration. Rajapaksa was elected with little support from minority parties and communities.

In the decades that have followed from the religious movement of Buddhist modernism launched by Dharmapala, Sinhala Buddhist nationalism has become embedded in the state system. It has served as a driving ideology for policies, particularly with respect to the conflict, and has provided impetus and legitimation for some of its more authoritarian or illiberal tendencies, particularly the resistance to power devolution, and indeed the increasing centralization of power over the past decades. From the Sinhala Only Act implemented under Bandarnaike came further laws that disenfranchised minorities and centralized state power, creating a structure that is intolerant to the grievances of minorities if not to minorities themselves. This includes the constitutions in the 1970s that granted new powers to the president and gave Buddhism a "foremost place" among religions, calling on the state to support Buddhism while simultaneously granting freedom to minority religions. In other words, Sinhala Buddhist nationalist ideology has shaped the political institutions and in so doing has become embedded in the state system in Sri Lanka, resulting in laws, policies, and institutions that ensure the supremacy of the Sinhala and justify the marginalization of minorities. This has been supported by and has in turn strengthened general social attitudes of intolerance and majoritarianism. To make the distinction David Little introduced in the first chapter of this volume, religion's role in manifesting intolerant attitudes and policies in

Sri Lanka is overt; minorities are not disenfranchised because of their religious identity or beliefs but rather Buddhism has been drawn upon as a warrant for intolerant policies, particularly the need to "protect" Buddhism. To address the grievances of minority communities who are made to feel under this system that they "live in Sri Lanka only due to Sinhalese Buddhist sufferance," this ideology will need to be challenged and transformed (DeVotta 2007, vi).

SACRED SPOILERS? MONKS AND THE PEACE PROCESS

Like the rise of Sinhala Buddhist nationalism as a political ideology exploited by politicians to legitimate their authority and appeal to the Sinhala masses, the monk's politically active role in society also arose out of Anagarika Dharmapala's Buddhist modernism movement. This program encouraged the monk to reclaim postcolonial prominence and embody social action for the local community.[9] The monk Rahula Walpola pushed further the Dharmapalic vision of the socially active village monk. His influential 1946 publication, *Bhiksuvage Urumaya*, encouraged monks to become involved in politics in the cities, arguing that monks had a special duty to ensure that the state was fulfilling its Buddhist duties (Seneviratne 2000, 191).[10]

Over the mid-century, monks began to run as politicians. The first monk to run and be elected in local elections was Venerable Walletota Pannadassi in Colombo in 1957 (Deegalle 2004). The first monk elected to parliament was Venerable Samitha Thero in 2001, a champion of peace who called on his fellow parliamentarians and *sangha* members to back the peace process unconditionally, and appealed to the latter to refrain from preaching divisive sermons (Deegalle 2004, 85). Ven. Samitha was not reelected in 2004, a year marked by the entrance of the monk-led Jathika Hela Urumaya (JHU).[11] This party fielded more than two hundred monks in the elections and won an impressive nine seats on a platform critical of the peace process and the "corrupt" nature of the main political parties and government, and sought to establish a righteous rule.

The entrance of the JHU into parliament has conjured a mixed response from the public, reflecting the discomfort many Sinhala feel about monk politicians. In October 2005 one of the parliamentarian monks who had led the call for monks to enter politics, Venerable Uduwe Dhammaloka, admitted publicly that it had been a mistake for monks to enter politics, and that in the future monks should focus on religious roles, which he felt would better serve the Sinhala public.[12] The JHU failed to win any seats in the 2006 local elections.[13] However, the JHU has continued to demonstrate its presence and influence in political affairs.

As monks became more politically active throughout the twentieth century, their political mobilization affected the dynamics around the conflict and peace processes. This is not to say, however, that the *sangha* operates as a hegemonic body.

The entire monastic community is divided by fraternity affiliation (*nikaya*), caste, wealth, and political ideology, all of which color dynamics within and between the three main schools (*nikayas)* that make up the Sri Lankan *sangha.* The internal differences manifest in the manner in which different groups of monks have mobilized for or against peace processes, or have identified with different and rival political parties.[14] It is accurate to assert, however, that the *sangha* has generally opposed negotiations seeking political devolution of power, a central demand of minority communities.

An example is in 1957 when Bandaranaike sought to ease ethnic tensions by entering into an agreement with the prominent Tamil leader S. J. V. Chelvanayagam to create local provincial councils. In response to this proposed agreement, a group of monks protested in front of Prime Minister Bandarnaike's house, spurning public opposition to the agreement and leading the prime minister to hastily abrogate the pact made with the Tamils. According to H. L. Seneviratne, "it is now widely accepted . . . that had the monks not prevented this agreement, the problem would have been nipped in the bud, and the country spared the trauma that has taken 60,000 lives" (Seneviratne 2001, 3; see also Tambiah 1992, 50). Bandaranaike was subsequently assassinated by a monk who felt he had too willingly capitulated to anti-Sinhala forces.

When Chandrika Kumaratunga ran on a peace platform in 1994, a group of monks toured the island explaining her devolution of power proposal and shoring up support for it (Seneviratne 2001). Notably, however, in 1997 monks led the opposition to President Kumaratunga's devolution proposals. In my own work, I have met monks who have coordinated pro-peace rallies in Colombo and around the country, and met with members of an interreligious group that brought *mahanayakas* to the north during the late 1970s and 1980s to build relationships with Tamil religious clergy. During the Norwegian-mediated process, the *mahanayakas* initially expressed support for the process, particularly after the LTTE dropped its demand for a separate state, but were quick to express concern when the proposals from the LTTE negotiating team were thought to backtrack to support policies that might threaten the unitary integrity of the island (Frydenlund 2005, 20).

Without doubt, the influence of the *sangha* on efforts to resolve the national conflict has been primarily counterconstructive. In interpreting the conflict through the lens of the Buddhist scripture and calling the Tamil rights movements an assault on Buddhism, political monks have played a role in framing a political and economic contest religiously, drawing upon deep sentiments in the Sinhala public. In her study, Iselin Frydenlund recounts sentiment expressed at myriad interviews with Buddhist monks who distinguished their position as pro-peace but were skeptical of past processes or solutions offered to achieve it (Frydenlund 2005, 17). As a result of their skepticism of these processes, they were more likely to direct public opinion to undermine them. Seeing themselves as stakeholders to the processes, they served as spoilers when they felt they were not engaged as such, and when the process failed to address their interests. In the end, perhaps, those interested in creating a sustainable peace in Sri Lanka will find they must understand the interests and motives of the various streams within the *sangha* in order to secure the support of significant monks and hence lend legitimacy to a reconciliation process that will inevitably involve political and social transformation.

Hence, measures must be taken to understand the experience and perspective of the oppositional monks; why and how they see themselves as protectors of Sinhala institution, religion, and nation; and which of their interests must be addressed in settlements. Their fears stem from very real experiences of marauding foreign powers that attacked—covertly and overtly—the Sinhala nation, culture, and religion. The reemergence of aggressive foreign Christian proselytizing groups, particularly in the aftermath of the 2004 tsunami, and continued Western funding to Christian faith-based humanitarian efforts feed their fears. These monks feel faced with a moral dilemma in which they feel compelled to take a stand. Though their active political involvement is still a controversial issue in Sri Lanka, the political monk is a phenomenon that is not going anywhere, and so must be reckoned with.

RELIGIOUS LEADERS AT THE GRASSROOTS: POSSIBILITIES AND REALITIES

In the grassroots, the diversity of religious leaders' responses to and roles in conflict and peace is made manifest. While the most strident religious voices in the public sphere, coming primarily from the JHU, supported the government's military efforts and have propagated suspicion toward other ethnic and religious groups, simultaneously and more quietly, myriad religious clergy are working throughout Sri Lanka to resolve local conflict, address human rights abuses, offer humanitarian aid, promote interethnic and interreligious reconciliation, and nurture a spiritual commitment to a multireligious Sri Lankan national identity. All of this work on the ground by religious clergy contributes to propelling dynamics toward ending the protracted ethnic conflict and offering healing to all of Sri Lanka's ethnic communities, each of whom has experienced trauma and suffering after decades of violence.

For example, there are several interreligious councils operating throughout Sri Lanka that appear to have often arisen organically as local religious clergy began to cooperate to address local concerns. These interreligious councils meet regularly to discuss local social and political issues; to actively address, mediate, and resolve local conflict; and to build interreligious understanding between themselves and their communities. They have mediated between conflicting communities in their provinces to deescalate rising tension and resolve disputes, particularly conflict with a religious dimension.[15]

The work of these councils highlights the particular leverage clergy have in addressing local conflict in Sri Lanka. Just as on the metasocial level, the Buddhist *sangha* has enormous influence in shaping public opinion, behavior, and political policy, so too the individual temple monks have influence in their local communities. To the extent to which these local monks can encourage peaceful coexistence and reconciliation, there can be local transformation that can create the environment for a successful and sustainable solution to the ethnic problem to take root, if not to mobilize a larger civil society movement for peace that might pierce the opaque bubble around the elite political and religious leadership. Local clergy from other traditions have similar leverage over local populations. As these clergy undertake activities to address the needs of the community, they are afforded greater trust and the sincerity of their interreligious commitment and message is amplified.

There are several ongoing projects in the civil and academic peace field that engage Buddhist monks. Some organizations and scholars are plumbing the depths of Buddhist philosophy and texts to discover how Buddhism defines the sources of conflict and hence what Buddhist peacemaking looks like in theory and practice, particularly when applied to Sri Lanka's ethnic conflict. The Buddhist faith-based development organization Sarvodaya, founded by lay Buddhist A. T. Ariyaratne, has assisted monks in working with other religious communities to support community development and social cohesion. Some social organizations directly engage Buddhist monks in their work, giving them the knowledge and tools, including Tamil language training, to help them reach out to other communities, understand their perspective, and work cooperatively to resolve ethnic tensions. Others, particularly those operating during the Norwegian-facilitated peace process, have analyzed the *sangha*'s power structures and decision-making and institutions in order to discover if and how federalism is complementary to Buddhism. These endeavors have powerful potential, often affirmed by monk participants and the community members who witness their work on the ground. The popular sentiment is that conflict resolution, peacemaking, and federalism are Western concepts and are thereby ideologically and indelibly Christian. The fact that the Christian church has often been on the forefront of peacemaking initiatives in Sri Lanka furthers this belief. To discover indigenous corollaries can hence assuage the fear that these peace and power devolution programs are remnants of colonial manipulation.

I offer these examples to demonstrate that the dynamics on the ground in terms of religion and the conflict are more varied than when seen from above. I assert that to the extent that some of these positive examples of religious movements for peace and reconciliation, for interreligious cooperation, for ethnoreligious tolerance, and for the articulation of faith-based principles for peace can be nurtured and expanded upon, they have a much better potential to directly challenge the religious narrative that deepens the ethnic divide and legitimates exclusionary policy than any secular ideology would. By first promoting tolerance, they can help create the impetus or space in which the political roots of Sri Lanka's conflict—lack of minority rights, poor governance, and so on—can be meaningfully and successfully addressed. In other words, just as the increasing majoritarian structure of the state was propelled by and encouraged the proliferation of attitudes of ethnic intolerance, which in turn led to the outbreak of violence, so too political restructuring will require attitudes of tolerance and will in turn seed these attitudes, making future violence less likely to break out, according to figure 1 in chapter 1 of this volume.

THE SPOILER AND THE RECONCILER

Sri Lanka aptly illustrates what Scott Appelby referred to as "the ambivalence of the sacred": the fact that a religion can propel both violence and humanitarian causes, both war and peace, both narrow communal self-interest and universal compassion, depending on the interests of those who wield religion's power to mobilize and legitimate (Appleby 2000). Buddhist actors and ideologies in Sri Lanka have propelled dynamics toward war in one context and intercommunal reconciliation in another. Attempts to make conclusions about how religion functions with respect to political dynamics are frustratingly stymied when confronted with the complicated reality, no more so than in environments of protracted conflict.

But let us return to this study's fundamental question, asking what it is that has propelled religious actors in Sri Lanka to act either for or against a peace process or a political project in pursuit of resolving the "national problem." The religious leaders I have spoken to, from those in rural villages to those high-ranking leaders in Colombo or Kandy, articulate political, economic, and social interests that underlie their positions with regard to the conflict while often applying religious principles or quoting scripture that supports or justifies their interests and positions. Those that support federalism and eschew violent military campaigns will draw on relevant religious principle to explain and argue for their position. Those that support the current governance system and backed the military campaign to defeat the LTTE also draw from appropriate religious argument. Either way, the political, social, economic, and religious argumentation is entangled and mutually informing.

Cynical observers of religious actors often paint them as ideologically driven to a degree that leaves little room for the rational give-and-take necessary for political negotiations. Religious claims to ultimate truth cannot be compromised after all. The reality, however, is that all extremist groups, both religious and political, often front stalwart positions, sometimes articulated in ideological extreme positions. When engaged, however, their interests are often more nuanced, and even religious arguments over "truth" change over time. Throughout the history of peace processes in Sri Lanka, the monks operated much like other stakeholder groups: they mobilized in support of peace processes when they felt the political leadership's interests were aligned with their own interests, and withdrawn their support and actively opposed peace processes when they felt they were failing to protect the interests of the *sangha* and the Sinhala community, which the *sangha* is tasked to protect. Prominent Buddhist monk elites have changed their positions as conditions have shifted, and even some of the previously nationalist monks have been willing to throw their support behind political negotiations to secure devolution when they have been assured that their concerns (protection of and access to Buddhist sacred sites in the North and East, or the unitary integrity of the island) are being addressed. Exposure to the content of negotiations in order to become familiar with the depth of the debate and to hear the interests and concerns of the other parties may help raise these religious leaders' comfort level. In the past, the *mahanayakas* and other monks have reacted to rumors or indirect sources on negotiations process, condemning them unfairly, until they have been briefed and engaged by the inside negotiators and mediators to correct their misunderstanding. Norway learned this during its process of facilitating the peace process, and so began regularly consulting with various streams within the *sangha*.[16]

Beyond their inclusion in peace and reconciliation processes as a means of ensuring their buy-in, religious elites have also become more actively supportive of peace processes when involved in unofficial dialogues with peers from other groups. Some members of the interfaith Congress of Religions in Colombo, who years ago were fairly skeptical of peace processes with the LTTE or of political devolution of power, have softened their position and now issue statements with their clergy colleagues that call on the government to pursue political policies that can address minority grievances.[17] What seems key here is sustained exposure to other viewpoints through dialogue, exposure to the negotiation process to understand what is being debated and how the interests of the Sinhala are being taken seriously, and authentic and direct avenues to submit their own concerns and viewpoints into the process.

It is also important to bear in mind that religious leadership is sensitive to hierarchy of authority within their institutions and to those whom they serve: the public. Some of the lower-ranking or younger monks who have participated in interreligious peace work have been ostracized by their teachers, which led some to withdraw from this work, or they have been criticized by the laity for stepping outside their appropriate role as monk, betraying Buddhism, or for being seduced and manipulated by Western nongovernmental organization (NGO) funding.[18] Similarly, monks have been encouraged or even ordered to work in some of these peace initiatives by teachers sympathetic to their goals.[19] When deciding whether or how to mobilize with respect to the conflict, monks carefully consider the potential response of their community, and that of the leadership above them, which can grant or take away their privileges and authority as clergy. Some, while sympathetic to the causes of the peace movement, are simply unwilling to shoulder the risks that accompany active peacebuilding or reconciliation work.

CONCLUSIONS

In the last stages of the war that ended in 2009, I had a sense that many monk voices for peace were being silenced in an environment in which the "militant monks," particularly those affiliated with the JHU, enjoyed an amplified voice in the public arena in which the overriding public perception that had evolved over the previous decades equated the "righteous Buddhist position" with support of the war, and in which NGO-coordinated "peace work" was decried as neocolonialism. During the period from 2008 to 2009, few prominent monks, including those affiliated with prominent interreligious work, were willing to criticize the government's military campaign. In this environment, monks were also less likely to become involved in peacemaking. Moreover, the *sangha* in Sri Lanka is reticent to create fissures within the monastic community by publicly condemning monk peers. This has prevented some monks throughout the *sangha* hierarchy who are in private conversation critical of the extremist or militant voices within the *sangha* from publicly condemning or challenging these views. This does not mean, however, that these monks are not engaging in internal dialogue with their peers. Indeed, following the 2009 battlefield defeat of the LTTE, some monks have become more publically critical of government action and policies.[20] Furthermore, with the threat of the island's physical division put to rest, monks have become more eager to reach out to minority ethnic communities in the east and north of the island to advance reconciliation. This includes initiatives led by some conservative Buddhist organizations.[21]

One thing is strikingly clear: the very things that make the *sangha* and Sinhala Buddhist Nationalist narrative a powerful force in propelling the conflict and shaping government policies and institutions also make it a potentially powerful force to achieve sustainable peace and reconciliation. Religious leaders' participation in promoting peace through political transformation and reconciliation will not in and of itself solve Sri Lanka's ethnic conflict, particularly the larger issues of political power sharing, good governance, and so forth. However, their greater involvement has the potential to greatly transform the ideologies that propel the violence and the increasingly centralized state system, as well as to mobilize a civil society movement for peace that can finally hold the fickle and often short-sighted political establishment accountable to those who face the violent or unjust results of decisions made in Colombo. This in turn will help promote a more deeply rooted democracy that can help foster a lasting peace in Sri Lanka.

NOTES

1. These statistics are taken from the 1981 census. Certainly, the numbers have changed since this time. However, as of the drafting of this chapter, the 1981 census was the last one conducted that is comprehensive of the north and east, areas in which the Liberation Tigers of Tamil Eelam (LTTE) operated. Access Sri Lanka's Department of Census and Statistics at www.statistics.gov.lk/.
2. Evidence for this dismissal is the manner in which ethnic identity often trumps in the Christian community, with Tamil Christian Bishops in the North who were sympathetic to LTTE causes in tension with Sinhala Bishops of the South.
3. There is one sense in which religion as a target of conflict has become more salient in recent years. There has been a significant increase in tensions between Buddhists and Christians in the country, with the latter accused of coercive proselytizing and churches targeted by arsons.
4. Just twenty-six miles to the northeast of Sri Lanka is the Indian state of Tamil Nadu, with a population of 60 million Tamils. By contrast, Sri Lanka serves as the sole Sinhala homeland.
5. Monks in particular were called to serve as these stewards of the Buddhist righteousness of the Sinhala and their political sphere.
6. Bartholomeusz (2002) explores how contemporary Buddhist-grounded justification of war in Sri Lanka drew from an existent just war theory in Theravada sources.
7. It is worth noting that religious legitimation of political rule and policy is a common phenomenon in much of the world, including the United States, where politicians seek to convey themselves as more authentically Christian and vie for support from Christian leadership.
8. Indeed, even those politicians who are not Buddhist will stage a publicized visit to a high-ranking Buddhist monk as a means to grant legitimacy to their authority. A perfect case in point was the visit by Pillyan, a former LTTE cadre who served as a high-ranking officer in the breakaway Karuna faction that partnered with the government and became a political party, to Buddhist temples immediately after his appointment as minister of the Eastern Province in 2008. This helped stem some suspicion toward him among the Sinhala South.
9. As Seneviratne (2000, 28) points out, the precolonial monk likely did not operate in society in the manner Dharmapala envisioned.
10. The politically active monk is still a controversial issue amongst Sinhala—many still think monks shouldn't be involved in the dirty realm of politics . . . it's not their place. Still, the politically active monk has become standard practice at this point.
11. While the JHU was founded by monks, it currently includes lay Buddhist members.

12. "Second Thoughts." *Lanka Business Online*, October 23, 2005.
13. Additionally, the Janatha Vimukthi Peramuna (JVP, People's Liberation Front) only succeeded in winning one seat. "Sri Lanka Snap Poll Possible as Ruling Party Sweeps Local Elections." *Agence France Presse*, April 2, 2006.
14. There are monks associated with the main political parties, including the United National Party, the Sri Lanka Freedom Party, and the JVP, and these parties will mobilize their monks to garner public support for party policies as needed (Frydenlund 2005, 14).
15. For example, in the Trincomalee area, when disputes have arisen regarding claims of Buddhist heritage sites in predominantly Muslim areas, the interreligious councils have been able to intervene to deescalate tensions.
16. As attested to me in various interviews with members of the Norwegian Foreign Ministry involved in the Sri Lankan peace process.
17. This is attested to by longtime observers of the Congress of Religions as articulated to me in interviews in November 2007.
18. This criticism often paints the peace activist monks as traitors to Buddhism, non-Buddhist, half-Christian (particularly when engaged in interreligious activities), or as paid off by NGO wealth. These criticisms delegitimate the monks' roles as authoritative Buddhist voices in support of peace. They also make them vulnerable to violence—several peace activist monks have been killed or have been forced to go into exile.
19. As attested to me in interviews with monks involved in reconciliation work in November 2010.
20. For example, following the arrest of the defeated presidential candidate Gen. Sarath Fonseka following the 2010 presidential election, two of the *mahanayakas* organized a protest calling for his release. This protest, under pressure from political elites, was called off.
21. As evidenced in my field interviews with monks from around Sri Lanka in November–December 2009 and in November 2010.

REFERENCES

Appleby, Scott. 2000. *The Ambivalence of the Sacred*. Lanham, MD: Rowman and Littlefield.

Bartholomeusz, Tessa. 2002. *In Defense of Dharma*. London: Routledge.

Bullis, Douglas, trans. 1999. *Mahavamsa*. Berkeley, CA: Asian Humanities Press.

Deegalle, Mahinda. 2004. "Politics of the Jathika Hela Urumaya Monks: Buddhism and Ethnicity in Contemporary Sri Lanka." *Contemporary Buddhism* 5:83–103.

DeVotta, Neil. 2007. "Sinhalese Buddhist Nationalist Ideology: Implications for Politics and Conflict Resolution in Sri Lanka." *Policy Studies*, no. 40. Washington, DC: East West Center.

Frydenlund, Iselin. 2005. *The Sangha and Its Relation to the Peace Process in Sri Lanka*. Oslo: International Peace Research Institute Oslo.

Little, David. 1994. *Sri Lanka: The Invention of Enmity.* Washington, DC: US Institute of Peace.

———. 1999. "Religion and Ethnicity in the Sri Lankan Civil War." In *Creating Peace in Sri Lanka*, edited by Robert Rotberg. Washington, DC: Brookings Institution Press.

Rotberg, Robert. 1999. *Creating Peace in Sri Lanka.* Washington, DC: Brookings Institution Press.

Seneviratne, H. L. 2000. *The Work of Kings.* Chicago: University of Chicago Press.

———. 2001. "Buddhist Monks and Ethnic Politics." *Anthropology Today* 17:15–21.

Smith, Bardwell, ed. 1978. *Religion and Legitimation of Power in Sri Lanka.* Chambersburg, PA: Anima Books.

Tambiah, Stanley. 1992. *Buddhism Betrayed?* Chicago: University of Chicago Press.

CHAPTER 11

PIETY AND POLITICS

Religious Leadership and the Conflict in Kashmir

SUMIT GANGULY AND PRAVEEN SWAMI

In 1912 the revivalist poet Maqbool Shah Kraalwari published *Greeznama*, an extended lament about the subversive syncretism of the Kashmiri peasantry:

> *They regard the mosque and the temple as equal,*
> *seeing no difference between muddy puddles and the ocean,*
> *They know not the sacred, honourable or the respectable* (Kraalwari 1912, 5).

Less than a century ago, the landscape Kraalwari described has disappeared: as the ugly shrine-land conflagration that set the state ablaze in 2008 demonstrated, mass politics in Jammu and Kashmir appears to be driven almost exclusively by questions of religious identity. Yet the fact remains that clerics and religious authority have had only a peripheral role in this political mobilization—and, as our survey of some religion-linked crises in Jammu and Kashmir will show, in earlier ones, too. We are confronted by the apparent paradox of a religion-driven politics that has almost no space for religious leaders. It is all the more intriguing if one considers the central place of religion in the making of the Kashmir conflict itself. In this chapter, we examine three contrasting crises in an effort to find an answer to this question. Much of the work on religion and politics in Jammu and Kashmir has focused on the two-decade-long insurgency that began in 1988.

First among these is the Hazratbal crisis of 1963–64, which was provoked by the disappearance of a holy relic from what is arguably Jammu and Kashmir's most revered shrine. In December 1963 the *moe-e-muqaddas*, reputed to be a hair of the Prophet Mohammad, disappeared from the shrine, provoking widespread violence and a generalized challenge to the legitimacy of Indian rule in Jammu and Kashmir. Indian investigators succeeded in tracing the relic and securing the imprimatur of prominent clerics for its legitimacy. However, a wide-ranging set of political reforms was needed to put the agitation to rest. Religious leaders had no role in this process whatsoever.

Second is the *Book of Knowledge* crisis, an Islamist mobilization that took place soon after the 1971 India-Pakistan war. In this case, a specific religious cause—the discovery of supposedly heretic images in an encyclopedia—provoked violence across Kashmir. However, the evolution of the crisis and its eventual outcome were shaped by politicians, not clerics or religious leaders. Political forces used the *Book of Knowledge* crisis as part of a competitive mass mobilization, and the eventual resolution of the crisis was brought about by elections.

Finally, we examine "Shrine war" of 2008—a dispute over the use of land by a trust managing a cave-temple in southern Kashmir, which led to a massive Hindu-Muslim conflagration that pitted Muslim-majority Kashmir and Hindu-majority Jammu against each other. Here too, we shall see, religious leadership had only a peripheral role, even though both the causes and the course of the mobilization centered on questions of faith.

We conclude that, historically, there has been no reason to turn to moderate religious heads for a resolution of political conflicts. Ever since the first decades of the last century, the mass political leadership in Jammu and Kashmir drew its legitimacy, at least in part, as a representative and champion of religious causes. Secular political mobilization and religious chauvinism were closely, often inextricably, enmeshed. Politicians—not priests—held the keys to the resolution of religion-driven conflicts, and continue to do so.

RELIGION AND THE KASHMIR DISPUTE

The origins of the Kashmir dispute are complex and can be traced to the decolonization process in South Asia.[1] It is of course well beyond the scope of this brief chapter to deal with the subject at any length. Instead only a synoptic account of its origins will be spelled out here. At the time of the close of colonial disengagement from the subcontinent, two classes of states existed under the aegis of the British Indian Empire. The first were the states of British India directly ruled from Whitehall through New Delhi. The second were the so-called princely states, which were nominally independent as long as they recognized the British Crown as the paramount authority in India. Some 562 in number, these rulers of these states had controlled all subjects barring foreign affairs, defense, and communications (see Ramusack 2004).

In the aftermath of World War II, faced with two irreconcilable nationalist movements, one based upon secular nationalism and the other on putatively primordial ties of faith, the British chose to partition the subcontinent. Lord Mountbatten, the last British viceroy, gave the rulers of the princely states a choice: they could accede to either India or Pakistan based upon their location and demographic composition. However, he conceded that certain "geographic compulsions" would have to be taken into account.[2]

The state of Jammu and Kashmir posed a unique problem. It had a Muslim-majority population, a Hindu monarch, and shared borders with the emergent states of India and Pakistan.[3] The monarch, Maharaja Hari Singh, was loath to join Pakistan for obvious reasons. Yet he was equally unwilling to cast his lot with India because he correctly feared that the Indian state would confiscate his vast landholdings (Ganguly 1997). As a consequence, even after the independence of India and Pakistan in August 1947, he refused to accede to either state.

In early October 1947 a tribal rebellion broke out in the western reaches of his state. Within days the Pakistani state entered the fray and assisted the rebels with weapons, logistics, and military personnel.[4] Owing to Pakistani support and the pusillanimity of the monarch's forces, the rebels and their supporters reached the outskirts of the capital city of Srinagar toward the end of October. In a panic, Maharaja Hari Singh appealed to Prime Minister Nehru of India for assistance. Nehru agreed to provide aid after two conditions had been met: in the absence of a referendum, he would seek the imprimatur of Sheikh Mohammed Abdullah, the leader of the largest popular and secular organization in the state, the Jammu and Kashmir National Conference, and the maharaja would also have to legally accede to India.[5] Once these conditions were met, Indian Army units were airlifted into Kashmir, thereby stopping the tribal and Pakistani advance but not before they had managed to seize about a third of the state's territory. Indian and Pakistani forces fought a bitter war until India referred the case to the UN Security Council on January 1, 1948. Subsequently, India and Pakistan have fought two more wars over the disputed territory in 1965 and in 1999. (In 1971 the two countries had gone to war, but not over the status of Kashmir [Sisson and Rose 1990.])

Within the portion of Jammu and Kashmir that it controlled, the Indian state allowed local political authorities substantial leeway—including substantial political corruption as long as they did not hint at secession. As a consequence, a coterie of individuals came to dominate the politics of the state (see Bhattacharjea 1994). To its credit, no regime in New Delhi sought to flood the region with settlers from other parts of India to change its demographic composition. Also, in an attempt to win the support of the citizens of this Muslim-majority state, it poured in vast development funds to improve the state's infrastructure.

Since 1989 India has been embattled in fighting a vicious ethnoreligious insurgency that has wracked the part of the state under its control. Among other things, the insurgency stemmed from the emergence of a new, politically sophisticated generation of Kashmiris who, unlike previous generations, were unwilling to tolerate the rampant political malfeasances that had characterized local politics (Ganguly 1996). Many of this generation were drawn to Islamist organizations such as the Jamaat-e-Islami and its student wing, the Islami Jamaat-e-Tulba, which from the mid-1970s launched a program of neofundamentalist mobilization that provided a core of cadre and support to jihadist groups. Later, Pakistani support transformed this discontent into a long-running military confrontation with the Indian state (see Sikand 2004).

Since the onset of the insurgency, the Indian state has managed to restore a modicum of both law and order in the state through an amalgam of the use of military force and the promise of political accommodation. However, it has yet to drain a reservoir of discontent that still seethes within much of the Muslim population of the state.

RELIGIOUS IDENTITY AND POLITICAL LEADERSHIP IN KASHMIR

No understanding of the relationship of modern politics and religious identity in Kashmir is possible without a careful engagement with its history. Economic discontent in the late nineteenth century prepared the ground for the emergence of mass politics in Jammu and Kashmir. In 1846 the East India Company signed the Treaty of Amritsar, which gave control of the territories that made up the preindependence state of Jammu and Kashmir to the Dogra monarch Maharaja Gulab Singh.

Less than a year after the Treaty of Amritsar was signed, Dogra tax policies led to a large-scale outflow of shawl workers to the Punjab plains, a development that decimated this economically vital industry. Widespread famine aggravated the situation and, in April 1865, Srinagar shawl workers rose in protest against the regime. "It was," F. M. Hassnain has argued, "perhaps the first organised demands day in the history of class struggle in India" (Hassnain 1988, 15). The shawl workers' revolt was brutally suppressed. Twenty-eight protestors were believed to have been killed by Dogra forces, and arrests and punitive fines were imposed on their leaders.

Despite some fitful efforts at administrative reform, working-class protests broke out with regularity in coming decades, mirroring trends in popular struggle across South Asia. The economic depression that followed the Great War of 1914–1918 further heightened these tensions. In 1924, for example, workers of the state-owned silk factory initiated a large-scale wage struggle, which again had to be suppressed by the use of brute force.

Kashmir's clerical establishment was ill-poised to take advantage of these conditions to expand its influence. Walter Lawrence, a British colonial administrator who was appointed to bring about major administrative changes at the end of the nineteenth century, observed that the Kashmir valley's Sunni-Muslim majority

> do not strike me as zealous or earnest in the profession of their faith and, except in their quarrels with the Shiahs [Shi'a], they seem free from all forms of fanaticism. It is true that they observe very strictly the fast of Ramzan, but they do not keep Friday as a day of rest and very few Kashmiris make the pilgrimage to Mecca, though the journey is now easy and does not cost more than Rs. 340. In 1892, twenty-one Kashmiris went to Mecca and this was an unusually large number. I do not base my ideas as to the laxness of Kashmiris in religious duties merely on my own observations. Holy men from Arabia have spoken to me with contempt of the feeble flame of Islam which burns in Kashmir and the local Mullahs talk with indignation of the apathy of the people. (1996, 285)

Dogra Jammu and Kashmir, though its ruling dynasty drew its legitimacy from Hinduism, gave institutional form to the practice of Islam. State-appointed clerics regulated everything from marriage to inheritance rights. However, their power was at best peripheral to the political life of the community. Lawrence found that "the leading Mullahs of the city, and occasionally a Mullah in the villages, exert some influence, but as a rule the ordinary Mullah is a man of no power" (1996, 291). He wrote:

> In the villages the Mullah acts as a Mufti [magistrate] in small cases and gives a decree. Thus the village Mullah can decide petty questions relating to the lawfulness of food and sometimes, if he is a man of some learning, he will give a decree regarding the division of land between members of a family. I have often read decrees given by the city Kazis [judges]. In one case which came before me the plaintiff produced one for possession of land. The defendant produced another for the possession of the same land, granted by the same Kazi. There was nothing strange in this, as the Kazi hears no evidence. He merely listens to the statement of his client and assuming that the statement is correct he gives his opinion. (1996, 296)

Lawrence offered two explanations for the marginal influence of the clerical establishment. First, he noted, peasant shrines built around syncretic practices, such as the veneration of holy relics and the worship of saints, had an influence "far greater than that exercised by mullahs in the mosque" (287). Second, he bluntly recorded that "the Mullah is ordinarily a man of no learning. In the *Lal Tahsil*, not one of the Mullahs can write" (290). People who could write—Indians trained in the new universities and colleges that had sprung up under imperial rule—thus emerged as leaders of the new mass politics in Kashmir.

By the time of the silk factory strike, the Dogra *durbar* (a court held by an Indian Prince) was under siege from this new class. Among its leading figures was Sheikh Mohammad Abdullah, the son of a peasant family who would have a central role in shaping Jammu and Kashmir's political future. Like many of the new class of educated young men emerging from Jammu and Kashmir, Sheikh Abdullah turned to Lahore for an education. He was influenced there by both secular-nationalist ideas and religious revivalism. Jammu and Kashmir, with its Hindu ruler and a predominantly Muslim population, was a place, historian Mridu Rai has noted, where "religion and politics became inextricably intertwined" (Rai 2004, 16–17).

Just before the silk factory strike, a group of Muslim clerical and business leaders submitted a memorandum that charged the Dogra monarchy with systematically excluding Muslims from governance and with obstructing their practice of their faith. It has been pointed out that Memorialists, as the authors of the 1924 memorandum were known, had overstated their case: Muslims did indeed occupy some positions of considerable influence, both in the coercive apparatus of the Dogra state and in its administrative organs, and there had been a considerable growth in the educational facilities available to them (Om 1982, 48, 107–8). Nonetheless, the fact remains that the traditional feudal elites, both Hindu and Muslim in the main the Hindu Pandit community but also some Rajput-caste notables of Jammu, were grossly overrepresented.

Abdullah, like many of his class and generation, cut his political teeth working on the Memorialist agenda. Among the most important of these was the Young Men's Muslim Association. Backed both by the new educated class and by influential clerics such as the Srinagar Mirwaiz Maulvi Mohammad Yusaf Shah, the Young Men's Association consisted of two major tendencies. One, represented by Abdullah, sought to use democratic and constitutional means to pressure the monarchy to bring about reforms for the advancement of Muslims. A minority, led by Ghulam Nabi Gilkar, sought to lead a revolution against Dogra rule intended to lead to the installation of a Muslim Sultan. In April 1931 an incident occurred that tipped the balance of power among the Young Men's Muslim Association in favor of the religious right. During Eid prayers that month, a Hindu police official in Jammu was alleged to have desecrated a copy of the Qu'ran. Gilkar pushed Abdullah to deliver a speech from a Srinagar mosque condemning the incident—after which violence broke out.

Religion, it thus became clear to the new leadership, could be a powerful tool for mobilization. In June 1931 the Young Men's Muslim Association met to elect its leaders. Toward the end of the meeting, Abdul Qadeer Ghazi Khan, a member of a clerical family with long-standing links to the Islamist ideologue Jamal-ud-Din Afghani Astarabadi, delivered a speech demanding an uprising against Hari Singh. Astarabadi had repeatedly called for jihad, which would free the world from British imperial rule; Khan hoped to bring about something of the kind within Jammu and Kashmir. Incarcerated for his seditious speech, Khan became a focal point for anti-Dogra sentiment in the Kashmir valley. Abdullah claimed that the cleric was being persecuted "for the cause of Islam and for the Muslim masses," and called for his supporters to be "prepared to be sacrificed for the sake of Islam" (Hassnain 1988, 45). On the day of Khan's trial, July 13, 1931, a fight broke out between protestors and policemen outside Srinagar's jail. What started as a minor scuffle rapidly escalated, and twenty-eight protestors were killed in the showdown that followed.

For the first time, events in Jammu and Kashmir generated a major pan-India political response. Muslim leaders from across India met at Shimla to express their outrage at the jail massacre and decided to call for a day of action against the monarchy. On September 22, the day chosen for this protest, thousands of people gathered at the Jamia Masjid in downtown Srinagar demanding the release of Sheikh Abdullah and Mufti Jalal-ud-Din, who had been incarcerated for their role in the violence that followed Khan's trial. Another massacre followed. As the protestors shouted "Islam zindabad [long live Islam]," the Maharaja's troops opened fire, killing at least twenty-five people (Hassnain 1988, 58).

After this second massacre, the Islamist character of the protest sharpened. Rioting directed at Hindu-owned businesses in urban Kashmir grew in scale.[6] Mirwaiz Yusaf Shah called for a jihad, leading thousands of his supporters to mass at the shrine of Dastagir Sahib in Srinagar armed with knives, swords, and guns (Hassnain 1988, 58). Soon, however, it became clear that the cleric had no desire to allow events to spiral out of hand. Using the services of several Muslim notables loyal to the throne, the monarch was able to defuse this second phase of protests and arrive at an accommodation with the Srinagar clerical establishment.

By September 1931 Hari Singh had succeeded in strengthening his accommodation with Yusaf Shah. It marked the end of the alliance between new and old elites in Kashmir. Abdullah and his supporters now formed a new organization, the All Jammu and Kashmir Muslim Conference. Yusaf Shah regularly charged this organization with being a front for the Ahmadiyya sect, deemed heretic by orthodox Sunni Muslims. Abdullah in turn claimed that the cleric had sold out to the Dogra monarchy.

Over the coming decade, the distance between the two groups steadily expanded. Abdullah's linkages with the all-India anti-imperial movement grew steadily, as did his attraction to the socialist ideas of the man who would become India's first prime minister, Jawaharlal Nehru. In June 1939 Sheikh Abdullah changed the name of the Muslim Conference, dropping the word that denoted its communal affiliation. It was now called the Jammu and Kashmir National Conference, signaling its commitment to represent all of the peoples of the state, irrespective of their faith. Over the next six years, the National Conference would increasingly align itself with the Indian National Congress. Abdullah's opponents, by contrast, would turn to the Muslim League, which was fighting for the creation of the state of Pakistan.

If the first decades of the twentieth century saw the emergence of new kinds of politics, they also witnessed the birth of a new form of faith. One major development was the arrival in Kashmir of the Jamaat Ahl-e-Hadis, a religious order that was created by followers of Sayyid Ahmad of Rai Bareilly. Ahmad died at Balakote in 1831, in what is present-day Pakistan-administered Kashmir, while waging an unsuccessful jihad against Maharaja Ranjit Singh's kingdom—a campaign that, the historian Ayesha Jalal has reminded us, still fires the imagination of numbers of Muslims in South Asia.[7]

Ahl-e-Hadith ideologues such as the clerics Siddiq Hasan Khan, Sanaullah Amritsari, and Nazir Husain rejected the accommodation Islam in India had made with its milieu. Muslims, they argued, must purge their practice of their faith of impious borrowings from Hinduism and return to the Qur'an and the Hadith—or traditions of the Prophet. Ahl-e-Hadith ideologues also called on Muslims to reject the four major schools of Islamic jurisprudence and instead model themselves on the companions of the Prophet.

Sayyed Hussain Shah Batku, a Delhi seminary student who carried the Ahl-e-Hadith message to Kashmir in 1925, denounced key practices of mainstream Islam in the state, such as the worship of shrines and veneration of relics. Along with his followers Anwar Shah Shopiani, Ghulam Nabi Mubaraki, and Sabzar Khan, Batku attacked traditionalists for following practices tainted by their Hindu heritage, such as the recitation of litanies before Namaaz. Not surprisingly, Batku came under sustained attack from traditionalist clerics who charged him with being an apostate and an infidel. The head priest of one of Kashmir's most revered shrines, the Khanqah-i-Maula, declared the Ahl-e-Hadith the *Dajjal*—or devil incarnate. Ahl-e-Hadith proselytizers faced a social boycott and were turned out of their mosques and neighborhoods. On some occasions, they faced violence (Wani 1997, 35–37).

Baktu's response was to cast himself as a defender of the faith, railing against heterodox Muslim sects such as the Ahmadis and the Shi'a, Hindu revivalists, and Christian missionaries, all of whom he claimed were working to expel Islam from Kashmir. Ahl-e Hadith clerics hit out at traditional Kashmiri mosques, saying their practice of singing litanies before congregational prayers in fact rendered them Hindu temples (see Khan 2000, 133, 138–51).

Within years of its arrival, the impact of the Ahl-e-Hadith was evident. Lawrence noted that "Wahabbi doctrines" had registered in the south Kashmir town of Shopian, where some two hundred families accepted the new religion. He noted that practitioners of peasant religion "declare that Wahabbi ideas are gaining ground" (Lawrence 1996, 285). However, he also noted the existence of counter-Salafi mobilization. "One idea commonly attributed by the orthodox Kashmiris to the Wahhabis," he wrote, "is that they deny the individual and exclusive right of a husband in his wife" (285). Despite its limited popular reach, the Ahl-e-Hadith had enormous ideological influence. As historian Chitralekha Zutshi has pointed out in her work, the "influence of the Ahl-e-Hadith on the conflicts over Kashmiri identities cannot be overemphasised" (Zutshi 2004, 150). Among other things, Yusaf Shah was thought to be a supporter of the Ahl-e-Hadith—thus giving the neoconservative religious school a point from which to influence mainstream Islam in Kashmir (ibid.). But while religion—in particular, neoconservative Islam—would play a critical role in shaping Jammu and Kashmir's ideological culture, it would be politicians, not clerics, who shaped the course of history.

THE HAZRATBAL CRISIS

The Hazratbal mosque stands gleaming on the east bank of the Dal Lake in Srinagar. In the course of Jammu and Kashmir's freedom movement, the shrine was appropriated by Sheikh Mohammad Abdullah—the Sher-i-Kashmir, or Lion of Kashmir, to his followers—as a counterweight to the Jamia Masjid mosque commanded by the cleric Mirwaiz Mohammad Farooq and his followers, the Bakras—so named for their goat-like long beards. It was home to perhaps the most revered holy relic in Jammu and Kashmir, the *moe-e-muqaddas*, a hair reputed to have belonged to the beard of the Prophet Mohammad. On December 27, 1963, the relic mysteriously disappeared from the shrine, provoking the first major crisis in Jammu and Kashmir since Pakistani irregulars had attacked it in 1947.

For the next seven days, a cross-party alliance of opposition figures known as the Action Committee emerged as the de facto administration of Jammu and Kashmir. Chaired by Maulana Mohammad Sayeed Masoodi, the Action Committee consisted both of National Conference figures, notably Sheikh Mohammad Abdullah's son, Farooq Abdullah—later chief minister—and also Islamists such as Mirwaiz Mohammad Farooq. Mobs attacked properties owned by the family of the New Delhi–backed chief minister, Bakshi Ghulam Mohammad. Even as the state government retreated behind well-guarded doors, the Action

Committee ran "an unauthorized parallel administration, controlling traffic prices and commerce" (Singh 1994, 265).

Just as suddenly as it disappeared, the *moe-e-muqaddas* was discovered by Indian investigators and restored to the shrine. B. N. Mullik, then-head of India's domestic covert intelligence service, has provided one of the few detailed accounts of the disappearance of the *moe-e-muqaddas* and its mysterious reappearance. Even the spymaster, however, shied away from spelling out the details (Mullik 1971, 87). One popular but empirically unfounded version of events is that the disappearance was engineered by Bakshi himself. The chief minister had resigned from office that October as part of a reorganization of the party apparatus, to be replaced by a relative lightweight, Khwaja Shamsuddin. Thirty-eight charges of corruption were eventually brought against Bakshi by a judicial investigator, of which fifteen were proven (Schofield 2003, 97). In the popular rendition of events, Bakshi hoped to use the chaos to establish his indispensability to the Indian state. There are several other anecdotal variations on this theme, none supported by any actual evidence.

One consequence of the cloak-and-dagger retrieval of the *moe-e-muqaddas* was that few on the streets of Srinagar were at first willing to believe that the hair authorities had produced was in fact the genuine relic. Agitators demanded that a *deedar*, a special exhibition of the relic sanctioned by custom, be held to establish its authenticity. Nehru, by senior Indian bureaucrat Y. D. Gundevia's account, personally interceded and overrode senior officials in the Union Ministry of Home Affairs who opposed the holding of a *deedar*. Maulana Masoodi, a prominent cleric, declared the relic to be genuine at the *deedar*, defusing the crisis. Things could well have gone the other way, Gundevia recalled: "As we went back to our aircraft to fly back to Delhi that afternoon, after a long silence [Nehru's Cabinet colleague and successor as Prime Minister, Lal Bahadur] Shastriji said to me, half musing to himself: 'Gundevia, what would have happened if the Maulana Saheb had declared, at that moment, that the *bal* [hair] wasn't genuine?' 'Don't think of it, for God's sake,' I said, 'it is all over!'" (Gundevia 1974, 1–82).

Barring this exercise of clerical authority, Islamic religious figures were to have no real role in the management of the Hazratbal crisis. Instead, political actors in New Delhi and Jammu and Kashmir now began to work to address the causes of the conflagration.

Prime Minister Jawaharlal Nehru understood that the crisis compelled him to "reconsider the basic premise and structure of the Kashmir policy" the Indian state had so far pursued (Behera 2000, 116). At an emergency subcommittee meeting of India's cabinet, he asserted that "if Kashmir is so destabilized that an ordinary incident of the theft of a relic provokes the people to the extent of trying to overthrow the government, it is time to adopt a new approach and to bring about a revolutionary change in our viewpoint" (Abdullah and Singh 1993, 147).

Ghulam Mohammad Sadiq, a lieutenant of Bakshi who had broken ranks with the chief minister shared this assessment. One of the beliefs which had under-pinned Indian policy, he argued, "is that the influence of Pakistan on the Kash-miri Muslims is fairly wide and firmly rooted" (Singh 1982, 267–68). From this assumption the government had developed "a primordial fear of the people." The *moe-e-muqaddas* agitation had torn apart the assumption that New Delhi could rule through "interested and self-seeking individuals."

One important outcome of the crisis was that it led New Delhi to release Sheikh Abdullah from jail. Abdullah had been arrested on charges of conspir-ing against the Indian state a decade earlier. However, Nehru now "realized that Sheikh Abdullah remained an important political force . . . [and that] it was nec-essary to release him to restore public confidence and reach a political accord" (Behera 2000, 116). Sadiq, who was chosen to succeed the effete Shamsuddin as chief minister in the wake of the crisis, supported this line of action, which he saw as part of a general "policy of liberalisation" (Bazaz 1978, 18).

Nehru, by some accounts, appears never to have been entirely convinced of the conspiracy charges in the first place, and saw Abdullah's release as the sym-bolic righting of an historic wrong. Gundevia has described the arrest and pros-ecution as a "coup," saying Nehru was never "convinced, at any stage, that Sheikh Abdullah was a communalist and was conspiring against India in league with the pro-Pakistan elements in Kashmir. . . . When I had the privilege of working very close to him, as Commonwealth Secretary and, later, as Foreign Secretary, I never heard Jawaharlal Nehru utter one unkind word against Sheikh, not to me and not in my hearing to anyone else," Gundevia recorded. He asserted that Nehru "never once maligned Sheikh Abdullah and never said one word against him" (Gundevia 1974, 118).

On April 8, 1964, Sheikh Abdullah became a free man. The Kashmir con-spiracy case was withdrawn.[8] The prolonged delays had become an embarrass-ment; one mainstream Indian newspaper had even proclaimed that while "Sheikh Abdullah [was] on trial, India [was] in the Dock" (Abdullah and Singh 1993, 144). In a classified note, Indian police official Surendra Nath recorded that "the case was withdrawn by the Government as a measure of normalisation and liber-alisation of the State['s] politics. It was hoped that this gesture would divert the attention and energy of a misguided section of people from clandestine and sub-versive activity to healthy political channels."[9]

In some senses, the *moe-e-muqaddas* crisis was just a metaphor for a larger crisis within Jammu and Kashmir politics. Its short-term resolution involved reli-gious leaders, notably in the legitimization of the restored relic. However, the cri-sis itself was born of specific political conditions. Indian policymakers came to understand at an early stage that its resolution would require political action, in this case the release of Sheikh Abdullah and, eventually, his return to power.

THE *BOOK OF KNOWLEDGE* CRISIS

Early in the 1970s India appeared to have settled the crisis in Jammu and Kashmir in its favor, once and for all. Pakistan had been sundered in two in 1971, its eastern wing having become the new nation-state of Bangladesh. If the war that gave birth to Bangladesh had made clear the decisive superiority of Indian arms, the Bengali-nationalist uprising that proceeded it tore apart Pakistan's foundational principle, that South Asia's Muslims were a nation.

Soon after the war, Prime Minister Indira Gandhi and Sheikh Mohammad Abdullah set about finalizing the terms of Jammu and Kashmir's accession to India. Few doubted that the outcome of their talks would favor India. It was not a prospect that motivated the religious right in Jammu and Kashmir.

In May 1973 a student in Anantnag was leafing through an old encyclopedia, Arthur Mee's *Book of Knowledge*, stored in the local college's library. He was appalled by one image he saw—a picture of the Archangel Gabriel dictating the text of the Qur'an to Mohammad. When clerics in Anantnag learned of the picture, it was denounced as blasphemous on the grounds that Islam prohibits the representation of the Prophet through graven images. College students in Anantnag went on strike, and the protests soon spread to Srinagar. Protestors demanded that the author of the encyclopedia be hanged—"a vain demand," Katherine Frank wryly noted, "since Arthur Mee had died in England in 1943" (Frank 2002, 365). The government of India banned sales of the encyclopedia, again a futile gesture, since it was no longer in print. However, protests continued, and the police eventually had to use fire to disperse violent crowds. At least four people died in the firing.

How does one account for the extraordinary outrage provoked by the *Book of Knowledge*? Some suspicion has always existed that the "discovery" of the encyclopedia cannot have been pure chance, for it had been in the town for decades, first in the collection of a school run by Christian missionaries and then at the Degree College's library. Whatever the truth, the fact is that the *Book of Knowledge* crisis must be read against a specific political circumstance: the steady growth of the Jamaat-e-Islami from the 1950s onward. Soon after independence, Yoginder Sikand has pointed out, the Jamaat-e-Islami had set up a wide network of schools to counteract what it believed was "an Indian onslaught in the cultural sphere" that caused "many young Kashmiris . . . to lose their Islamic moorings" (Sikand 2002, 733).

Jamaat schools—like its industrial-scale production of propagandistic literature—also represented a political project. Sikand cites one insider as suggesting that the schools were "set up in order to lead a silent revolution, to keep alive the memory of Kashmiri independence and of India's brutal occupation of the state." Moreover:

It was widely believed in JIJK [Jamaat-e-Islami] circles that a carefully planned Indian conspiracy was at work to destroy the Islamic identity of the Kashmiris, through Hinduizing the school syllabus and spreading immorality and vice among the youth. It was alleged that the government of India had dispatched a team to Andalusia, headed by the Kashmiri Pandit [politician] D. P. Dhar, to investigate how Islam was driven out of Spain and to suggest measures as to how the Spanish experiment could be repeated in Kashmir, too. Faced with what it saw as these menacing threats, the JIJK felt the compelling need for a comprehensive educational system of its own to save the Kashmiri Muslim youth from Indian cultural imperialism. (Sikand 2002, 733–34)

No hard evidence exists that Jamaat cadre spearheaded the *Book of Knowledge* riots: investigation records maintained by the Jammu and Kashmir police for this period are sketchy at best. For policymakers in both New Delhi and Srinagar, the message of the *Book of Knowledge* riots would have been unmistakable: while the war of 1971 may have proved the undoing of Pakistan, anti-India forces within Jammu and Kashmir were far from spent. As during the Hazratbal crisis, Islamists had demonstrated their ideological authority as well as the existence of an urban constituency who believed that their faith was under attack in India. All through 1974 the point was hammered home as cadre loyal to the Srinagar-based cleric Mirwaiz Mohammad Farooq clashed with workers of Sheikh Abdullah's Plebiscite Front rivals, claiming that their rival was on the edge of betraying Kashmir's claims to nationhood (Schofield 2003, 125).

Amid this street drama, Indira Gandhi began a series of closed-doors meetings with Abdullah in an effort to marginalize the Mirwaiz and the Jamaat-e-Islami. Her principal adviser on Jammu and Kashmir, G. Parthasarathi, held a parallel series of discussions with Abdullah's key lieutenant, Mirza Afzal Beg. Sheikh Abdullah pushed hard for fresh elections to be held in Jammu and Kashmir, hoping that a poll victory would enhance his bargaining position. Indira Gandhi would have none of it but offered him the chief minister's position in place of Syed Mir Qasim, who served as chief minister from 1971–75 (Frank 2002, 366). Sheikh Abdullah took the bait. Qasim resigned on February 23, 1975. The next day Indira Gandhi made public the six-point formula that Beg and Parthasarathi had signed in secrecy four months earlier.

The Beg-Parthasarathi Agreement, as it came to be known, affirmed that New Delhi would "continue to have power to make laws relating to the prevention of activities directed towards disclaiming, questioning or disrupting the sovereignty and territorial integrity of India or bringing about cession of a part of the territory of India or secession of a part of the territory of India from the Union." While such laws already existed, the agreement represented a commitment by

Sheikh Abdullah that he would no longer seek independence. The Delhi Agreement went on to assert that Jammu and Kashmir was "a constituent unit of the Union of India." This, again, was not a novel formula; Sheikh Abdullah had said as much on several occasions. It did, however, mark a formal renunciation of the Plebiscite Front's raison d'être and paved the way for its return to mainstream politics. Critically, the Delhi Agreement mandated that "provisions of the Constitution of India already applied to the state of Jammu and Kashmir without adaptation or modification are unalterable" (Beg and Parthasarathi 1974).

In effect, this meant that Sheikh Abdullah concurred with the restructuring of Jammu and Kashmir's relationship with India, much of which had been carried out while he was in jail. No agreement could be arrived at on the sixth issue before Beg and Parthasarathi, Sheikh Abdullah's demand that the governor and chief minister of Jammu and Kashmir be called its sadr-e-riyasat and wazir-e-azam, or president and prime minister, as had been the situation prior to 1965. It was therefore "remitted to the Principals" and was never to be discussed again until the late 1990s.

From 1975 to 1977 Indira Gandhi's regime suspended India's democratic institutions and engaged in a brutal crackdown against political opponents (Hart 1976). Although the emergency had nothing to do with Jammu and Kashmir, the Jamaat-e-Islami had been proscribed along with several other communal organizations of both the Hindu and Islamist right. Much of the organization's leadership was jailed, and its publications were suppressed. As such, the Jamaat and its clerical allies had little opportunity to protest the Abdullah–Indira Gandhi deal. Not surprisingly, Indira Gandhi's crackdown on the Jamaat-e-Islami had Sheikh Abdullah's enthusiastic endorsement. In one speech he had described the Islamist organization's schools as "the real source for spreading communal poison" (Behera 2000, 143). Some 125 Jamaat-run schools, with more than 550 teachers and 25,000 students, were banned. So were another 1,000 evening schools run by the organization which reached out to an estimated 50,000 boys and girls (Sikand 2002, 736).

In March 1977, however, Indira Gandhi withdrew the emergency and called general elections. She was defeated. The coming to power of the Janata Party, a coalition spanning socialists, centrists, and Hindu chauvinists, provoked a crisis within the Jammu and Kashmir Assembly, and elections in the state had to be called early.

Having emerged more or less unscathed from the emergency, and wearing the halo of political martyrdom, the Jamaat-e-Islami sought to capitalize on the new situation. It allied itself with the Janata Party both at the national level and in Jammu and Kashmir. Sheikh Abdullah responded to the threat with unconcealed appeals to communal sentiment. A vote for the Jamaat-e-Islami, Sheikh Abdullah claimed, was a vote for the Jana Sangh, a Hindu chauvinist constituent of the Janata Party whose "hands were still red with the blood of Muslims" (Behera 2000, 143). Islam, National Conference leaders insisted, would be in danger if the Jamaat-Janata alliance took power. Beg went one step further and appropriated the pro-Pakistan position traditionally taken by Mirwaiz Farooq. At rally after rally, he produced a green handkerchief with Pakistani rock-salt—as opposed to Indian sea-salt—wrapped in it, signaling support for that country to his audience (Schofield 2003, 125). National Conference cadre administered oaths on the Qur'an to potential voters, through which they pledged their commitment to the party. Clerics were imported from Uttar Pradesh and Bihar to campaign in Muslim-majority areas of Jammu. Sheikh Abdullah, wary of the consequences of pushing New Delhi too hard, was carefully to assert that "Kashmir was a part of India and Kashmiris were Indians," but added that "if we are not assured of a place of honour and dignity in India, we shall not hesitate to secede" (Behera 2000, 140).

Sheikh Abdullah's incendiary campaign paid off: the National Conference won forty-seven of seventy-five seats in the Jammu and Kashmir Assembly, a decisive majority. Moreover, the National Conference secured more than 46 percent of the popular vote, an exceptionally high proportion in Indian elections. By contrast, the Jamaat-e-Islami could secure just one of the nineteen seats it contested and received only 3.59 percent of the statewide vote (Election Commission of India, n.d.). This was a poorer performance than even the fledgling Janata Party, which picked up thirteen seats and secured 23.7 percent of the popular vote. However, Sheikh Abdullah's victory had come at a price. His aggressive use of Islamist themes and images during the campaign had cost him support in Jammu, particularly among Hindus. Just one of the seven seats the National Conference picked up in Jammu, that of Ramban, had a Hindu majority (ibid.). In effect, the National Conference had abandoned its historic project of building itself into a spokesperson for the entire state and had retreated instead to its heartland in the valley. More importantly, the party had opened the gates for the large-scale use of religion in mass politics, a weapon that, in time, others would also learn to use.

For the moment, however, Sheikh Abdullah's rule seemed unshakable. Despite the anger of Islamists such as Mohammad Farooq and the despair of figures such as Altaf Khan, Sheikh Abdullah's return to political center stage put an end to visible anti-India protest. While the Sher-i-Kashmir himself was to regret his capitulation to New Delhi and his decision to ally with the congress, on the substance of the agreement there could be no withdrawal (Schofield 2003, 122). Until Sheikh Abdullah's death in 1982, the secessionists would continue to stage an unhappy retreat.

As with the Hazratbal riots, the *Book of Knowledge* crisis was also centered on a religious theme. However, both its genesis and its resolution were political. Clerics played some role in precipitating the early violence that characterized the movement, but the principal actors who gave it shape and content—Indira

Gandhi, Sheikh Abdullah, and his Jamaat-e-Islami opponents—were all political groupings. In the short term, the crisis was resolved by the use of the state's coercive instruments, specifically the use of lethal force against rioters. In the long term, though, New Delhi made concessions to a political ally in Kashmir, which it empowered against its Islamist opponents.

In both of the crises we have examined so far, Islam in the Kashmir valley was the sole religious force driving major political mobilizations. We shall now turn to a third crisis, in which the Jammu region's Hindus were pitted against the Kashmir valley's Muslims, to see if even this confrontational religious dynamic gave religious leaders a significant role in politics.

KASHMIR'S "SHRINE WAR"

Pakistani flags fluttered from the top of the clock tower in Srinagar's Lal Chowk on India's independence day in 2008. In the worst years of the two-decade-long Pakistan-backed jihad, Indian forces in Srinagar had ensured the national flag flew from Lal Chowk each independence day. As usual, Central Reserve Police Force (CRPF) personnel hoisted the Indian flag on the clock tower on the morning of August 15. Later that afternoon, though, Islamist protestors marched on Lal Chowk. With strict orders not to fire on unarmed protestors, and without backup to block the march, CRPF personnel brought down the Indian flag and withdrew (Ghosh 2008). Elsewhere in Srinagar, mobs destroyed police and CRPF posts, attacked police stations, and burned down the offices of pro-India politicians (Irfan 2008a). Six weeks of protests had succeeded in bringing about what a two-decade jihad in Jammu and Kashmir had not achieved. How did this come about, and who were the actors who achieved it?

If nothing else, the genesis of the shrine-land war demonstrates that seismic consequences can result from the smallest of causes. In the summer of 2004 Jammu and Kashmir's chief minister, Mufti Mohammad Saeed, and its federally appointed governor, S. K. Sinha, locked horns over the management of the Amarnath Yatra—an annual pilgrimage to a cave-temple in the mountains above the town of Pahalgam. Saeed shot down Sinha's decision to extend the pilgrimage to eight weeks from four. Five Hindu cabinet ministers from the Jammu region—all members of Saeed's coalition partners, the congress—submitted their resignations in protest (Puri 2005).

Amid this feud, the Jammu and Kashmir High Court ordered the government to give the Shri Amarnath Shrine Board (SASB), which manages the pilgrimage, the right to use forestland to provide shelter and sanitation for pilgrims. It took another two years of legal wrangling, though, before the SASB was finally given permission for "raising pre-fabricated structures only for camping purposes of pilgrims without going in for construction of permanent structures." The government order granting permission made clear that that the "proprietary status of [the] forest land shall remain unchanged" (Swami 2008a).

Islamist patriarch Syed Ali Shah Geelani of the hardline Tehreek-i-Hurriyat, though, mobilized against the order, claiming it was part of a conspiracy to settle Hindus in the region. At one press conference, he warned that Sinha had been working "on an agenda of changing the demography of the state." He warned, "I caution my nation that if we don't wake up in time, India and its stooges will succeed and we will be displaced" (Majid 2008). Later he asserted that the land-use rights granted to the SASB were part of a covert enterprise code-named Operation Yatra, which was "devised on the lines of Israel's strategy of settlement in Palestine" (Irfan 2008b). The SASB, he went on, was "pursuing the similar method to settle Hindus here." He was later to hold out dark hints that a genocide of Kashmiri Muslims, modeled on the Partition of India pogroms, was being planned (Fayyaz 2008a).

Geelani's position stemmed from his long-standing belief that Islam and Hinduism were locked in an irreducible civilizational opposition. At an October 26 rally in Srinagar, Geelani had made clear this position, saying that "the people of state should, as their religious duty, raise voice against India's aggression." This duty, he argued, stemmed from the fact that to "practice Islam completely under the subjugation of India is impossible because human beings in practice worship those whose rules they abide by" (Dar 2007). Geelani had long located the legitimacy of the secessionist movement in Jammu and Kashmir in the supposed oppositional dualities of Hindus and Muslims. In matters of faith, belief, and customs, he argued in his prison diaries, Hindus and Muslims are set irrevocably apart because they are divided by such matters as food, clothing, and lifestyles. He described it as being as difficult for Muslims to live in a Hindu milieu as "for a fish to stay alive in a desert." Muslims, he argued, cannot live harmoniously with a Hindu majority without their own religion and traditions coming under a grave threat, one major factor being Hinduism's capacity to assimilate other religions. For Islam to be preserved and promoted in Kashmir, it is necessary for it to be separated from India (Sikand 1998).

Matters came to a head when Saeed's People's Democratic Party (PDP), whose ministers had supported the land-use orders in the state cabinet, threw their weight behind Islamist calls for them to be revoked. PDP leaders were driven by the fact that a significant part of their constituency was affiliated with Kashmir's religious right. However, their congress coalition partners were unable to meet their demand, afraid it would undermine their position among their core constituency of Jammu Hindus. Sinha's successor as governor, N. N. Vohra, in his capacity as head of the shrine board, attempted to resolve the stalemate. He offered to surrender the land-use rights if the state government itself would provide all facilities to pilgrims, as it had been doing since 1979. Hoping to avert a showdown with the PDP, Chief Minister Ghulam Nabi Azad agreed. Later, under pressure from the party's central leadership in New Delhi to save the congress's alliance with the PDP, Azad revoked the land-use order altogether. However, the PDP pulled out of government days before a deadline it had set to resolve the crisis (Dogra 2008).

Now a second phase of the crisis began as Hindu chauvinist groups in Jammu began an agitation demanding the land back. Elements among them threatened to blockade traffic to Kashmir. It is unclear that there was, in fact, a significant blockade.[10] But the threat itself provided leverage to Geelani, and Mirwaiz Umar Farooq, a Srinagar-based cleric who chairs the rival All Parties Hurriyat Conference (APHC).

Acting on a call from the Pakistan-based United Jihad Council, both groups organized a march across the Line of Control, which divides Indian-administered and Pakistan-administered Kashmir, saying the economic blockade necessitated the opening of traffic from Srinagar to Muzaffarabad.[11] India had, in fact, been calling for free trade along the route, a demand Pakistan had rejected. However, the defiance of the Line of Control was an act the state simply could not countenance. To no one's surprise, force was used to stop the marchers: three people were killed, including a mid-ranking APHC leader. More than twenty other people died in subsequent clashes between police or soldiers and the protestors, often a consequence of attacks on the bunkers of police and army personnel by enraged mobs (Fayyaz 2008b).

Ever since 2002, when levels of jihadist violence in Jammu and Kashmir began to decline, Indian policymakers had assumed that the anti-India movement in the region would also slowly disappear. It was a seismic error of judgment. Faith and xenophobia became the twin poles of a long-running and powerful effective Islamist campaign that began in 2005, after it became evident to Islamists that the jihad on which their political position had been predicated was in terminal decline. Economic change and the social dislocation it had brought about provided the firmament for their revival. Islamists began to make the wider case that the secularization of culture in Kashmir—in turn the consequence of economic growth—constituted a civilizational threat.

Later Islamists leveraged the uncovering of a prostitution racket in Srinagar to argue that secularism and modernity were responsible for and an Indian conspiracy to undermine Jammu and Kashmir's Islamic character. Pro-Islamist scholar Hameeda Nayeem even claimed the scandal pointed "unequivocally towards a policy-based state patronage [of prostitution]" (Nayeem 2006). Significantly, the prostitution protests saw the first large-scale Islamist mob violence that went unchecked by the state. Geelani's supporters were allowed to gather at the home of alleged Srinagar prostitution-ring madam Sabina Bulla and raze the home to the ground. Mobs also attacked the homes of politicians charged with having used her services (Swami 2008e).

In the summer of 2007, the rape and murder of north Kashmir teenager Tabinda Gani was used to initiate a xenophobic campaign against the presence of migrant workers in the state. Addressing a June 24, 2007, rally at the town of Langate, Geelani said that "hundreds of thousands of non-state subjects had been pushed into Kashmir under a long-term plan to crush the Kashmiris."[12] He claimed that "the majority of these non-state subjects are professional criminals and should be driven out of Kashmir in a civilised way." His political ally, Hilal War, claimed that migrant workers' slums were "centres of all kinds of illegal business."[13] Language such as this inspired a serious of terrorist attacks on migrants, the last of which was the bombing of a bus carrying workers from Srinagar just as the shrine board protests began (Swami 2008e).

From these events Islamists learned that the objective conditions existed for xenophobic politics to succeed. Even on the eve of the shrine board protests, Islamists mobilized against a career counselor who, they claimed, had been dispatched to Srinagar schools to seduce students into a career of vice. An Anantnag schoolteacher also came under attack after a video surfaced showing that a group of his students had danced to pop film music on a holiday in Anantnag (Swami 2008d).

Part of the reason for Geelani's success was the absence of secular voices—either in political life or among public intellectuals—to challenge his contentions. No political group condemned his actions. Indeed, elements in the congress made opportunistic use of his mobilization. The PDP politicians, too, sought to appropriate Geelani's rhetoric in an effort to draw the electoral endorsement of his supporters. So, too, did the National Conference. All parties, as events have shown, miscalculated, to be swept away by the Islamist tide they failed to stem when it was just a trickle.

Across the Pir Panjal Mountains in Jammu, a near-identical chauvinist mobilization was under way—one that was even more invisible to analysts and the government than its Islamist counterpart. In the build-up to the 2002 elections, the Bharatiya Janata Party (BJP) found itself discredited by its failure to contain terrorism. Much of the Hindutva movement's cadre turned to a new grouping, the Jammu State Morcha (JSM). JSM leaders wanted a new, Hindu-majority state carved out of Jammu and Kashmir. In the end, both the JSM and the BJP were wiped out in the elections, winning just one seat each.

A new generation of Hindutva leaders then took control of Hindu neoconservative politics in Jammu. Soon after the congress–PDP government came to power, this new Hindutva leadership unleashed its first mass mobilizations. PDP leader and former chief minister Mufti Mohammad Saeed's calls for demilitarization and self-rule, Hindutva leaders claimed, pointing to the expulsion of Pandits from Kashmir at the outset of the jihad, proved that Saeed was now preparing the ground for the expulsion of Hindus—and Hinduism—from Jammu.

From 2003 Hindutva groups sought to forge these anxieties into a concrete political mobilization around the issue of cattle slaughter. Hindutva cadre would interdict trucks carrying cattle and use their capture to stage protests. It was not as if the anti-cow-slaughter movement had stumbled on a great secret. For decades, cow-owning farmers—generally Hindus—had sold to traders from Punjab and Rajasthan old livestock that no longer earned them an income. In turn, the traders sold their herds to cattle traffickers on India's eastern border, who fed the demand for meat among the poor of Bangladesh. But Hindutva groups understood that the cow was a potent—and politically profitable—metaphor. In December 2007, for example, Vishwa Hindu Parishad (VHP, a Hindu organization) and Bajrang Dal cadre organized large-scale protests against the reported sacrificial slaughter of cows at the villages of Bali Charna, in the Satwari area of Jammu, and Chilog, near Kathua District's Bani town.[14] Riots had also taken place in the villages around Jammu's Pargwal area in March 2005, after Hindutva activists made bizarre claims that a cow had been raped.[15]

It should be noted, however, that religious leaders had a peripheral role in these mobilizations. For example, south Kashmir-based Jamiat Ahl-e-Hadis neofundamentalist activist Maqbool Akhrani mobilized against migrant workers in 2006; the workers were part of a campaign by India's intelligence services to "divert attention from real issues and that is why new things like country made liquor are pushed into the valley" (Bhat 2006). As noted earlier, similar xenophobic claims informed the shrine war. However, Akhrani and the Jamiat Ahl-e-Hadis, although they participated in the anti-shrine-land mobilization, were at best marginal to its course. Indeed, senior Ahl-e-Hadith leaders continued to engage with the Jammu and Kashmir government to build a denominational university and refused to condemn Gov. S. K. Sinha (Swami 2008c). Kashmir's quasi-official grand mufti, Maulvi Mohammad Bashir-ud-Din, also made interventions in the course of the shrine war.[16]

However, it bears note that—like the Jamiat Ahl-e-Hadis leadership—Bashir-ud-Din did not address a single rally of consequence. That task was left to leaders of the Tehreek-i-Hurriyat and APHC, none of whom bar Mirwaiz Farooq was a religious leader—and even in this one case, a religious leader with influence only in a small part of Srinagar. Hindu religious leaders, such as Swami Dinesh Bharati, who played roles in the Hindu chauvinist agitation there, were also leaders of obscure denominations and temples and had no real clerical authority.[17] No figure associated with major temples, such as the priests of the Mata Vaishno Devi or Raghunath Mandir, appear to have participated in the protests.

Although it is still unclear just what consequences the shrine war might have for Jammu and Kashmir, though, this much is clear: politicians, not priests, both initiated the conflict and controlled its working. It is clear there were no clerics with influence of an order who could have prevented its outbreak or tempered its course.

CONCLUSIONS

Our examination of the three cases leads us to three inexorable conclusions. First, religion and politics are inextricably intertwined in Jammu and Kashmir. The ethnoreligious demography of the state, its fraught history in the context of Indo-Pakistani relations and its significance for a constitutionally secular Indian polity ensures that most political issues will inevitably take on a religious coloration.

Second, both secular and religiously oriented politicians have on many occasions exploited and manipulated religious sentiments to advance personal political agendas. This propensity to exploit religious issues to advance short-term and parochial agendas has proven to be explosive and has had deleterious consequences for political development in the state.

Finally, it is far from clear that religious authorities have played a central role in either promoting or dampening religious tensions, even though the neofundamentalist religious movements they lead have contributed significantly to the sharpening of ethnic-religious group boundaries. Their roles, for the most part, have been on the margins of these conflicts. They have rarely, if ever, precipitated in any of the crises that have wracked the state and have played very limited roles in containing them once they ensued. As a consequence, and despite the salience of religion in the politics of Jammu and Kashmir, it appears that in many ways this case constitutes an important outlier in this volume.

NOTES

1. For two discussions, see Brines (1968) and Ganguly (2001); for some historical background to the conflict, see Hodson (1969).
2. Namely, that if a princely state was well within one of the two emergent states, it would be forced to accede to the relevant state regardless of the monarch's preferences or its demographic composition. On this subject, see Campbell-Johnson (1953).
3. In recent years a controversy has arisen about whether or not the state shared borders with the two emergent states. The controversy stems from the writings of Alastair Lamb, see Lamb (1994); for an Indian rejoinder to Lamb see Jha (1996); for a careful assessment of the evidence and a refutation of Lamb's claims see Illahi (2003).

4. The evidence of Pakistani involvement in the rebellion can be found in Khan (1975).
5. On the significance of Sheikh Mohammed Abdullah, see Das Gupta (1968).
6. For an account of the rioting, see Swarup and Aggarwal (1992, 72–74).
7. For the origins of the Ahl-e-Hadith, see Jalal (2008, 64).
8. Contrary to the assertion of one scholar, Sheikh Abdullah was not actually exonerated of the charges against him, at least in a legal sense see (Schofield 2003, 91). The state merely dropped the prosecution against him, leaving the question of his guilt unresolved. See [SECRET], *Report on Pakistani Organized Subversion, Sabotage and Infiltration in Jammu and Kashmir* (Jammu and Kashmir: Criminal Investigation Department, 1966), 27–28; also see Gundevia (1974, 118).
9. [SECRET], *Report on Pakistani Organized Subversion.*
10. "Centre: No Economic Blockade of Valley, Pak Cashing in on Turmoil," *Indian Express* (New Delhi), August 17, 2008. www.indianexpress.com/printerFriendly /349694.html. Also see Singh (2008).
11. "March towards Muzaffarabad: UJC," *Rising Kashmir* (Srinagar), August 7, 2008.
12. "Non-Kashmiris Should Be Seen Off: Geelani," *Greater Kashmir* (Srinagar), July 25, 2007, 3.
13. "Construction Works to Be Hit by Labourers Exodus," *Daily Excelsior* (Jammu), August 4, 2007, 1.
14. "Tension over Cow Sacrifice," *Daily Telegraph* (Kolkata), December 23, 2008. www.telegraphindia.com/1071223/jsp/nation/story_8700385.jsp.
15. "'Unnatural Act' with Cow Leads to Protests in Akhnoor," *Expressindia.com*, March 28, 2005. www.expressindia.com/news/fullstory.php?newsid=44002.
16. "Lift Blockade or We Lift Durbar," *Rising Kashmir* (Srinagar), August 3, 2008.
17. "Dinesh Bharti's Detention under PSA Ordered," *Daily Excelsior* (Jammu), August 26, 2008, 1.

REFERENCES

Abdullah, Sheikh Mohammad, and Khushwant Singh. 1993. *Flames of the Chinar.* New Delhi: Viking.
Bazaz, Prem Nath. 1978. *Democracy through Intimidation and Terror.* New Delhi: Heritage.
Beg, Mirza Mohammad Abdullah, and G. Parthasarathi. 1974. "Agreed Conclusions," *South Asian Terrorism Portal*, New Delhi, November 13. www.satp.org/satporgtp /countries/india/states/jandk/documents/papers/sheikh_indira_accord_1975 .htm.
Behera, Navnita Chadha. 2000. *State, Identity and Violence: Jammu, Kashmir and Ladakh.* New Delhi: Manohar.
Bhat, Hilal. 2006. "Bihari Labourers Producing Desi Liquor in South Kashmir." *Greater Kashmir* (Srinagar), June 29, 3.

Bhattacharjea, Ajit. 1994. *Kashmir: The Wounded Valley*. New Dehli: UBS Publisher Distributors.

Brines, Russell. 1968. *The Indo-Pakistani Conflict*. New York: Pall Mall.

Campbell-Johnson, Alan. 1953. *Mission with Mountbatten*. New York: Dutton.

Dar, A. M. 2007. "Geelani Slams Mainstream Politicians." *Greater Kashmir* (Srinagar) October 27.

Das Gupta, Jyoti Bhusan. 1968. *Jammu and Kashmir*. The Hague: Martinus Nijhoff.

Dogra, Chander Suta. 2008. "Echoes in Hell." *Outlook* (New Delhi), August 18.

Election Commission of India. n.d. "Key Highlights of General Election, 1977, to the Legislative Assembly of Jammu and Kashmir." New Delhi: Election Commission of India.

Fayyaz, Ahmad Ali. 2008a. "Stronger Geelani's New Slogan: Ham Pakistani Hain." *Daily Excelsior* (Jammu), August 19, 1.

———. 2008b. "Toll Reaches 21 as One More Killed in CRPF Firing." *The Daily Excelsior* (Jammu), August 15, 1.

Frank, Katherine. 2002. *Indira: The Life of Indira Nehru Gandhi*. Boston: Houghton Mifflin.

Ganguly, Sumit. 1996. "Explaining the Kashmir Insurgency: Political Mobilization and Institutional Decay." *International Security* 21:76–107.

———. 1997. *The Crisis in Kashmir: Portents of War, Hopes of Peace*. New York: Cambridge University Press.

———. 2001. *Conflict Unending: Indo-Pakistani Tensions since 1947*. New York: Columbia University Press.

Ghosh, Avijit. 2008. "Tricolour at 8 a.m., Flags of Separatists at 4.00 p.m." *Times of India* (Mumbai), August 16. http://timesofindia.indiatimes.com/JK_Tricolour _at_8am_separatist_flags_at_4pm/articleshow/3369371.cms.

Gundevia, Y. D. 1974. "On Sheikh Abdullah." In *The Testament of Sheikh Abdullah*. New Delhi: Palit and Palit.

Hart, Henry. 1976. *Indira Gandhi's India: A Political System Re-Appraised*. Boulder, CO: Westview Press.

Hassnain, F. M. 1988. *Freedom Struggle in Kashmir*. New Delhi: Rima Publishing House.

Hodson, H. V. 1969. *The Great Divide: Britain, Indian, Pakistan*. London: Hutchinson.

Illahi, Shereen. 2003. "The Radcliffe Boundary Commission and the Fate of Kashmir." *The India Review* 2:77–102.

Irfan, Hakeem. 2008a. "Angry Mobs Storm CRPF Bunkers, Police Stations." *Rising Kashmir* (Srinagar), August 14. www.risingkashmir.com/index.php?option=com _content&task=view&id=5879&Itemid=1.

———. 2008b. "Operation Yatra Devised on Israeli Lines: Geelani." *Rising Kashmir* (Srinagar), June 13.

Jalal, Ayesha. 2008. *Partisans of Allah*. Cambridge, MA: Harvard University Press.

Jha, Prem Shankar. 1996. *Kashmir 1947: Rival Versions of History*. Bombay: Oxford University Press.

Khan, Akbar. 1975. *Raiders in Kashmir*. Islamabad: National Book Foundation.

Khan, Bashir Ahmad. 2000. "The Ahl-i Hadith: A Socio-Religious Reform Movement in Kashmir." *The Muslim World* 90:133–51.

Kraalwari, Maqbool Shah. 1912. *Greeznama [The Peasant's Tale]*. Srinagar: Privately printed.

Lamb, Alastair. 1994. *Kashmir: Birth of a Tragedy*. Hertingfordbury: Roxford Books.

Lawrence, Walter. 1996. *The Valley of Kashmir*. Jammu: Kashmir Kitab Ghar.

Majid, Zulfikar. 2008. "I Caution My Nation: Wake Up: Geelani." *Kashmir Press Service*, June 24. http://kashmirpress.com/the-news/1-latest-news/166-i-caution-my-nation-wake-up-geelani.

Mullik, B. N. 1971. *Chinese Betrayal: My Years with Nehru*. Bombay: Allied Publishers.

Nayeem, Hameeda. 2006. "Unite, in Humanity." *Indian Express* (New Delhi), May 11, 6.

Om, Hari. 1982. *Mulism of Jammu & Kashmir: A Study of the Spread of Education and Consciousness, 1857–1925*. New Delhi: Archives Publishers.

Puri, Luv. 2005. "Amarnath Yatra: Court Vests Authority with Shrine Board." *The Hindu* (Chennai), April 17. www.hindu.com/2005/04/17/stories/2005041706750700.htm.

Rai, Mridu. 2004. *Hindu Rulers, Muslim Subjects: Islam, Rights and the History of Kashmir*. Princeton, NJ: Princeton University Press.

Ramusack, Barbara N. 2004. *The Indian Princes and Their States*. Cambridge: Cambridge University Press.

Schofield, Victoria. 2003. *Kashmir in Conflict: India, Pakistan and the Unending War*. Minneapolis: IB Tauris.

Sikand, Yoginder. 1998. "For Islam and Kashmir: The Prison Diaries of Sayyed 'Ali Gilani of the Jama'at-i-Islami of Jammu and Kashmir." *The Journal of Muslim Minority Affairs* 18: 243.

———. 2002. "The Emergence and Development of the Jamaat-e-Islami of Jammu and Kashmir." *Modern Asian Studies* 36:733.

———. 2004. "Kashmir: From Nationalist Liberation to Islamist Jihad." In *Muslims in India since 1947: Islamic Perspectives on Inter-Faith Relations*, edited by Yoginder Sikand. London: Routledge Curzon.

Singh, Harmeet. 2008. "Army Controls Highway, Traffic Restored," *Greater Kashmir* (Srinagar), August 4. www.greaterkashmir.com/news/2008/Aug/4/army-controls-highway-traffic-restored-45.asp.

Singh, Karan. 1982. *Heir Apparent: An Autobiography*. New Delhi: Oxford University Press.

———. 1994. *Autobiography*. New Delhi: Oxford University Press.

Sisson, Richard, and Leo Rose. 1990. *War and Secession*. Berkeley: University of California Press.

Swami, Praveen. 2008a. "Anatomy of the Shrine Board Crisis." *The Hindu* (Chennai), June 30. www.hindu.com/2008/06/30/stories/2008063059891300.htm.

———. 2008b. "Bombing in Srinagar a Response to Islamist Calls." *The Hindu* (Chennai), July 25. www.hindu.com/2008/07/25/stories/2008072556861500.htm.

———. 2008c. "Islamic University Falls Victim to Kashmir's Shrine War." *The Hindu* (Chennai), August 21. www.hindu.com/2008/08/21/stories/2008082155121100 .htm.

———. 2008d. "Kashmir: The War for Hearts and Minds." *The Hindu* (Chennai), June 4. www.hindu.com/2008/06/04/stories/2008060455311000.htm.

———. 2008e. "Righteousness, Religion and Right-wing Politics." *The Hindu* (Chennai), May 15. www.hindu.com/2006/05/15/stories/2006051504021000.htm.

Swarup, Devendra, and Sushil Aggarwal. 1992. *The Roots of the Kashmir Problem: The Continuing Battle between Secularism and Communal Separatism*. New Delhi: Manthan Prakashan.

Wani, Mushtaq Ahmad, 1997. *Muslim Religious Trends in Kashmir in Modern Times*. Patna: Khuda Bakhsh Oriental Public Library.

Zutshi, Chitralekha. 2004. *Languages of Belonging*. Oxford: Oxford University Press.

CONCLUSION

⤳

From Terror to Tolerance to Coexistence in Deeply Divided Societies

TIMOTHY D. SISK

Conflict emanating from "internal" wars—conflicts within states—remains the principal, immediate threat to international peace and security into the opening decades of the twenty-first century. Today's most violent crises most occur in countries riven by a volatile mix of factors that give rise to violence, often including religious drivers or manifestations of deep social divisions. Indeed, most country-specific conflict assessment instruments in use in the policy arena today are driven by the reality of analyzing intersections between "need, greed, and creed" (Arnson and Zartman 2005). Thus, as this volume shows, religion cannot be fully isolated as a singular "root cause" of violence because the interactions among belief, social, economic, and political processes are deeply complex and case-contingent. At the same time, the history of the twentieth century would also suggest that there is no reason for complacency in the prevention of mass atrocities and genocide, often justified or loosely inspired by systems of belief and (typically extremist) interpretation of religious doctrine.

The study of "ethnic conflict" that burgeoned in the immediate post–Cold War era has been eclipsed—as several authors in this volume refer—by a narrow set of factors focusing on economic drivers of conflict (Collier et al. 2003). The research presented in this book shows that focusing solely, or even primarily, on the material causes of conflict in divided societies mistakenly discounts the role of religion in the organization, justification, and manifestation of grievances grounded in the material *and* social aspects of conflict. There is fallacy in reducing conflict to the material; religious leaders directly influence conflict causes, trajectories, and outcomes in deeply divided societies.

This volume contributes to our understanding by exploring in comparative analysis how religious belief has affected the trajectory of recent conflicts in war-torn countries such as Iraq, Lebanon, Nigeria, and of conflicts that were putatively settled but still show deep divisions, such as Northern Ireland, and situations where intercommunal strife has escalated in recent years (for example, Kyrgyzstan or Egypt). Religious belief and religious behavior continue to matter in the oscillation of these conflict-riven countries between war and peace. And they affect the extent to which there is doctrinal justification of terror—either by insurgents, as in the case of the terror of insurgents (e.g., mass bombings, as in Iraq today) or by the state thorough other forms of mass violence, such as genocide.

Religious leaders are in many ways reflective of the broader social forces in which they are embedded, and they are rarely able to mobilize with hateful motives or advance the causes of peace when these underlying social conditions are prohibitive. The case of Francois Bazaramba, an ex-Baptist pastor accused of organizing killings in the Rwanda genocide of 1994, illustrates and reinforces the essential finding that in some circumstances, indeed, religious leaders may well provide the underlying moral or ideological justification or "hateful motive" for mass killing. Bazaramba's trial began in Finland in September 2009, where he is accused of planning, leading, and carrying out the 1994 genocide that killed eight hundred thousand or more in one hundred days.[1] According to journalist Bob Allen's account.

> [In Rwanda], both groups lived in totally integrated communities, until a propaganda campaign incited local citizens to root the Tutsis out as part of their civic duty. Churches were not immune from the tensions ... South African Missiological Society, missiologist J. J. Kritzinger said that while most Hutu and Tutsi Christians fellowshipped warmly on the personal level, most accepted the prevailing wisdom that Hutus were not as capable as Tutsis to govern the country and thus divided themselves between "us" and "them." Churches did not challenge those stereotypes, Kritzinger said, until it was too late. (Allen 2009)

This anecdote and the cases in this book underscore that religious roles in conflict are essentially instrumental and not directly causal in terms of mass social violence. Thus, greater clarity is needed in both the analysis and understanding of the role of clergy and nonclerical leaders in fanning the flames of violence. At the same time, there is the need for better appreciation of the roles that religious leaders play in defending tolerance and promoting peace when social conditions for these more positive roles are present. As these chapters show, across the Abrahamic traditions and, indeed, in other religious orientations, such as Buddhism, there is no shortage of evidence that shows the multiple and sometimes contradictory roles that religious elites play in the escalation and de-escalation of conflict (see Wellman 2007).

The conceptual framework and findings presented in this research yield rich insights too complex to be simply summarized in a simple message; instead, as presented in the introduction, the approach to this volume is to explore the findings of cross-case analysis through a few contingent generalizations on critical questions. This concluding chapter seeks to distill some of the findings of the research presented in this volume in relation to four questions touched upon in the various chapters. What are the relationships among religion, national identity, and state character and authority, and how does religious belief affect the dynamics of conflict in deeply divided societies within the state? How do religious leaders affect social forces and, through social mobilization, help define intolerant or tolerant national identities? How do religious leaders rhetorically justify or mobilize for conflict in situations of violent struggle or affirmatively advocate for peace? What are the implications for better understanding the roles of religious leaders in peacemaking?

RELIGION, NATIONALISM, AND THE STATE

As David Little finds in his examination of liberal and illiberal regimes, "religion and ethnicity are themselves reciprocally influenced by the character and practice of the state." The interplay between religion, ethnicity, and state authority is central to an analysis of the prospects for conflict and the prospects for peace. The chapters in this volume support Little's conceptual framework on the character of the regime and the enabling conditions for religious intolerance in illiberal regimes, in which the changing role of the conceptualization of the nation has been influenced in conflict by religious belief. The implication of this research is that the role of the state in defining a liberal, tolerant religious character for the nation is, at the end of the day, pivotal. It is in the nationalistic setting of these conflicts that religion plays a direct role in defining the extent to which national identities are more exclusive or inclusive and to the connections among religion, state authority, and specific policies. The complex interplay between the articulation of the identity of the "nation" and "state" determines the ways in which the legitimacy of the nation and the terms of citizenship in the state are defined.

The cases in this book differ over the relative influence of religious and state actors in this interplay. As George Irani notes in his analysis of the role of religion in the Lebanese civil war, religious identity as such was salient because religion was used in an ethnic sense. Indeed, the ways in which religious actors define the parameters of the nation and the source of legitimacy and purpose of the state is the thread that links each of the case studies in this book. This nationalist construction of the state—and the ways in which some states, such as Nigeria, continue to wrestle with this construction during bouts of religiously described violence—is at the heart of religion's role in deeply divided societies.

However, what emerges most strikingly from these case studies is how conflict settings move over time across the spectrum of nationalism and extremism, and how changes in domestic institutions of the state shape the ways in which religious and political elites find common cause in ways that contribute to conflict dynamics through a higher justification of the nature of difference within society. Whether countries move toward greater tolerance and political inclusivity, as in Northern Ireland, or toward war and further entrenchment of ethnic hegemony, as in Sri Lanka, depends much on the ways in which religion and state authority have had mutually reinforcing influences—away from and toward peace—over time.

The role that the structure of state institutions allows for, or provides barriers to, the use of religious rhetoric as a vehicle for defining the boundaries of the nation is critical. When the basic legitimacy and defining parameters of the nation and of state is the subject of conflict, as is the case in divided societies, this political competition is often aided by a turn to religious belief and justification for the boundaries of the nation. That is because beliefs in religious or ethnic identity are so much at issue in defining political authority and power (as in Sudan, as described in Carolyn Fluehr-Lobban's account of the interplay between religion and essentially authoritarian politics in Sudan over the enforcement of Shari'a law in the South). She writes that "weak leaders devolve to opportunism permitting their survival while strong leaders gain their position and voice within authoritarian and increasingly illegitimate circles of power." Many of the cases in this book demonstrate a strong incentive by authoritarian political elites to define state authority in religious terms and to justify political legitimacy in appeal to higher religious justification. Religious diversity or tolerance is therefore deemed a threat to the extant legitimacy and order.

Religious belief and state power thus combine to create "outbidding" conditions through which, for political survival or aggrandizement, elites turn to conflictive, justificatory, and usually nationalist rhetoric. The decisions of elites on whether and how to frame national identity in religious terms have a strong bearing on the ways in which state authority is organized and deployed. This in turn affects how those outside these religious-national interpretations perceive and react to the state. This dynamic is nowhere more evident than in the polarized relations between Israel and the Palestinians, in which material deprivation, global influences, and institutional crises have resulted in deep-rooted fissures in both communities that are principal barriers to the peace process. As Micheline

Ishay contends, "a hegemonic crisis within Israeli and Palestinian society has led to the rising popularity of religious and ultranationalist parties."

The religious dimensions of nationalist identity are often highly accentuated in the process of rapid democratization or ongoing crises and sequences of extended democratization processes where there is the absence of consolidation. As Rosalind Hackett observes of tumultuous Nigeria, "decades of mistrust and interreligious tensions plus the need to promote one's own religious organization in a highly competitive religious environment undermines the need to work together in the national interest." At the same time, Nigeria's vibrant civil society arena does provide space for some manifestations of religious action that underscore the essential commitment to coexistence that is part of Nigeria's complicated efforts to promote intercommunal peace at national, regional, and local levels (especially in key areas such as Kaduna and Plateau states). Nigeria needs to move beyond religious balancing in its state–society relations and address more effectively the underlying causes of media insensitivities, marginalization, and managing disputes over resources and development.

The recent escalation of violence along the Sunni–Shi'a divide in Islam, as Nader Hashemi observes, is highly contextual and should be seen in part as a function of the contest over the state in a region in which state authority has been captured along ethnoreligious lines. The close relationship between Muslim sectarian discourses is juxtaposed against secularist orientations; at the heart of these debates is the politics of group identity in a rapidly changing environment. Religious sectarianism is about ethnic identity mobilization in the context of rapid economic, political, and regional realpolitik shifts. Hashemi notes in concluding the analysis of these tensions across the region that "democratization is highly varied, fragile, and vulnerable to manipulation of religion by incumbent elites." The persistence of [nondemocratic regimes] is the biggest contributing factor that perpetuates sectarian conflict and affects the behavior of religious leaders. Until it is tackled, meaningful peace and mitigating violence over the long term will be extremely difficult."

Likewise, in Tajikistan, the context of rapid democratization and civil war created the conditions for rapid mobilization along Islamist lines. The conflict itself eventually resulted in a peace agreement; however, that agreement did not allow for sufficient redefinition of national identity that would allow for fully participation by Islamist orientations. There is still insufficient trust that an Islamist victory at the polls would not yield an Islamist state. As Karina Korostelina notes, "tolerance toward others was based on the willingness to preserve a negative peace and prevent further violence and not on the readiness to peacefully exist and cooperate with the former enemy. . . . Tajikistan has a long way to go to achieve the second type of tolerance."

RELIGIOUS ELITES IN CONFLICT DYNAMICS:
SPOILER AND CONCILIATORS

The focus on leaders or elites in the exacerbation of intergroup conflict raises the question of causality: Do elites shape attitudes of their publics, or are they "mirrors" of society and thus not autonomous in justifying, providing injunctions, mobilizing, or making sense when it comes to intergroup conflict? The case study of Kashmir in this volume would suggest the latter because religious leaders have had remarkably low-profile roles in the conflict context, despite the fact that many of the escalation incidences have been tied to religiously related precipitants. This inability to determine how much influence elites may have does not detract from the many examples, as seen in this volume, in which there is an interactive relationship between elites and the broader public. There may be greater limits to the elasticity of religious ideas for peace than for conflict. For example, Mari Fitzduff shows in her analysis of Northern Ireland that religious leaders were often unable to get out in front of their congregations in support of cross-communal community relations work for fear that they would lose their own internal credibility. She writes that "the inability of the major churches to produce significant leadership among their ranks that was theologically and socially transformative and inclusive raises questions about the ability of large institutions to move at a pace that is significantly beyond that of their many followers, given that their power and influence is dependent upon the retention of such followers."

It is clear that across many of these cases, elites have framed and shaped the terms of intergroup interaction in a way that has contributed to mass intolerance, as Susan Hayward's analysis of Buddhism in Sri Lanka reflects. Strikingly, she notes that the "very things that make the *sangha* and Sinhala Buddhist narrative a powerful force in propelling the conflict and shaping government politics and institutions also make it a powerfully important force to achieve peace.... [Religious leaders'] greater involvement has the potential to greatly transform the ideologies that propel the violence and the increasingly centralized and authoritarian state system." At least one critical difference among religious traditions with implications for the "autonomy" of elites is the extent to which religious organization is hierarchical (as in the Vatican role in the Lebanese civil war) or nonhierarchical, as in the case of the analysis of Sunni–Shi'a relations across the Middle East. Generally, those religious traditions with less hierarchy may be more susceptible to internal "outbidding" by alternative contenders claiming to be the authoritative voice of a "multivocal" religion.

One of the findings that emerge from this research is the need to have a clearer understanding of the wide range of types of religious leaders and the ways in which they interact with social conflict dynamics. Deeply divided societies see a range of religious actors, and it is important to understand their various roles as potential spoiler or conciliators. For example, in related research on South Africa, Pierre du Toit and Hennie Kotzé find a deep disconnection in that country between secular, modernist elites and traditionally oriented masses (du Toit and Kotzé Zoll 2011). Their survey research reveals how religious notions of "evil" emanating from practices of witchcraft constrain the consolidation of an otherwise celebrated "coexistence" in the wake of apartheid. Views of evil in the community constrain the state's ability to prevent intergroup violence (especially against immigrants).

These summary findings about the varieties and roles of religious leaders emerge in this research.

- Religious leaders cannot be defined narrowly on whether or not they are ordained clergy—there are many other avenues by which religiously driven individuals have influence. There are religious academic scholars, for example, or religious leaders who are also parliamentarians. This suggests that a focus of analytical priority is on those religious elites who are directly politically active, and those political elites who are overtly religious in their orientation.
- There are both men and women clergy, and the case studies reveal both influential men and women religious actors. In Sri Lanka, as Susan Hayward's chapter finds, there are both Catholic and Buddhist nuns—so there are women clergy in this case. What makes someone a "religious leader" is not necessarily their title of reverend or imam or mahanayeke, which would certainly limit the analysis to mostly men, but their influence and authority as a religiously driven civil society (or political-social) actor.
- Political elites are often removed from the effects of the war; those at the grassroots who actually know and feel the situation on the ground can bring that perspective and pressure to bear on the political elites—not just in an effort to force them to be more moderate—to ensure the decisions made in peace agreements are fair, just, equitable, and responsive to the suffering on the ground. In the religious realm, grassroots religious leadership can put pressure on the officials regarding the conflict.
- Local religious actors who can marshal a great deal of public support and mobilize a great number of people may in the end be able to influence political elite just as much as religious elite simply by bringing together a lot of people in a movement. For example, Shi'a Muqtada Al-Sadr in Iraq, who is studying to become an ayatollah and whose religious ranking is fairly low, certainly has become a powerful religiopolitical leader in the volatile democratization process following the 2003 multinational invasion.
- Leaders in faith-based development/relief/advocacy/peace nongovernmental organizations are typically at the forefront of peacemaking. For example, in the Catholic Church in Colombia there is a justice and peace department in

which many lay women and men lead and direct the Church's peace work. Religiously driven civil society leaders who head secular peace organizations are also very active in their religious communities, interact with their religious leadership, and are generally known to be religiously driven in their work.

Three summary findings arise from the comparative research on the roles of the various religious leaders on conflict dynamics in divided societies. First, it is critical to look within religious differences and consider that sectarian conflict can be as deadly as interreligious tension. In this book the analysis on Northern Ireland and Shi'a–Sunni relations would argue for a better understanding of the manifestations of sectarianism and understanding of how these overlap with other critical variables, particularly economic opportunity (Stewart and Langer 2007). Struggles within religious discourse also define the extent of tolerance and the degree of extremism. The key insights from this research reinforce the concern with vitriolic forms of speech that differentiate and inflame differences along religious lines: the chapters each present a concern with how religious leaders define a "hateful motive" (see chapter 1). This function, especially, is seen in the admonition in some religious orientations to terrorism as divinely justified through the articulation and defining of the "infidel." Extremist religious tendencies prone to violence tend to articulate that the modern religious mainstream has deviated from a true, authentic path; such deviation from authenticity is heretical, leading to severe intrareligious tensions and ultimately to intolerance and the implicit or explicit justification of violence.

Second, global dynamics have profound local effects, and vice versa. The case studies in this book do not exist in a country-level vacuum, and as Micheline Ishay's chapter reveals, globalization and transnational patterns of economic flows and of ideas have had a profound effect on the emergence of extremism in both the Israeli and Palestinian communities. Saudi Arabia has had a significant influence on Sunni Muslims, the Vatican on Catholics, Iran on the Shi'a, and Israel on global Judaism. Likewise, Karina Korostelina's chapter on Tajikistan underscores the context of post-Soviet democratization as setting the stage for the rise of an Islamist challenge to the state and eventually to civil war. The analysis of Northern Ireland reveals how the changing nature of economic success in Ireland—which stemmed from globalization—made the calculus of passion during the Troubles change over time.

Third, leadership—agency—matters in framing or defining the discourse of overall political culture regarding conflict or tolerance and coexistence because religious appeals are seen as a higher-order identity than those that otherwise might be more inclusive (such as a national identity). Religious authority and religious leaders can define through their reference to the religious cannon or to interpretation and moral reasoning the terms of conflict, tolerance, or—more positively—coexistence. Much depends in some cases on the actual local-level relationships between religious elites and society; in sum, religious elites are more likely to reflect social forces than to shape them.

IMPLICATIONS FOR PEACEMAKING IN DIVIDED SOCIETIES

What are the implications for the better understanding of the roles of religious leaders in peacemaking? All of this points to a critical finding: during conflict or in the wake of violent interactions, it is less likely that religious leaders will, or can, articulate the justification for peace unless or until the social, political, and economic conditions are permissive. While there may be a few courageous clerics seeking to bridge intergroup divides, for the most part religious leaders are reflective of the broader context in which they exist. Belief may prevent them from pursuing tolerance across lines of conflict, in addition to the practical incentives to articulate what their congregations want to hear.

The Nigeria case study by Rosalind Hackett reaffirms how religious leaders have at times sharpened divisions and prevented greater national integration. In the transition from conflict to peace, religious leaders have participated directly and indirectly as "spoilers" and as facilitators; in this period their roles may change (as was the case in South Africa). During these times, religious leaders may help in rearticulating the terms of religious tolerance, and may well settle on a minimal form of tolerance (Tolerance I in David Little's terms) and not advocate for, or allow for, greater national integration as a result of the lingering tensions of prior conflicts (as George Irani's chapter on Lebanon attests). Over time, however, through the manipulation of discursive practices and, critically, through symbolic acts, religious elites may tip the balance from tolerance as a minimal condition to coexistence in which religious differences are not reified as ethnic representation in the state.

Clearly, these case studies provide evidence that religious leaders have very little opportunity to promote peace when the social, economic, and political conditions are prohibitive. Even when religious rhetoric has been at the heart of the turn to war, as in Sudan and Sri Lanka, religious action can still contribute to peace. As Carolyn Fluehr-Lobban observes of Sudan, "unlike the politics who have lost legitimacy with the masses, religious leaders across the spectrum of belief and custom have yet to locate and fulfill the role they might play with the mass of Sudanese spiritually depleted by decades of war and conflict." This research reveals that international engagement to promote local peacekmaking by religious leaders should focus on both the normative articulation of "tolerance" as a minimal concept and "coexistence" as a more enduring national-integration goal. Lebanon, for example, seems to be stuck in the former rather than the latter, with considerable implications for conflict vulnerability and for economic opportunity.[2] An approach is needed that facilitates the negotiation across and within religious divides of the imperatives of tolerance on the basis of religion and belief and that supersedes the equation of religious identity with ethnic representation.[3]

The critical question regarding rights is often debated in terms of defamation of religion, as the Nigeria case study by Rosalind Hackett shows. Debates also swirl around the limits of free expression—for example, in the Danish-published "Mohammed Cartoons" controversy or the denialist conference on the holocaust in Iran. What is the appropriate balance between free association, "defamation of religion," and speech that incites hatred or provides direct incitement or injunctions to violence? The UN High Commissioner for Human Rights special rapporteurs on religious freedoms, expression, and racism together emphasize that the critical concern is in fact one of religious incitement:

> Whereas the debate concerning the dissemination of expressions which may offend certain believers has throughout the last ten years evolved around the notion of "defamation of religions," we welcome the fact that the debate seems to be shifting to the concept of "incitement to racial or religious hatred," sometimes also referred to as "hate speech."
>
> Indeed, the difficulties in providing an objective definition of the term "defamation of religions" at the international level make the whole concept open to abuse. . . . There are numerous examples of persecution of religious minorities or dissenters, but also of atheists and non-theists, as a result of legislation on religious offences or overzealous application of laws that are fairly neutral. (Muigai, Jahangir, and La Rue 2009)

The case studies show that in terms of rights-based discourses, social justice is often a cross-cutting value within and across religious traditions. The language of rights in terms of social justice may thus bridge various traditions and values and allow for a common language that emphasizes the imperative of tolerance in deeply divided societies. In turn, the focus on rights of religious freedom—articulated in critical global instruments such as the ICCPR (see chapter 1)—can relate to the focus on national identities that transcend religious particularism through a focus on issues such as the plight of the poor. Practically, this means that the creation and sustaining of locally contextualized interreligious councils is an important way to create structured bargaining across group lines and, indeed, for the international community to actively engage, and often (through development assistance) build the capacity of ongoing, structured religious dialogue.

In framing the discourse, international participants typically stress rights-based approaches in terms of hard international law—for example, in questions of abrogation of rights of freedom of belief—and in terms of soft law, such as common principles in running religious dialogues or in engaging religious leaders. Today, whether in Sri Lanka in focusing on the rights of the defeated Tamil minority, or in Sudan where the focus is on the applicability of Shari'a and the relationship between religion and the state, the language of rights focuses on critical linkages between the state and nondominant religious communities. These challenges will resolve in both Sudan and the newly recognized South Sudan. Exclusion, discrimination, denial of dignity and status, and direct repression in turn lead to frustration, reaction, and violent responses by persecuted religious minorities. Unless states can be distinct from and mediate religious differences and provide for a minimal basis of respect for rights, the persistence of conflict is likely. Practically, this means that international engagement should be premised upon a constant and unwavering reference to the international norms and ways to engender compliance by state authorities. Indeed, the result of this approach has been the waning of debates about the applicability of Shari'a to non-Muslims, as the case studies of Sudan and Nigeria in this volume suggest.

However, a focus on rights is only half of the peacemaking story. The other half is to consciously build a common identity that transcends religion and embraces a multireligious view of the state. This suggests that further advances in democratization are essential, despite the ironic findings that democratization processes themselves can exacerbate religious tensions. Religiously divided societies are typically structured around "parallelism," in which groups share the same national identity but rarely interact. This parallelism is often constitutionally enshrined in power-sharing arrangements (as the case study on Lebanon shows, often with the explicit help and interest of religious elites), with the consequence of perpetuating political coalition-making along religious lines and inhibiting the social integration needed to move from minimalist tolerance to a more affirmative principle of coexistence. Such a condition of power-sharing, while common, often lays the basis for conflict when economic or social differences persist or the demographics of voting lead to political exclusion. How to move beyond this minimal state of tolerance to a more enduring form of coexistence remains a puzzle. As a start, however, it is essential that groups in conflict embrace symbolic politics and policy actions that affirm "parity of esteem" or the legal and operational existence of equality of dignity and coexistence contribute to successful conflict management in divided societies. Another point of departure is to be aware of the conflict-inducing nature of proselytization and identification of ways to manage rapid transformation of religious demographics.

Religious leaders clearly have a direct role in the movement of divided societies away from minimalist constructions of tolerance toward a deeper notion of coexistence. Douglas Johnston has articulated the conditions under which religious leaders may contribute to this pursuit of coexistence: religious leaders may harbor credibility as trusted interlocutors associated with a value system that provides opportunities for persuasion and a "moral warrant" for peace. As well, religious leaders may have the ability to "humanize" situations, to mobilize local capacities. Finally, when engaged in peacemaking, many enter with an enduring sense of perseverance.[4] In Kashmir, for example, the chapter by Ganguly and Swami suggests that an essential part of the potential contribution of religion to management of this enduring conflict is the focus on a parity of esteem, or overarching identity, in the terms of "Kashmiriat." How can a prior history of respect and coexistence be recreated after decades of conflict? Mari Fitzduff finds that those religious leaders who were successful in buttressing the peace process in Northern Ireland were able to leverage the status of the Church and the continued community respect for religious institutions primarily through their pastoral roles. When religious leaders backed the politically reached cease-fire agreement, they provided the moral authority to allow political elites to pursue settlement through negotiation.

The consequence of rights-based approaches and norms, symbols, and measures that promote parity of esteem are seen in societies that also witness the evolution of an institutionally structured, integrated civil society that cuts across religious, sectarian, and doctrinal lines.[5] When such integrated civil societies exist, the propensity for intergroup conflict diminishes. Monitoring of religious messages should indeed focus on identification of language that is condemning of other faiths, that sharpens ethnic divisions, or that glorifies violence as a duty of devotion. This means that in terms of conflict prevention, a focus on continuing, institutionalized forms of religious dialogue are critical to marginalize, more broadly, those who would articulate difference and division within communities and bolster a political culture of multireligiosity. Religious peacemaking should therefore focus in principle and first and foremost on the definition, meaning, and boundaries among religion and ethnicity and the "nation," an articulation of the role of the state in ensuring tolerance and freedom from discrimination on the basis of religion or belief as an intermediary goal, and the practical and operational measures through which state and society embrace and pursue a broader definition of "tolerance" that affirms the principles of "coexistence."

NOTES

1. Finland exercises universal jurisdiction in genocide cases. For a scholarly treatment of the role of religion (in particular, Christianity) in the Rwandan genocide, see Longman (2009).
2. On the inhibiting effects of confessionalism on human development, see the UNDP *2008–2009 National Human Development Report for Lebanon: Toward a Citizen's State*. Available at www.undp.org.lb/communication/publications/index.cfm.
3. This argument is based in part on the international normative framework of the UN Declaration on the Elimination of all Forms of Intolerance and

Discrimination based on Religion or Belief (A/RES/36/55 25 November 1981). For further analysis, resources, and a bibliography, see the University of Minnesota's Human Rights Library resource site, available at www1.umn.edu/humanrts /edumat/studyguides/religion.html.

4. See the case studies in Johnston (2003).
5. Varshney's (2002) work on India's communal strife has affirmed this conclusion.

REFERENCES

Allen, Bob. 2009. "Former Rwanda Baptist Pastor on Trial for Genocide." *Associated Baptist Press*, September 2. www.abpnews.com/index.php?option=com_content& task=view&id=4365&Itemid=53.

Arnson, Cynthia J., and I. William Zartman. 2005. *Rethinking the Economics of War: The Intersection of Need, Creed, and Greed*. Washington, DC: Woodrow Wilson Center Press.

Collier, Paul, Lani Elliot, Harvard Hegre, Anke Hoeffler, Marta Reynal-Querol, and Nicholas Sambinis. 2003. *Breaking the Conflict Trap: Civil War and Development Policy*. Washington, DC: World Bank; and Oxford: Oxford University Press.

du Toit, Pierre, and Hennie Kotzé. 2011. *Liberal Democracy and Peace in South Africa: The Pursuit of Freedom as Dignity*. London: Palgrave MacMillan.

Johnston, Douglas. 2003. *Trumping Realpolitik: Faith-based Diplomacy*. New York: Oxford University Press.

Longman, Timothy. 2009. *Christianity and Genocide in Rwanda*. Cambridge: Cambridge University Press.

Muigai, Githu, Asma Jahangir, and Frank La Rue. 2009. "Freedom of Expression and Incitement to Racial or Religious Hatred." Durban Review Conference, Geneva, April 22. www2.ohchr.org/english/issues/religion/docs/SRJointstatement22April 09.pdf.

Stewart, Frances, and Arnim Langer. 2007. "Horizontal Inequalities: Persistence and Change." CRISE Working Paper #39, August. Oxford: Queen Elizabeth House. www.crise.ox.ac.uk/pubs/workingpaper39.pdf.

Varshney, Ashutosh. 2002. *Ethnic Conflict and Civic Life: Hindus and Muslims in India*. New Haven, CT: Yale University Press.

Wellman, James K., ed. 2007. *Belief and Bloodshed: Religion and Violence across Time and Tradition*. Lanham, MD: Rowman and Littlefield.

CONTRIBUTORS

Mari Fitzduff is professor and former director of the international master of arts program Coexistence and Conflict at Brandeis University. From 1997 to 2003 she held a chair of Conflict Studies at the University of Ulster where she was director of UNU/INCORE, which addresses the management of ethnic, political, and religious conflict through an integrated approach using research, training, policy, program, and practice development. From 1990 to 1997 she was chief executive of the Northern Ireland Community Relations Council, which works with government, statutory bodies, trade unions, churches, community groups, security groups, ex-prisoners, businesses, and politicians to develop programs and training to address issues of conflict resolution in Northern Ireland.

Professor Fitzduff has also worked on programs that address conflict and diversity issues in many countries, including the Basque Country, Sri Lanka, Middle East, and Indonesia, and she serves as an international expert for many governments and international organizations on issues of conflict and coexistence, including the United Nations, the World Bank, the Commonwealth, the European Union, and the British Council. Her publications include *Beyond Violence: Conflict Resolution Processes in Northern Ireland*, winner of an American Library Notable Publications Award; *Community Conflict Skills*, published in 1988 and now in its fourth edition; and *NGO's at the Table*, which she coedited with Cheyanne Church. Her most recent publication is *The Psychology of War, Conflict Resolution and Peace*, a three-volume series that she coedited with Chris Stout.

Carolyn Fluehr-Lobban is a professor of anthropology at Rhode Island College, where she teaches courses in anthropology and Islamic, African, and Afro-American studies. She received her bachelor's and master's degrees from Temple University and her doctorate in anthropology and African Studies from Northwestern University in 1973. At Rhode Island College she received both the Award for Distinguished Teaching and the Award for Distinguished Scholarship. Over three decades she has lived and conducted research in Sudan, and in North Africa for six years. She is a founder and twice past president of the Sudan Studies Association and is currently conducting research in Sudan under a two-year grant from the US Institute of Peace.

She is the author or editor of eleven books, including *Islamic Societies in Practice*, *Islamic Law and Society in the Sudan*, and *Historical Dictionary of the Sudan* (coauthored). She translated the writings of Egyptian liberal-humanist intellectual Muhammad Sa'id al-Ashmawy from Arabic to English in *Against Islamic Extremism*. She is also the editor of *Ethics and the Profession of Anthropology: Dialogue for Ethically Conscious Practice*. Recent works include *Race and Identity in the Nile Valley*, coedited with Kharyssa Rhodes; *Race and Racism: An Introduction*; and *Female Well-Being: Toward a Global Theory of Social Change*, coauthored and coedited with Janet M. Billson.

Sumit Ganguly is a professor of political science and holds the Rabindranath Tagore Chair in Indian Cultures and Civilizations at Indiana University, Bloomington. Professor Ganguly has previously taught at James Madison College, Michigan State University, Hunter College, the Graduate School of the City University of New York, and the University of Texas at Austin. He has also been a fellow and a guest scholar at the Woodrow Wilson International Center for Scholars in Washington, DC, and a visiting fellow at the Center for International Security and Cooperation at Stanford University. He is the author, coauthor, editor, or coeditor of fifteen books on South Asian politics. His latest books are *The State of India's Democracy* (edited with Larry Diamond and Marc Plattner) and *India, Pakistan, and the Bomb* (cowritten with S. Paul Kapur). Professor Ganguly serves on the editorial boards of *Asian Affairs*, *Asian Survey*, *Current History*, *Journal of Democracy*, *Journal of Strategic Studies*, and *Security Studies*. He is also the founding editor of the only referreed social science journal devoted to the study of contemporary India, *The India Review*, and he is one of the editors of the *International Studies Quarterly*.

Rosalind I. J. Hackett is a distinguished professor in the humanities at the University of Tennessee, Knoxville, where she teaches religious studies and anthropology. In the early 1980s she taught at the University of Calabar in Nigeria. She has published widely on religion in Africa, notably on new religious movements, as well as on art, media, gender, conflict, and religious freedom in the African context. In 2005 she was elected president of the International Association for the History of Religions. She has published an edited volume, *Proselytization Revisited: Rights Talk, Free Markets, and Culture Wars*, and is bringing to completion a book titled *Nigeria: Religion in the Balance*.

Nader Hashemi is an assistant professor at the Josef Korbel School of International Studies, University of Denver. He received his PhD from the Department of Political Science at the University of Toronto. His research interests lie at the intersection of political theory and comparative politics of the developing world with a regional specialization in the Middle East and the Islamic world. Specific research areas include secularism and its discontents in Muslim societies, Western and modern Islamic political thought, religion–state relations, the politics of Islamic fundamentalism, and the history and development of liberal democracy. His writings have appeared in *Journal of Church and State*, *Third World Quarterly*, *Queen's Quarterly*, *Global Dialogue*, *Tikkun*, *The Nation*, *Chicago Tribune*, *The Daily Star* (Beirut), *The Globe and Mail*, and *Toronto Star*. He is the author of *The Great Problem of Our Time: Rethinking the Relationship between Islam, Secularism and Liberal Democracy*. Previously he was an Andrew W. Mellon Postdoctoral Fellow at Northwestern University and a visiting assistant professor at the UCLA International Institute.

Susan Hayward joined the US Institute of Peace (USIP) in August 2007 as a program officer in the religion and peacemaking program. She specializes in the role of religious leaders and communities in motivating violence and peace processes, and the development of conflict prevention, resolution, and reconciliation programs specifically targeting the religious sector. Prior to joining USIP, Susan worked as a short-term religious peacemaking program development consultant for the Academy of Educational Development in Colombo, Sri Lanka, as a fellow of the program on negotiation at Harvard Law School. She has experience consulting on religious peacemaking in the Conflict Resolution Program at The Carter Center in Atlanta, Georgia. Susan has also conducted political asylum, refugee policy, and human rights work in Minneapolis and Washington, DC.

She studied Buddhism in Nepal and is currently pursuing ministerial ordination in the United Church of Christ. Her recent research work has focused on religious dynamics in the conflict and efforts toward peace in Sri Lanka, Northern Uganda, and, most recently, Colombia. Hayward holds a bachelor of arts degree in comparative religion from Tufts University, a master of law and diplomacy from the Fletcher School at Tufts, and a master of divinity from Harvard Divinity School.

Scott W. Hibbard is an associate professor in the Department of Political Science at DePaul University, where he teaches courses on American foreign policy, Middle East politics, and international relations. He spent the 2009–10 academic year teaching at the American University of Cairo as part of a Fulbright Award from the Department of State. Hibbard received his doctorate from Johns Hopkins

University (2005), and he holds advanced degrees from the London School of Economics and Political Science (MSc Political Theory, 1989), and Georgetown University (MA Liberal Studies, 1988). Hibbard also worked in the US government for twelve years, including five years as a program officer at the US Institute of Peace (1992–97) and seven years as a legislative aide in the US Congress (1985–92). Hibbard is the author of *Religious Politics and Secular States: Egypt, India and the United States* and coauthor (with David Little) of *Islamic Activism and US Foreign Policy*.

George Emile Irani is professor at the American University of Kuwait. Prior to this appointment, he was director for the Africa and the Middle East program at the Toledo International Center for Peace (CITPAX) in Madrid, Spain. Until June 2005 he was a professor in the peace and conflict studies division at Royal Roads University in Victoria, Canada. Prior to that, he was senior policy analyst with the US Commission on International Religious Freedom. In 1997–98, Dr. Irani was Jennings Randolph Senior Fellow at the US Institute of Peace (USIP), where he conducted research on rituals as methods of conflict control and reduction in the Middle East. Dr. Irani serves as a senior fellow with the Strategic Studies Department, Joint Special Operations University under contract with Science Application International Corporation. Between 1993 and 1997, Irani was assistant professor in political science at the Lebanese American University in Beirut (Lebanon), where he organized two international conferences funded by USIP.

Irani is the author of *The Papacy and the Middle East: The Role of the Holy See in the Arab-Israeli Conflict*, which has been translated in French, Italian, Arabic, and Portuguese. Together with Laurie King-Irani, he coedited the book *Acknowledgment, Forgiveness and Reconciliation: Lessons from Lebanon* published by the Lebanese American University. Together with Vamik Volkan and Judy Carter, Dr. Irani has published a book titled *Regional and Ethnic Conflicts: Perspectives from the Frontlines*. He holds a laurea in political science from the Universita Cattolica del Sacro Cuore (Milano, Italy) and an MA and PhD in international relations from the University of Southern California.

Micheline Ishay is professor and director of the international human rights program at the Josef Korbel School of International Studies at the University of Denver. She is the author or editor of several articles and books, such as *Internationalism and Its Betrayal: The Nationalism Reader*. Her *History of Human Rights: From Ancient Times to the Era of Globalization* has been translated into several languages and was chosen by the *Philadelphia Inquirer* as one of the ten top nonfiction books of 2004. She has also published *Human Rights Reader: From Ancient Times to the Present* and is currently working on two new book projects—*The Future of Human Rights* and *Israelis and Palestinians: Beyond a Two-State Solution*—that she began while serving as Lady Davis Professor at the University of Jerusalem in 2006. She travels widely in Europe, the United States, and the Middle East and speaks on a variety of topics ranging from current political issues to political theory, to human rights to American foreign policy.

Karina Korostelina is an associate professor at the Institute for Conflict Analysis and Resolution at George Mason University and a fellow of the European Research Center of Migration and Ethnic Relations. She is a leading expert on identity-based conflicts, ethnic conflicts, the relationships between Muslim and non-Muslim populations, and conflict resolution and peacebuilding. Her recent interests include the study of civilian devastation and the role of history education in conflict and postconflict societies. She was a Fulbright New Century Scholar and has participated in the regional scholar-exchange program administered by the Kennan Institute; Woodrow Wilson Center, Washington, DC; and in the CRC nationalism session at the Curriculum Resource Center of the Central European University. Karina has received grants from the MacArthur Foundation, Soros Foundation, US Institute of Peace, US National Academy of Education, Spenser Foundation, Bureau of Educational and Cultural Affairs of USDS, INTAS, IREX, and the Council of Europe. Her books include *Social Identity and Conflict* and, coauthored, *Identity, Morality, and Threat.*

David Little, Professor Emeritus at the Harvard Divinity School (HDS), came to the divinity school in 1999 and was, from 1999 to 2005, the T. J. Dermot Dunphy Professor of the Practice in Religion, Ethnicity, and International Conflict. Before joining HDS, he was senior scholar in religion, ethics, and human rights at the US Institute of Peace (USIP) in Washington, DC, where he directed the working group on religion, ideology, and peace, which conducted a study of religion, nationalism, and intolerance in reference to the UN Declaration on the Elimination of Intolerance and Discrimination. From 1996 to 1998 he was on the State Department advisory committee on religious freedom abroad. He writes in the areas of moral philosophy, moral theology, history of ethics, and the sociology of religion, with an interest in comparative ethics, human rights, religious liberty, and ethics and international affairs. He is author with Scott W. Hibbard of *Islamic Activism and US Foreign Policy*, and author of two volumes in the USIP series on religion, nationalism, and intolerance.

Timothy D. Sisk is a professor at the Josef Korbel School of International Studies, University of Denver, and director of the Center for Sustainable Development and International Peace (SDIP), a research and policy institute at the school, and director of the Korbel School's program in humanitarian assistance. His research focuses on the nexus between democracy and governance and the management of conflict in deeply divided societies, especially those emerging from civil war. He has conducted extensive research on the role of international and regional organizations, particularly the United Nations, on peace operations, peacemaking, and peacebuilding. He is also the editor, with Tom Farer, of the journal of the Academic Council of the United Nations System (ACUNS), *Global Governance: A Review of Multilateralism and International Organizations*. He is an associate fellow of the Geneva Centre for Security Policy in Geneva, Switzerland. Sisk's latest scholarly book is titled *International Mediation in Civil Wars: Bargaining with Bullets*. Two other books for which he is the editor also recently appeared: *From War to Democracy: Dilemmas of Peacebuilding* (with Anna Jarstad) and *The Dilemmas of Statebuilding: Confronting the Contradictions of Postwar Peace Operations* (with Roland Paris). Prior to joining the University of Denver in 1998, he was a program officer in the grant program of the US Institute of Peace in Washington, DC, and, prior to that, a staff member for US senator Dale Bumpers (D-Arkansas). Sisk earned a PhD with distinction in political science (comparative politics, research methods) from George Washington University in 1992, an MA in international journalism (1984), and a BA in foreign service and German (1982).

Praveen Swami is diplomatic editor of *The Daily Telegraph*, London, and writes on international strategic and security issues. Earlier, he was associate editor of *The Hindu*, for which he reported on the conflict in Jammu and Kashmir, the Maoist insurgency in India, and Islamist groups. He reported on Jammu and Kashmir, Punjab, and security issues for much of the 1990s before becoming Mumbai bureau chief in 1998. Swami also served as a producer for an independent television network, where he worked on projects related to terrorism in Punjab. He has won several awards for his work. He received the Sanskriti Samman award in 1999 for a series of investigative stories on Indian military and intelligence failures preceding and during the Kargil War. His work on the Indian army's counterterrorist operations won him the Prem Bhatia Memorial Award for Political Journalism in 2003. In 2006 he won the Indian Express-Ramnath Goenka Excellence in Journalism prize. Swami was a Jennings Randolph senior fellow at the US Institute of Peace in Washington, DC, in 2004–5.

INDEX